T5-AWI-746

EDUCATION IN LATIN AMERICA

Education in Latin America

Edited by Colin Brock and Hugh Lawlor

CROOM HELM
London • Sydney • Dover, New Hampshire

©1985 Colin Brock and Hugh Lawlor
Croom Helm Ltd, Provident House, Burrell Row,
Beckenham, Kent BR3 1AT

Croom Helm Australia Pty Ltd, First Floor,
139 King Street, Sydney, NSW 2001, Australia

British Library Cataloguing in Publication Data

Education in Latin America.
   1. Education–Latin America
   I. Brock, Colin II. Lawlor, Hugh
   370'.98   LA541
   ISBN 0-7099-3273-1

Croom Helm, 51 Washington Street, Dover,
New Hampshire 03820, USA

Library of Congress Cataloging in Publication Data
Main entry under title:

Education in Latin America.

   Bibliography: p.
   1. Education–Latin America– Addresses, essays,
lectures. I. Brock, Colin. II. Lawlor, Hugh.
LA541.E277   1985   370'.98   85-3750
ISBN 0-7099-3273-1

Printed and bound in Great Britain
by Billing & Sons Limited, Worcester.

CONTENTS

PREFACE

PREFACE

When inviting the contributors to write on particular
themes and places for this volume we aimed to achieve a
balance between the components of Latin America and a range of
educational issues and problems. We are grateful to each of
our colleagues for their responses to our various requests and
as editors accept full responsibility for any resulting imbalances or emphases.

It was never our intention to attempt a blanket coverage
of educational issues in Latin America. This would have been
neither appropriate nor possible. Selection is inevitable,
and our major decision in this respect was to concentrate on
formal educational provision, national units, and critical
analysis.

A geographical sequence has been preferred to a sectoral
succession. Following a regional contextual profile, we
begin our national cases in the Latin Caribbean and move on
to selected themes from Central America and the Andean states.
As the giant and in some respects primate state of South
America, particular attention is then focused on Brazil. Extending south into the temperate zone, Brazil is followed in
our sequence by two states, the bulk of whose populations
reside in this zone and, whose official educational policy in
recent times has been strongly influenced by Brazilian
practices. In each and every country included here, we have
opted for a contribution on what we consider to be an aspect
of education of some distinctive contemporary significance.

We would like to thank all the contributors and to
express our gratitude to Margot Lawlor for the skill and
alacrity with which she has typed the camera-ready copy.

Colin Brock and Hugh Lawlor

Chapter One

LATIN AMERICA: AN EDUCATIONAL PROFILE

Colin Brock

Latin America was once portrayed by an eminent geographer
as being a 'harmony of contrasts'.   Such a phrase could well
be used to epitomise its educational character.
      Unlike Africa and Asia - the other components of the so-
called 'Third World' - Latin America has no clear cut
geographical definition, though the major part of it, South
America, is a continent in its own right.   Most of Central
America is a component of Latin America, though Mexico is
occasionally included in definitions of North America.   The
islands of the Caribbean region, known as the West Indies,
include parts of Latin America such as Cuba and the Dominican
Republic as well as nations historically related more to
Britain, France and the Netherlands than to Hispanic or
Lusitanian metropoles.   None the less, one international
classification includes the entire Americas minus Canada and
the USA in 'Latin America', and sub-divides the region into:
Tropical South America;   Temperate South America;   Middle
America;   Caribbean.
      Given that Latin America is generally regarded as being
part of the 'Third World', the fact that many of the formal
education systems of this region derive from the same formative period of national political development as do the major
European systems is a significant consideration.   The age of
the emergence of nation states in Europe, deriving from the
philosophical challenge of the 'Age of Enlightenment' is
shared by the formation of many of the states of Latin America
through their revolutionary wars of independence from Spain.
Indeed, it is perhaps ironical that the contemporary external
power in the region, the USA, emerged at much the same time
and through a similar process, though primarily a colony and
cultural offshoot of Britain rather than Spain.   Herein lies
the major division of the New World into Anglo America and
Latin America.
      So the nations of Latin America, while having been sub-
ject to European colonialism in its various forms like most
other countries of the 'Third World', have a generic relation-

Fig. 1: Latin America

Source: adapted from Map 1 in: Wynia, G. W. (1984), The Politics of Latin American Development, Cambridge University Press.

Note: countries on this map not normally considered to be part of Latin America are: Belize, Guyana, Suriname and the Department of France known as French Guiana.

ship with their European counterparts that differs from the
European cultural overlay and colonial legacies in Africa and
Asia.   To many parts of Latin America the cultural dualism
deriving from colonialism seems to be in respect of the long-
standing paternalistic and economic influence of the USA
rather than Europe.   One must not forget, however, that the
indigenous Amerindian peoples of Latin America were placed in
a similar position in relation to European political economic
and cultural domination as that experienced by Africans and
Asians in their homelands.   Nowadays of course,it is internal
colonialism to which the Amerindians are subjected.

With few exceptions,/the missions of the Catholic Church ¥
that accompanied and followed the Iberian conquest of the
region, concentrated on the establishment of highly selective
and academic educational foundations.   Schools, seminaries
and universities were central features of the towns and cities
from which the colonial territories were controlled and
administered.   The rural/urban dichotomy in education, while
a virtually global phenomenon, has particularly deep roots in
Latin America.   This is not just a question of human ecological context but also a structural feature.   The formative
influence on the nascent educational systems of the newly
founded Latin American republics of the nineteenth century was
that of Napoleonic France.   Tiers of interlocked and hierarchical responsibility extended from national to regional to
local scale of territorial administration, and in each of
these levels from urban to rural.   As a consequence of a
combination of élitist educational philosophy, oppressive
political control and economic constraint, the ideals of
universal educational provision enshrined in the republican
constitutions of Latin America have still to be realised in
most countries of the region even at the primary level.   Indeed, the incapacity of most of these systems, after about 150
years of political independence, in respect of servicing the
mass of the population as well as the complex labour needs of
national economies, provides a sobering example to younger
developing countries with high expectations of education in
terms of development.

During a century and a half, the history of educational
development in Latin America has exhibited alternating phases
of growth and retrenchment that have been remarkably concord-
ant throughout the region.   The periods of growth are
characterised by an expansion of state provision under populist or socialistic governments, while in between, the private
sector has been favoured by more conservative regimes.   The
nature of the policy does not seem to have related necessarily
to the degree of autocracy, oligarchy or military control
present during such phases, all three being common, almost
endemic features of Latin American political history.   The
pattern has probably more to do with the strong influence on
the region of the outside world in economic terms, and of the

3

USA in particular.   Despite the relatively early acquisition
of political independence, the emerging economies of the Latin
American republics were drawn into a position of dependency
within the world economic order developed by the requirements
of the industrialising nations of Western Europe, especially
Britain.   Although very little of the British Empire existed
in Central and South America, British investment in and
exploitation of the resources of the region was paramount in
the nineteenth century.   Along with this came a significant
number of British professional, technical and entrepreneurial
settlers, and the model of the English 'public school', still
favoured by some Latin American élites.   Large numbers of
immigrants came also from other parts of Western Europe, and
especially to the temperate zone comprising southern Brazil,
Paraguay, Uruguay, Argentina and Chile.   Some, especially
the Germans and Italians were sufficiently numerous, culturally cohesive and influential to add new dimensions to the
emerging patterns of educational provision.

The condition of dependency, whether political, economic
or cultural requires not only external domination but also the
collusion of the local élite.   Given the generic relationship between the nation states of Europe and the emergence of
the Latin American republics, it is not surprising that a
condition of structural dependency was created, the study of
which has provided the substance of dependency theory.   The
provision and operation of education has played a significant
role in Latin American dependency, and continues to do so.
Networks of political and cultural control emanate from the
cities through a web of increasingly deficient school provision, with local political figures in general assuring the
effective maintenance of the status quo.   Local mayors are
in effect caciques, keeping their power by negotiating between
their populations and the agencies of municipal, provincial
and national control for mutually acceptable ends.   An
example would be the provision of the means to construct or
develop a village school in return for the acceptance of a
particular teacher selected on grounds of politics or nepot-
ism.   A gradient of increasing incompleteness of even the
primary sector descends from town, through village to the
rural periphery, thus providing the educational dimension of
the marginalisation of a significant proportion of the population of Latin America.   This is the typical situation,
deriving from a symbiosis of political neglect and environ-
mental constraint, but there are other variants.   For example,
the so-called decentralisation mechanisms of some of the
reactionary regimes of the present day, while promoted under
a spurious liberal rationale are in practice a system to
ensure the extension of central control of education.   At the
other end of the political spectrum, the equalisation of educational opportunity as between urban and rural sectors
through massive investment in physical and human resources

provides a government with a more efficient control mechanism, however altruistic the reform.

Clearly then, Latin American educational systems have been part of as well as influenced by the structures and dynamics of dependency.   Since about 1920, however, the origin   of the most influential external influences has shifted.   The dominance of Western European nations, and especially Britain, over the Latin American economies was severely weakened by the action and aftermath of the Great War of 1914-18.   Some states in the region succeeded to a degree in gaining greater control over their own economies by import substitution,   diversification and industrialisation, but such developments were moderated by the increased influence of the USA and the onset of the world economic depression.   Progressive educational trends inspired by Dewey's thinking and destined to have influence world-wide, played their part in one of the expansionist periods of provision.   In addition to providing additional schools, more imaginative innovations in areas such as adult and rural education took place and have continued to have some influence despite several alternations in the political climate in the meantime.   One suspects that the ideas and operations of Paulo Freire and his successors in the adult literacy movement in Latin America owe more than a little to the vision of José Vasconcelos and his establishment of 'Cultural Missions' in Mexico in the 1920's.

Although the World War of 1939-45, like its predecessor, provided a brief opportunity to Latin American states to diversify their economies and break loose from their structural dependency, it also saw the emergence of the USA as the undisputed leader of the nations of the world at least in economic terms.   Given the historic Monrovian vision of that country as the guarantor of Western hemispheric freedom from Old World colonial oppression and infiltration, and the rise of the USSR to superpower status, the stage was set for a readjustment rather than a weakening of Latin American dependency.   At the same time, the educational ideas of the newly founded United Nations Organisation, through its agency UNESCO, encouraged the provision of universal primary education in accordance with its Charter.

While the significance of a certain style of educational development for hemispheric solidarity under US patronage was not lost on the leadership of that country, the role of a different style of educational philosophy and investment was seen as crucial by those who sought to resolve the gross disparities and injustices of the human condition in Latin America through socialism.   Within the context of the postwar economic boom, the USA launched the 'Alliance for Progress' which included massive projects of educational aid.   These had the effect of a quantitative expansion of provision, but without challenging the long-standing structural inequities of the formal education systems of Latin America.   Much of the improvement was in fact appropriated by the already privileged élites and middle classes who were in a position to determine the nature of increased educational provision.   Unlike the mass of the population, they already enjoyed universal primary education and so priority was given to investment in the expansion of the secondary and tertiary sectors.   Since access to these sectors is consequent upon successful completion of the primary programme, and for various reasons of deprivation and constraint only a tiny fraction of the masses achieve this, they have been effectively debarred from significant benefit.   At the secondary level, the expansion accommodated increased enrolment of middle class females which in respect of the sexism endemic in Latin American societies did represent some sort of improvement.   However, the tertiary sector gained most from the massive injection of public money into education, and the situation here was even more invidious.   Entry to this sector has always been very competitive in Latin America, and one of the most important functions of private schooling has been to prepare for university selection.   The consequence of expanding the tertiary sector has been to enable an increased proportion of the products of private schooling to enter.   In general, therefore, the educational outcome of largely US investment in increased provision has been to widen the gap between the privileged minority and the underprivileged majority in Latin American society.   During the same period certain demographic trends have compounded the problem of educational provision for the masses.   A continued high birth-rate in most countries of the region obviously places most strain on the already incomplete and underfunded primary sector, and massive migration from rural to urban areas often involving 'illegal' settlement adds a new dimension to the educational profile that most Latin American governments have hardly begun to cope with.

The Latin American republics came into being as revolutionary responses to the oppression and neglect of Iberian colonial rule.   The general and educational ideals of this movement have been sustained by political radicals through the generations, and have from time to time enjoyed periods of implementation and innovation.   One of the aftermaths of the Mexican revolution in this respect has been mentioned above. In the period since 1945 there has been first a phase when radical challenges to the structural inertia of Latin American educational provision gained some ground, and more recently a period of strong, often military reaction in favour of the traditional inequities.   Given the extreme and in practice irrelevant nature of formal systems of state education in this region, it is perhaps not surprising that some of the most radical contemporary critics of this mode of provision, such as Ivan Illich and Paulo Freire, are Latin Americans.   Their priorities lie not in formal schooling but in non-formal, adult and continuing education.   Unlike the features of educational expansion under US funding, the combating of mass illiteracy has been a feature of regimes seeking to widen educational access and public awareness. Notably successful in this respect has been the Cuban revolution which has by most criteria sustained itself since 1959. Literacy campaigns have also been a priority of the more recent Nicaraguan socialist regime, and have enjoyed periods of support in various countries of the region, notably in Chile under Allende from 1970-73.

In general, however, education in Latin America remains under the influence of dependency and inertia, and exhibits today the same broad characteristics as 100 years ago. These are:

a. in most countries, incomplete systems even at primary level, despite their constitutional obligations, and the objectives of the Santiago Plan of 1963;

b. problems of enrolment at primary level, especially in the rural sector and in the barrios and favelas of the cities;

c. very high levels of repeating and wastage at primary level caused by inappropriate curriculum content and excessively strict examinations for promotion from one year to the next;

d. inadequate provision of public secondary schooling, except in the middle class sectors of the urban population, and even here the same sort of curricula and promotional problems as found at primary level;

e. a relatively large and thriving private sector serving the needs of the various élites and gaining a disproportionate share of university places;

f. a traditionally academic tertiary sector, which despite some diversification in recent decades remains in most countries insufficiently technical;

g. low teacher quality at all levels, especially in the rural sector, and a lack of professional status and identity for this occupation;

h. a strong correspondence between the quality of educational provision and the patterns of social class whereby the mass of the population is severely disadvantaged - this also tends to be linked indirectly with patterns of race and ethnicity thus producing multiple disadvantage for groups of non-European origin, mainly Amerindians and Blacks;

i. a poor correspondence between formal education and the occupational structure;

j. severe female disadvantage outside of the middle classes and élites;

k. increasing rates of illiteracy in most countries, with rural populations and females most disadvantaged in this respect.

There are of course exceptions where most or even all of

these problems do not apply, notably Cuba and Costa Rica, or where genuine and vigorous attempts are being made to combat them, as for example in Mexico and Venezuela.   But in much of the region the current phase of reactionary military regimes operating under a shared philosophy of 'National Security' is having the effect of increasing the inequities and disparities outlined above, as well as the operational role of education as a mechanism of social and political control.   Whether the return of Argentina to a democratic system heralds a new phase, with the possibility of improving the educational profile, depends largely on hemispheric politics.

Chapter Two

EDUCATION AND REVOLUTION IN SOCIALIST CUBA: THE PROMISE OF DEMOCRATISATION

Mark Richmond

It is widely acknowledged, by friend and foe alike, that the field of education has witnessed some of Cuba's most dramatic, substantial and significant advances since 1959. Indeed, along with remarkable achievements in public health, the educational revolution now serves as the standard-bearer of the Revolution as a whole. Inspired by this success, Fidel Castro has grown ambitious for Cuba to become nothing less than a world educational power before the turn of the century.

Such grandiose ambitions imply tremendous costs, efforts, and sacrifices for a small country, but for Cuba's leaders these will be more than offset if, by pleasing established allies, winning new friends, and earning much-needed foreign exchange, educational and related manpower programmes help to ensure the survival and development of the Revolution. A beginning has already been made through overseas civilian aid programmes, which include specifically educational components such as the detachments of literacy workers in Nicaragua and Angola, as well as the hiring-out of skilled human capital to other countries.[1] Not least there is Cuba's hospitality to thousands of foreign students enrolled in her schools, institutes, and universities.[2] However, while the success of such schemes for exporting the educational revolution will depend greatly upon the international political situation and the state of the world economy, particularly as they affect Latin America and the Caribbean, the perceived legitimacy of Cuba's role as a world educational power will rest ultimately upon her capacity to sustain and develop her domestic educational performance.[3]

Part of the genius of Cuba's educational revolution has been the ability to pursue potentially conflicting aims simultaneously and successfully, though with shifts of emphasis over time, and to devise particular educational forms and practices which serve <u>all</u> these aims at one and the same time. Long-established, prominent features of Cuba's new educational system include the redesign of education so as

to make its contribution more relevant and useful to national
economic development; the attempt to engender a 'new man'
largely through the socialist education of the new generations;
the implementation of various schemes for combining study with
productive work; and the re-orientation of education in a
more scientific-technological direction.

None the less, although many of these and other developments have been radical, innovative and imaginative in the
perspective of Cuban history, in the context of Latin American
cultural traditions, and in the circumstances of underdevelopment, they must all take second place to the democratisation
of education as the foremost accomplishment of Cuba's educational revolution. A focus on the democratisation of Cuban
education not only reflects its fundamental importance during
the past twenty-five years but also emerges from a recognition
that it may well have recently entered a fresh stage in which
'qualitative development' rather than 'quantitative growth'
will become its most representative characteristic.[4]

THE DEMOCRATISATION OF CUBAN EDUCATION:
MAIN CONCEPTUAL FEATURES

The concept of 'democratisation of education' is highly
normative and susceptible to wide-ranging interpretation; it
is essential, therefore, to clarify any particularities of
understanding and usage when examining a given country's
performance in this area. Specific interpretations of democratisation of education, embodied in government policy and
practice, are shaped by many factors: educational and non-
educational; domestic and foreign; short-term and long-term.
The ideological frame of reference of the Cuban leadership,
for example, has strongly influenced the selection and definition of the educational inequalities to be dealt with. However, policies promoting educational democratisation have been
affected by the pursuit of other ideological goals as well as
by pragmatic responses to world events and genuine resource
shortages. In addition, Cuban understanding of the complexity of educational democratisation has probably been deepened
not only by lessons drawn from domestic practice but also by
awareness of trends abroad during a period of intense interest
in reducing educational inequalities in both developed and
underdeveloped countries.[5] The Cuban experience itself, of
course, has become part of the international debate.

From the outset of this analysis, it is important to note
that while the democratisation of education in Cuba has been
pursued as an end in itself, as a basic ideological commitment,
it has also served as an instrument for the achievement of
other revolutionary goals and educational objectives. For
example, as Carnoy and Werthein point out, 'Mass education
became the means to mass economic participation and mobilisation'.[6] Furthermore, while the policy of democratising

education has clearly enjoyed huge popular support, the drive
and initiative behind it have not come from below but from a
revolutionary leadership which has retained tight control over
policy-formation and decision-making.

Cuba has adopted a global approach to the democratisation
of education. This can be understood in two main senses.
First, the approach is global in that every type and level of
education has been thrown open to the Revolution's egalitarian
impulse. Second, it is global in that this educational
policy is considered an integral part of a strategy of planned
social transformation which involves the participation of the
whole population in the construction and enjoyment of a
radically new society free from exploitation and destructive
divisions.

At the heart of the Cuban strategy for democratising
education has been the promise to guarantee equality of access
to education for all Cubans. Seeking to distinguish itself
from all previous Cuban governments, the revolutionary leadership has consistently interpreted this commitment to mean that
the equal right to education must be substantive, not simply
formal. To its great credit, the Cuban regime has not shrunk
from the implications of this interpretation, namely, in order
to guarantee the end it must also guarantee the means.[7] Thus,
education in Cuba is free, that is the costs of education are
not borne directly by the individual or his/her parents but
by the whole society. In addition, the government has
engineered a massive expansion of educational provision, as
measured by financial, material and human indices. In
comparative-historical perspective, the level of educational
provision and the speed with which it has been delivered have
been remarkable.

Another aspect of the policy of equalising access to
education has been the guarantee of equality of educational
opportunity through the eradication of all discrimination
based on economic standing, sex, race, or place of residence.
The government has placed its considerable weight behind the
removal of all forms of official and public discrimination in
education based on these criteria which, either singly or more
usually through mutual reinforcement, had had such an adverse
effect upon educational opportunities before 1959. Today,
Cuba's educational institutions are typically multi-racial,
co-educational and contain students drawn from diverse social
and cultural backgrounds.

Equality of educational opportunity has been further
promoted by the expansion of educational provision and by the
broader egalitarian strategies and programmes adopted by the
regime. While the momentum of the early wave of redistributive policies has not been sustained, and though social
inequalities have probably been growing in recent years, the
egalitarian principle is still strong. This is especially so
in the field of education, making any attempted justification

11

of unequal access to education a difficult task indeed. In
addition, it should be noted that the universalisation of
state education by mid-1961 effectively removed one traditional support of unequal educational opportunities, private
schooling.

The democratisation of education in Cuba has not been
formulated as a policy for securing higher levels of individual social mobility. Such individual advance has undoubtedly occurred but the main thrust of the policy has been to
raise the general level of educational attainment and social
well-being of all Cubans. The democratisation of education
has been conceived as a social enterprise dedicated to
national and collective goals, not as a device for selfish
opportunism.[8] This policy has demanded a re-education of
public opinion about the responsibilities which educational
progress entails:

> '... the revolution set out to change the country's
> attitude toward education. In the new view, education
> was not something that could be taken or left, according
> to individual desire or whim. It was a vital national
> necessity, a duty as much as a right.'[9]

Thus, Cubans have acquired a social obligation to raise
their individual levels of educational attainment so as to
make a greater contribution to the society which made the
right to education effective. Precisely how many young
Cubans have 'internalised' the idea of education as a duty is
impossible to say, but it is a principle which pervades the
whole educational system, serving as a norm which exacts
public displays of conformity at the very least. Furthermore, education as a social obligation is expressed not only
through the duty to learn but also through the duty to teach.
Significantly, government calls for people to teach others at
lower educational levels. Many individuals in non-formal
educational settings in Cuba or even abroad, have been
personally associated with efforts to remove a blockage in the
process of democratising education caused by teacher shortage.
Of course, various political pressures and material incentives
may be involved in the motivations of such volunteers, but so
also may be the social duty to teach: some most certainly
consider it a revolutionary duty.

A closely related phenomenon, the technique of student
mobilisation based on voluntarism and the ideal of service,
has been a recurrent feature of the democratisation of education in Cuba. It is a well-tested method for meeting 'extraordinary' challenges considered vital by Cuba's leaders.
Rapid student mobilisations for solving urgent non-educational
problems, such as labour shortages at harvest time, have been
partly justified on educational grounds in that they serve to
reduce the gap between school and society; in addition, such

mobilisations have been 'routinised' to some extent through,
for example, the regular 'school to the countryside' schemes.
However, student mobilisation for solving problems of educational access have also been important.   This has been true
from the student brigades in the 1961 Literacy Campaign,
through to the Manuel Ascunce Domenech Student-Teacher
Detachment, whose efforts facilitated the great expansion of
post-primary education in the 1970's.

With one out of two Cubans over five years of age now
engaged in some form of organised study, education as an item
of social consumption has become part of the Cuban way of
life.   According to Lehmann, Cuba 'is a society where education has become something of a popular cult.'[10]   Education
has become 'popular' in another sense of the word.   For an
essential feature of the process of democratising Cuban
education has been the mass mobilisation of hundreds of
thousands of Cubans in the pursuit of national educational
goals and in the implementation of educational policies.   This
popular participation has been largely channelled through a
variety of institutions and organisations, such as the School
Councils;   the political organisations - the Communist Party
and the Young Communists - the trade unions and their national
umbrella organisation, the Confederation of Cuban Workers
(CTC);   youth organisations such as the Pioneers and the
unions of students;   and the mass organisations such as the
Federation of Cuban Women and the Committees for the Defence
of the Revolution and their base organisations - for example
the Militant Mothers of Education Movement and the Exemplary
Parents Movement.   Whilst mobilising their membership for the
implementation of government educational policies and for day-
to-day educational work in the schools and the community,
these organisations also encourage and help their members to
raise their own educational levels.   Thus, one way in which
Cuba's democratisation of education must be understood is
that, through mass mobilisation and the activities of numerous
organisations, the schools are 'invaded' by the wider society.

Ultimately, however, the democratisation of education in
Cuba today must be evaluated in terms of the goal which that
process serves, namely, the democratisation of society.   This
complex question can be approached in several ways.   We might
look at the curriculum, for example, to see how, through deliberate efforts to inculcate egalitarian values and democratic
principles within a communist ethos, the foundations might be
laid for the growth of attitudes, orientations and behaviour
conducive to the desired form of active, namely productive
citizenship.   This adaptation of the curriculum to the
requirements of ideological preparation and revolutionary
socialisation has been linked to hopes of creating a 'new man'.
However, this aspect of educational democratisation has yet to
prove itself.   On the other hand, we might examine the efforts
to reshape the social relations of schooling so that they

become more appropriate to a socialist society. These
efforts include schemes to reduce authoritarian patterns in
teaching, to move away from intellectualism, verbalism and
memorisation towards more active, independent, student-centred
learning, to create new types of schools in which more
co-operative behaviour can develop, and to overcome resilient,
historically-rooted divisions between theory and practice,
manual and intellectual labour, school and life and, above all,
study and work. The concern and disappointment expressed by
some foreign observers[11] regarding the insufficiently democratic aspects of the social relations of schooling in Cuba
today, are partly shared by Cuban educational authorities.
The latter, however, seem unconvinced by models and arguments
which do not appear to recognise the need for discipline, hard
work and respect for authority.

Another facet of the relationship between educational
democratisation and the democratisation of society is revealed
through efforts to promote national economic development by
means of educational policies. The potential for contradiction here is considerable, since Cuba has sought to improve
productivity and efficiency through advances in the general
educational level of the population, that is to say, through
the democratisation of education. None the less, it has
found it necessary to create cadres of highly skilled and
qualified industrial, scientific, administrative and political
leaders. This demand for high-level manpower, in conjunction
with a continuing strong emphasis on grades, examinations and
competitive academic entry into highly-prized careers, not to
mention the growth of élite institutions such as the Lenin
School, raises major questions about the compatibility between
educational and social trends towards élitism and democratisation in modern Cuba. For the moment, these contradictions
seem neither debilitating nor destructive. In view of the
thorough politicisation of decision-making in Cuba, however,
it seems likely that their resolution in the long-term will
depend mainly upon the distribution of political power. Consequently, this analysis of the democratisation of Cuban
education will conclude with a discussion of the relationship
between rising educational levels and popular participation in
the decision-making process.

The foregoing conceptual and thematic analysis is intended
to prepare for an examination of the application of the policy
of democratising education during the past twenty-five years
and the effects of this policy on certain sectors of Cuban
society.

MAIN PHASES OF DEVELOPMENT IN THE DEMOCRATISATION OF CUBAN
EDUCATION

The democratisation of education since 1959 has experienced three main phases of development which correspond to the

stages through which the entire educational system has passed.
In identifying these phases and their leading features, one
does not intend to deny the existence of numerous continuities
nor to obscure the more subtle changes of emphasis and direction that have occurred from one year or even one month to
another. Also, for reasons of brevity, this chapter will
focus on the most distinctive features of the democratisation
of education in each period.

Phase One: 1959-1971/72

Casas has characterised this period as one of reform and
of 'la democratisation quantitative de l'education',[12] while
Martuza points to 'experimentation and somewhat uneven
growth'.[13] The clear educational priority of the new regime
was to provide the basics of a sound education to as many
Cubans as possible; the means adopted were, on the one hand,
the rapid and massive expansion of access to free public
schooling, especially at the primary level and, on the other
hand, the attack on adult illiteracy and the creation of
nationwide facilities for adult education.

By effectively guaranteeing the equal right to education
and by attacking social and educational inequalities which
restricted access and opportunity, Cuba's leaders hoped that
mass education would help create a truly national community
dedicated to radical social change and rapid economic development. In addition, the new regime would consolidate and
expand its base of popular support by being seen to keep its
promises, by satisfying a growing demand for education -
formerly a relatively scarce social good - and by reaching the
whole population with its political and ideological messages.

The 1961 Literacy Campaign and its achievements have been
described on many occasions and so a detailed analysis will
not be offered here.[14] The bare facts are simple but
impressive: 929,207 illiterates were identified, the great
majority living in rural areas; a diverse voluntary teaching
force of over 280,000 was amassed; and a total of 707,212 of
the illiterates contacted were made 'literate' during the
campaign, thereby reducing the national illiteracy rate from
23.6 per cent in 1953 to 3.9 per cent in 1961. None the less
doubts have been raised about this figure as a measure of
functional literacy. In addition, the overall rate of
illiteracy reduction under the Revolution has been put into
sharper focus by Mesa-Lago, who points out, using projections
of illiteracy trends and an official 12.9 per cent illiteracy
rate revealed by the 1970 census, that:

'... the annual average rate of illiteracy reduction in
1953-70 was 0.68 per cent as compared to 0.51 per cent
in 1943-58, an important improvement indeed but not as
remarkable as originally thought.'[15]

Mesa-Lago is more impressed by the reduced gap between
the urban and rural illiteracy rates, from 12 per cent and
42 per cent respectively in 1953 to 7 per cent and 22 per cent
in 1970, though he notes that 'the relative positions remained
almost unchanged for a rural/urban ration of 3.5 to 1.0 in
1953 and 3.1 to 1.0 in 1970.'[16]
These facts are important to bear in mind when evaluating
Cuban progress in reducing illiteracy, but the Literacy
Campaign itself was successful on several levels. According
to Armando Hart, in a speech marking the twentieth anniversary
of the Literacy Campaign:

> '... the most important lesson of that colossal under-
> taking lies in the fact that the tasks involved in build-
> ing socialism, especially in the fields of education,
> culture and ideology, can only be carried out success-
> fully by means of the active and dynamic participation
> of the masses as a whole.'[17]

Indeed, the techniques of mass mobilisation and organisation focused on the attainment of a specific goal were first
worked out during the Literacy Campaign. Hart also points
out that the campaign saw the mass organisations 'cut their
first teeth' on a mass mobilisation exercise. Among its
many achievements, the campaign helped to integrate almost the
entire population into the revolutionary process, and in so
doing it linked the Revolution with a strong sense of national
identity and pride. Ultimately, the campaign was an enormous
political success for the Revolution and its leadership;
through it, perhaps for the first time, the Revolution assumed
the dimensions of a national mass movement.
After 1961, a number of seguimiento (follow-up) courses
and other adult education programmes were set up to allow not
only new literates but also undereducated adults to raise
their educational levels. Gradually, a national system of
adult 'worker-peasant' education emerged offering courses in a
flexible range of non-formal settings, with much assistance
from trade unions and mass organisations. Adults thus obtained the opportunity to seek a third-grade education and upwards,
the sixth grade being the eventual target for all Cubans to
achieve. High enrolment rates of about 500,000 per year, on
average, were secured in the 1960's, although enrolments
declined after 1967/68, probably reflecting the success of
many initial participants. According to Valdés, 1.7 million
adults reached sixth grade standard by 1968.[18] An important
feature of the democratisation of adult education was the
opportunity for study to be continued through successive
academic levels. Eventually, the idea of the 'universalisation of the university' was conceived according to which
workers would constitute 50 per cent of total university enrolment.

Education and Revolution in Socialist Cuba:
The Promise of Democratisation

With regard to primary schooling, in 1956/57 only 56.4 per cent of school-age children (6-12 years) were enrolled; by 1971/72, 96.4 per cent of this age bracket were enrolled. Clearly a substantial effort had been launched in order to universalise primary schooling. Further evidence of expansion at this level, especially in rural areas, can be seen in Fig. 1.

Some of the early increase in public primary school enrolment was due to the absorption of the private education sector. In 1958, Cuba had 665 private primary schools with an estimated enrolment of 120,000 and a teaching force of about 7,000;[19] but most of the increase flowed directly from the government's policies for expanding educational access and provision. A great propaganda exercise was mounted to explain the need to have all school-age children enrolled in school and to offer those young people who had never attended or had dropped out early the chance to continue their education. The government enlisted the support of the whole society in this effort, with the mass organisations playing a major role in contacting parents, checking on attendance, and helping with the general educational work of the schools. This mass mobilisation was complemented by the rapid expansion of the teaching force, especially through the appeal to young Cubans who had completed only a few years of schooling themselves to volunteer for teaching duties. These inexperienced, barely trained, but often enthusiastic young teachers, many destined for rural service, were vital for the democratisation policy. They were needed not only to cope with the growth in enrolment and in the number of schools, but also to replace the many thousands of qualified teachers who either refused to teach in the new educational system or had already fled into exile.[21]

Not only were an ever increasing number of children enrolled in primary schools but they also received more hours of instruction, mainly through the lengthening of the school year.[22] Curricula reorganisations and extensions of the syllabus, coupled with the adoption and implementation of the polytechnical principle at all levels of schooling, meant that primary school children began to experience a 'proletarianised' education which was part of the broader interpretation of democratisation of education in socialist Cuba.

Primary education undoubtedly progressed in many directions during this first period, with greatest emphasis being placed on enrolment as the key variable for measuring the democratisation of access. However, what happened in the schools and how long the students remained there became sources of increasing anxiety to Cuba's educational and political leaders. In particular, the low internal efficiency and quality of primary schooling were reflected in the recurrent problems of high rates of drop-out and repetition. Indeed, during the first five years of the Revolution, a drop-out rate

Fig. 1:   Basic Yearly Data on Primary Education, 1958-1972

ACADEMIC YEAR	TOTAL PRIMARY			URBAN PRIMARY			RURAL PRIMARY		
	Schools	Teachers	Enrolment	Schools	Teachers	Enrolment	Schools	Teachers	Enrolment
1958-59	7 567	17 355	717 417	2 678	12 019	500 567	4 889	5 336	226 850
1959-60	10 381	24 443	1 092 264	2 026	14 135	631 881	8 355	10 308	460 383
1960-61	12 248	29 924	1 136 277	2 943	15 812	653 320	9 305	14 112	482 957
1961-62	12 843	33 916	1 166 267	2 709	19 272	646 497	10 134	14 644	519 770
1962-63	13 780	36 613	1 207 286	2 643	20 752	651 841	11 146	15 816	555 445
1963-64	13 845	37 041	1 280 664	2 656	21 171	712 973	11 189	15 870	567 691
1964-65	13 999	38 473	1 323 925	2 604	22 155	756 370	11 395	16 318	567 555
1965-66	14 141	41 922	1 321 768	2 599	24 988	748 423	11 542	16 934	573 345
1966-67	14 442	43 056	1 353 899	2 632	25 760	775 024	11 810	17 296	578 875
1967-68	14 568	46 910	1 391 597	2 440	28 406	805 852	12 128	18 504	585 745
1968-69	14 806	48 642	1 457 217	2 454	30 069	855 301	12 352	18 573	601 916
1969-70	15 012	55 854	1 558 145	2 520	34 154	926 240	12 492	21 700	631 905
1970-71	15 190	60 592	1 664 634	2 607	36 091	994 693	12 585	24 501	669 941
1971-72	15 369	65 189	1 759 161	2 638	38 025	1 053 549	12 731	27 164	705 618

Sources: 1.   Cuba, JUCEPLAN, Dirección Central de Estadística (1970), Compendio Estadístico de Cuba, Tables XII.1-XII.5, pp. 212-220 (in Dahlman (1973), op. cit., p. 68). 2. Cuba, Comité Estatal de Estadísticas (1980), Anuario Estadístico de Cuba, Table 10, p. 219.

of about 80 per cent was recorded between each cohort starting
first grade and reaching sixth grade.[23]   Negotiating the
first grade proved to be a major stumbling block for many
pupils, although as the 1960's progressed, a larger proportion
of students managed to get through the first few grades.
However, if high drop-out rates were to be expected during the
initial phase of rapid, massive growth, the persistence of
high drop-out levels in the late 1960's and early 1970's
clearly showed that problems of internal efficiency were far
from resolution.   For example, of the 387,000 pupils who enrolled in the first primary grade in 1965/66, only 124,000
survived to enrol in the sixth grade and of these, only 82,300
graduated;   that is to say, only 21.3 per cent of the original
enrolment.   Furthermore, this national rate hid the fact that
urban schools enjoyed a cohort graduation rate of 34.2 per
cent for that year while rural schools could only graduate
11.7 per cent.[24]   Repetition also remained a severe problem:
in 1971/72, over half the children enrolled in primary schools
were over-age repeaters.[25]

Clearly, regular promotion from one primary grade to
another and eventual graduation after six years were exceptional rather than typical in Cuba's much expanded educational
system.   Despite the large investment of educational inputs
and despite some headway in terms of initial enrolment and
attendance, the whole democratisation programme of universalising primary schooling was being undermined.   It was becoming
clear that democratisation of access had to involve progress
through, as well as enrolment in, schools.   This, in turn,
demanded that the problems of low quality, especially in
respect of teachers, and poor internal efficiency be solved as
quickly as possible, for the pressure of numbers at primary
levels could only increase given the high birth-rate of the
1960's.[26]

The national obsession with the 1970 sugar harvest probably distracted attention from many other problems, including
those in education.   With the failure of the harvest and the
strategy it represented, a mood of self-criticism swept
through the entire revolutionary leadership and educational
performance came under sharper scrutiny.   Various options
were in principle available.   With the opportunity costs of
the hugh expansion of education being considerable, one possible alternative was to pull back from rapid growth at lower
educational levels and to adopt a more gradual approach, with
less risk of qualitative damage.   On the other hand, instead
of mass education, a stronger promotion of the training of
high-level manpower could have become the chief focus of
educational policy.   Cuba's leaders, however, saw no inevitable incompatibility between these options and, with renewed
determination, set out to solve the crisis in education by
fighting on several fronts simultaneously.   In so doing, the
leadership reconfirmed its commitment to the democratisation

of education from the bottom up.   Of course, this decision
also made good political sense, since the people's expectations had already been raised.

The policy of democratising education was not in serious
jeopardy, however, for additional reasons.   One lesson
derived from the sugar harvest failure, the danger of taking
short cuts, alerted Cuba's leaders to the need to rethink the
tempo and time-scale of revolutionary change, especially
regarding the transformation of the consciousness of ordinary
Cubans.   The creation of the 'new man', it was acknowledged,
would be a long-term process of education, socialisation and
ideological immersion.   The role of formal education in this
process would be vital, but schooling was also expected to
make a contribution yielding more immediate results.   If the
creation of the 'new man' was put on the 'back burner', a
hotter flame would be applied to the process of economic
development.   Of special importance for the success of this
process would be the regular supply of trained manpower at all
levels.   Bottled up within the primary schools were large
numbers of young people whose energies and abilities had to be
developed and made available either for immediate useful
employment or for additional education and training.   It was
recognised, therefore, that greater success in the democratisation of education was indispensable for the attempt to overcome underdevelopment and to move towards a more advanced
social system.   This meant: accommodating larger enrolments;
securing qualitative improvements and higher levels of internal efficiency;   and facilitating student flow through the
educational system.   However, more rather than less investment in education would be required to achieve this success.
Out of this predicament came Castro's solution: 'the application of the principle of universal study is possible only to
the extent that work is also made universal'.[27]   Thus, if
education was to be free and open to all, this democratisation
had to be paid for.   It had to be paid for not only through
the quantity and quality of the educational system's output of
human capital but also through the actual productive output of
students from the primary school onwards.   In this way, the
two leading themes of the first period, quantitative expansion
and the search for educational forms suited to the Revolution,
came together in the early 1970's.

Phase Two: 1971/72-1980/81

The main features of the second phase are as follows:
continued expansion of enrolments not only at the primary
level but also, and especially, at secondary levels of schooling;   considerable improvements in the internal efficiency of
Cuba's schools and greater continuity or flow between one
cycle, level, or type of education and another, both of these
developments helping to produce a different enrolment pyramid;

the universalisation of some form of combination of study and
productive work; a radical reform of the entire educational
system in accordance with 'the methodological and organisational principles of socialist pedagogy';[28] and a closer
relationship between educational output and the manpower needs
of a planned economy. Clearly, there has been a mixture of
quantitative and qualitative changes.

Two public events mark the end of the first phase and the
beginning of the second phase of the democratisation of Cuban
education. On the one hand, the First National Congress of
Education and Culture was held in 1971 and during its proceed-
ings numerous deficiencies in the educational system were
highlighted, including the maintenance of an old-fashioned
curriculum; inefficiency in the organisation of the school
system and in the use of time; poor levels of teacher preparation coupled with teacher shortages; the use of outdated,
ideologically inappropriate texts; poor co-ordination; a
failure to keep up with scientific-technological developments;
enrolment bulges in primary schools caused mainly by late
starters and over-age repeaters; and the unsatisfactory operation of the 'school to the countryside' scheme.

On the other hand, official disenchantment with educational performance could have received no clearer expression
than Castro's speech at the Second Congress of the Young
Communists in April 1972. Amongst other things, Castro
criticised the failure of the schools to produce enough graduates oriented towards the sorts of skills and careers most
needed for economic development. He also drew sharp attention to the problems of attendance, drop-out and repetition,
the small proportion of teachers who were suitably trained,
and the inadequate level of consciousness of many students as
revealed by their attitudes and behaviour. Castro's speech
alerted everyone in Cuba, but especially the educational
bureaucracy and teachers, to the necessity of a major educational shake-up. Soon after, a systematic process of educational diagnosis and prognosis was begun, orchestrated by the
Ministry of Education, with help and advice from Cuban and
East European educational specialists.

The Plan de Perfeccionamiento del Sistema Nacional de
Educación (the Improvement Plan of the National System of
Education) which emerged from this process was put into operation through Ministerial Resolutions issued in April 1975 and
October 1976.[29] The Improvement Plan was to be fully implemented during the six years ending in the 1980/81 school year.
The process of formulating and implementing the Plan occurred
during a period of intense debate and extensive change concerning the direction of the Revolution, the functioning of
the economy, and the institutional structure of the state.
Crucial events and developments were the adoption of the
socialist principle of distribution at the Thirteenth Congress
of the Confederation of Cuban Workers (CTC) in 1973; the

Education and Revolution in Socialist Cuba:
The Promise of Democratisation

First Congress of the Cuban Communist Party (PCC) in 1975; the adoption of a new Constitution, the inauguration of the new political system of Poder Popular (People's Power), and the installation of a new political-administrative division of the country; acceptance, after much public discussion of the Family Code; and the application of the new System of Economic Management and Planning.

So great and far-reaching were the educational changes introduced by the Improvement Plan and stimulated by the wider institutionalisation process that Casas,[30] following Castro's lead, has described them as a 'revolution' in education, though 'radical reform' seems a more acceptable term.   The Minister of Education Fernández has described the Plan in these terms:

> 'The transformations produced in the Cuban educational system... are not simple quantitative modifications, nor partial reforms, nor equivalent to a substitution of antiquated teaching methods by other more modern ones; they represent, in reality, deep changes in the education of the new generations.   The essence, objectives and goal of education have been radically transformed.'[31]

While the fundamental objective of the Improvement Plan was 'to make education conform to the society we are building',[32] that is, the construction of socialism, it was designed in such a way as to carry the democratisation of education into a higher stage of achievement and success in association with other educational policies shaped by the same basic purpose.

Changes attributable mainly to the Improvement Plan include the following: the introduction of over 1,350 new school programmes;   the thorough revision of curricula and of hundreds of textbooks and teachers' manuals;   the application of new teaching methods and evaluation techniques, with more emphasis upon the encouragement of independent student learning, better use of teaching materials, and the clarification of teaching and learning objectives;   the reorganisation of the structure and cycles of schooling with a view to improving the acquisition of basic skills and the sequence of learning, especially in scientific subjects;   the achievement of a smoother flow through the educational system, with fewer bulges induced by poor promotion and graduation rates;   the improvement of the quality of schooling through the up-grading and training of teaching staff;[33] rapid school construction, especially to cope with increased enrolments at secondary levels,[34] and to pay for all this, an increase in the state budget allocation to education from 350 million pesos in 1971/72 to 1,340.8 million pesos in 1980/81.[35]   Through these and related quantitative and qualitative changes, the democratisation of education in Cuba has overcome many, though not all, of the problems evident in the 1960's.

Perhaps the most noteworthy indication of substantial progress in the democratisation of Cuban education during this period is the change in the enrolment pyramid, from an extremely broad-based shape to one resembling those to be found in more developed countries. (See Fig. 2)

Fig. 2: The Cuban Enrolment Pyramid (Enrolment Percentages in Primary, Secondary and Higher Education, Selected Years)

Sector/Years	1959-60	1975-76	1982-83
Higher	2.2	3.2	6.0
Secondary	7.8	23.9	40.4
Primary	90.0	72.9	53.6

Source: Jiménez, G. (1984), Current Total Enrolment: 3 Times Greater than 1959, Granma Weekly Review, January 29.

- - - - -

The slimming down of primary enrolments derived partly from a reduced birth-rate following the 1960's baby boom and partly from greater internal efficiency bringing the disappearance of the bulge in primary enrolment caused by low promotion and graduation rates. Close to 100 per cent enrolment and attendance rates for the 6-12 years age-group are now regularly recorded, promotion rates now reach 93 per cent, and improved graduation rates are reflected in the fact that between 1975/76 and 1979/80, over 1,290,000 pupils graduated from the sixth grade, 3,000 more than during the first fifteen years of the Revolution.[36] Primary enrolment peaked at 1,801,191 in 1974/75 and has fallen regularly ever since, to 1,468,538 in 1980/81.[37]

The changed shape of the enrolment pyramid also reflects the growth of intermediate education and university enrolments during the 1970's (see Fig. 3). This in turn reflects the guarantee by the government, as part of its commitment to educational democratisation, of continuity of schooling at post-primary levels. The expansion of intermediate education points to improvements in internal efficiency at this level too, though not quite to the same degree as primary schooling. Thus, by 1981, 84 per cent of 13-16 year-olds were enrolled in some type of secondary school,[38] though drop-out and repetition problems have not been totally eliminated. A ninth grade of education, however, has been effectively guaranteed.

Fig. 3: Enrolment in Intermediate Education, 1971/72-1980/81

School Year	Basic Secondary	Pre-University	Teacher Training	Technical-Vocational	Total
1971-72	186 115	15 695	50 040	30 429	282 279
1972-73	200 448	22 033	59 980	41 940	324 401
1973-74	239 437	26 152	72 996	59 959	398 544
1974-75	307 209	30 315	88 137	94 634	520 295
1975-76	382 643	37 672	94 229	114 653	629 197
1976-77	485 878	49 231	111 500	159 440	806 049
1977-78	556 845	88 743	123 684	194 032	963 304
1978-79	645 944	113 344	116 737	198 261	1 074 286
1979-80	690 503	135 349	109 905	214 615	1 150 372
1980-81	677 590	159 671	112 065	228 487	1 177 813

Source: Cuba, Comité Estatal de Estadísticas (1980), Anuario Estadístico de Cuba, 1980.
Cuadros 7, 11, 12, 13.

Clearly, to accommodate the huge increase in secondary
enrolments, a corresponding investment of human and material
resources was needed.   Initial ambitions of housing all basic
secondary and pre-university students in 'schools in the
countryside' were not realised, however, largely for economic
reasons.[39]   Similarly, the rate of growth of secondary enrolment outpaced the government's ability to supply scholarships,
especially during a period of growing economic difficulty.[40]
Nevertheless, the regime deserves much credit for the way it
managed to ensure continuity of schooling despite several
handicaps.   Of crucial importance was the supply of teachers
to staff the new secondary schools.   Many of the new teachers
were pre-university students in the Manuel Ascunce Domenech
Detachment, who taught basic secondary pupils whilst they
pursued their own studies and undertook in-service training
courses.   At a mass graduation ceremony in July 1981, 10,653
members of the Detachment received their teaching certifi-
cates.[41]   Without these student-teacher volunteers, it is unlikely that the growth of secondary education and the guarantee of continuity could have been secured.   However, the use
of young, under-trained teachers may have compromised some of
the qualitative improvements sought by the Improvement Plan.
      Important changes also occurred at the university level,
with enrolment increasing from 36,877 in 1971/72 to 151,733 in
1980/81 and the university share of total educational enrolment rising to about 6 per cent.   About half this enrolment
was comprised of workers taking preparation courses under
university auspices.   The policy of universalising the university involved not only the 'intellectualisation of the
workers' but also the 'proletarianisation of the students',
who were required to engage in some form of productive work
for twenty hours per week, thereby repaying part of the cost
of their education.
      In general, by the close of the second period, the demo-
cratisation of Cuban education was showing real results,
though problems and shortcomings remained.   The 1981 census
revealed an average educational level of 6.4 years of schooling and an illiteracy rate of only 1.9 per cent of the 10-49
year-old population 'apt for study'.[42]   With regard to the
problem of drop-out and repetition at primary level, it is now
being confidently asserted that:

> 'The number of students behind in their schooling has
> been reduced significantly and we can now say that it
> does not exist as a social phenomenon.'[43]

Continuity of study beyond the sixth grade was guaranteed
and the universalisation of at least basic secondary schooling
was being achieved, with the 'battle for the ninth grade'
being the next target of the adult education system.   Some
indication of how the educational level of the population has

changed over the period of the last three national censuses
can be seen in Fig. 4.   Using 1953 census data and a Cuban
pre-census survey of 1979, Brundenius has painted the following slightly different but helpful picture: (See also Fig. 5)

> '... the illiteracy rate decreased from 23.9 per cent to
> 5.6 per cent, the share of the population having more
> than six years of schooling increased from one-fourth to
> almost two-thirds; and the most spectacular growth
> occurred in the category having more than nine years of
> education, which increased from 6 per cent to 41 per
> cent.'[44]

Phase Three: 1980/81 onwards

While much remains to be done, the scheduled implementation of the Improvement Plan by the 1980/81 school year serves
as a convenient point of division for identifying the third
phase of the educational revolution in general and the democratisation of education in particular.

Cuba's educational leaders expect the most distinguishing
feature of the third phase will be the 'qualitative development' of education.   What they have in mind is that, through
an on-going struggle between the old and the new on the level
of ideas, methods and practice, the Cuban educational system
will not only improve but also change its character into one
which more fully expresses its socialist foundation and
orientation.[45] They are aware that the emergence of this new
kind of education will depend largely upon the capacity of
Cuba's teachers to thoroughly absorb and then put into operation the principles of socialist pedagogy.[46]   This will not
only involve a large amount of formal ideological training in
Marxism-Leninism but it will also demand that all teaching and
learning, from the top to the bottom of the educational system,
will be suffused with the Marxist-Leninist world view. It is
open to debate, of course, whether this process of 'qualitative development' will lead to the creation of a 'new man' as
conceived by Guevara and Castro in the 1960's, or even of a
'new bureaucratised man'.

As part of the struggle for 'qualitative development', a
number of educational changes and trends are likely to emerge
in coming years.   For example, the number of primary school
enrolments and sixth grade graduations will not be repeated,
for several reasons.   The Cuban birth-rate has declined
considerably, in fact down to 1.1 per cent per annum according
to the 1981 census, and sustained improvement in internal
efficiency means that bulges in enrolment due to drop-out and
repetition are unlikely to recur.   Similarly, the expansion
of enrolment at basic secondary level has already peaked, but
growth in enrolment and graduation is to be expected at pre-
university and technical-vocational levels.   The expansion of

Fig. 4: Population Six Years Old or Over According to School Level
(According to 1953, 1970 and 1981 Censuses)

School Level	Population (000)			Percentage		
	1953	1970	1981	1953	1970	1981
Sixth Grade and below	4396.2	6019.9	5232.5	89.0	84.5	59.2
General Intermediate	491.2	1000.4	3316.3	9.9	14.0	37.6
Higher	53.5	80.1	288.0	1.1	1.1	3.2
Not given	-	28.7	-	-	0.4	-
TOTAL	4940.9	7129.1	8836.8	100	100	100

Source: Granma Weekly Review, December 18, 1983

enrolment at Cuba's universities may serve to characterise
this period just as primary level expansion did the first
phase and intermediate level expansion did the second. However, university growth is most unlikely to proceed to levels
comparable to those reached lower down the educational ladder.
The expense of university training, especially in science and
technology, will be prohibitive, and creating facilities and
providing qualified teachers to cope with the baby boom cohort
would soon lead to wasteful overcapacity once it had passed
through. None the less, the expansion of university enrolment will test the strength of the government's commitment to
guarantee continuity of schooling. Finally, the field of
adult education has witnessed several 'once-and-for-all'
accomplishments such as the attainment by a large proportion
of the population of functional literacy and a sixth grade
education. By 1990, it is anticipated that the average educational level in Cuba will be nine years of schooling.

Cuba's educational system will continue to be the scene
of a battle for greater quality. This battle will be fought
on two fronts: internal efficiency and external efficiency.
The former will require further improvement in the quality of
teachers through a more rigorous process of preparation and
in-service training in teaching method, a better grounding in
the theory and practice of socialist pedagogy, and greater
insistence that teachers exhibit a demanding attitude,
encourage high standards, and develop the all-round educational work of the school. Internal efficiency improvements will
also demand better school buildings and facilities; better
student discipline and behaviour; the maintenance of high
standards of promotion and graduation; and the application of
more advanced learning strategies which require more independent learning and more school activities involving experimental
methods and problem-solving.[47]

External efficiency, on the other hand, will be measured
by the output of the educational system in terms of students'
entry into higher educational levels or into employment where
further skill training will permit greater contributions to be
made to social and economic development. Of particular
importance will be the forging of stronger links between
schools and various types of productive work units and the
closer integration of educational enrolment and graduation
patterns (for example, in technical-vocational and scientific
areas), manpower requirements, and economic planning. One
field deserving more analysis will be the relationship between
higher levels of education and training and increases in work-
place productivity.[48] In addition, the question of schooling's external efficiency is likely to figure in the aforementioned export of human capital as Cuba seeks to realise the
ambition to become a world educational power.

Problems, of course, continue to stand in the way of these
improvements, some of a subjective kind such as old-fashioned

teacher attitudes, others of a more objective nature such as
material shortages and socio-cultural patterns which still
give rise to drop-out, repetition and behavioural difficulties.[49] A clearer perspective on the various challenges
facing Cuban education will hopefully emerge from the following section, which examines how certain social sectors have
been affected by the educational revolution and the democratisation of education during the past twenty-five years.

THE DEMOCRATISATION OF CUBAN EDUCATION: MAIN SOCIAL TARGETS

> 'I consider myself the best friend of the poor man, the
> best friend of the Cuban campesino, the best friend of
> the workers, the unemployed and the thousands of bare-
> foot children, without teachers or schools, the best
> friend of the discriminated black and the best friend of
> the discriminated woman too.'[50]

In this early, rather populistic statement, Castro
identified the particular social groups destined to become the
key targets of Cuba's social and educational revolution. The
revolutionary era began with policies being defined mainly in
terms of getting rid of various inequalities and injustices
inherited from the old regime. It was only later that a more
positive, coherent formulation of, say, educational goals and
pedagogical methods were worked out satisfactorily in terms of
'building socialism'. However, the continuity of the leadership's commitment to egalitarian policies is clear, although,
as we shall see, this commitment has been constrained by
numerous forces.[51]
In terms of the educational revolution, the members of
Cuba's disadvantaged social sectors have benefited primarily
from the general policy of educational democratisation through
increases in access, provision and continuity of study in the
national system of free public schooling. The removal of
discriminatory barriers has further promoted equality of
educational opportunity for these groups. In addition, broad
egalitarian policies have helped to limit, but not eliminate,
the socio-economic inequalities which tend to adversely affect
the educational rights and performance of certain sectors of
society. A comprehensive analysis of the social impact of
the democratisation of Cuban education is beyond the scope of
this chapter. Consequently, certain critical issues and
achievements will be selected for discussion, with an emphasis
on more recent post-revolutionary developments.

Race and the Democratisation of Cuban Education

Before the Revolution, despite constitutional guarantees
supposedly in operation, the educational rights and opportunities of Cuba's black and mulatto population were sharply

limited due to racial discrimination and prejudice in conjunction with other disadvantages, especially those based on social
class.   On the basis of census data, however, Masferrer and
Mesa-Lago have concluded that during the half-century prior to
the Revolution, 'the rate of literacy among blacks was gradually increasing and the gap between whites and blacks was
decreasing slowly'.[52]   Nevertheless, there can be little
doubt that the pre-revolutionary level of racial disadvantage
was very high, as is indicated by the types of occupation
which education, or lack of education, prepared blacks and
mulattoes for.   Mesa-Lago, interpreting the 1943 census,
found that:

> '... non-white workers (predominantly Negroes and mulat-
> toes) were consistently under-represented in occupations
> requiring advanced training (e.g. medicine, law, banking)
> but were over-represented in low-skill occupations (e.g.
> domestic services).' [53]

In 1959, the new revolutionary government came to power
intent upon removing all forms of open racial discrimination,
especially that which had afflicted the educational system.
However, very little information is available concerning race
and education in contemporary Cuba.   The Cuban authorities
have been rather sensitive about the race question and noticeably reluctant to publish hard data on this matter.   On the
other hand, they have not been reticent in proclaiming the end
of open racial discrimination, the equalisation of educational
opportunity regardless of racial origin, and the success of
the schools as the main agency for transforming social relations through the cultivation of values, attitudes and behaviours free from racial prejudice.   Children and young people
from different races mix together in all educational settings,
from day-care centres onwards, and it is felt that such educational institutions as the boarding schools in the countryside
allow racial mixing and equal treatment to take place in ways
which can offset the possibly adverse effects of the home and
community social environment.   However, the actual social
impact of these policies and schemes is unclear despite the
claims and assurances routinely offered by Cuban educators.
For example, as Paulston says: 'we know next to nothing from
field research about the effectiveness of their educational
programmes in changing behaviours'.[54]
     Nevertheless, blacks and mulattoes have undoubtedly
benefited from the Revolution's egalitarian policies, particularly the democratisation of education:

> 'The campaign against illiteracy proved to be particular-
> ly beneficial to blacks, because they constituted the
> largest illiterate group.   The establishment of compul-
> sory elementary education;   the expansion of elementary,

secondary and boarding school facilities; the increased
number of scholarships granted to black children - all
aided in improving noticeably the educational level of
this group.'[55]

Alongside these clear advances, however, are certain
regrettable question marks. According to the 1981 census,
for example, whites constitute 66 per cent, blacks 12 per cent,
mulattoes 21.9 per cent and Asians 0.1 per cent of the Cuban
population.[56] On past experience, however, no correlations
between race and such indicators as literacy or years of
schooling will be forthcoming from the Cuban authorities.
Pérez has noted that 'no data on race and education from the
1970 census have ever been released',[57] though such data were
collected. In this way, Cuba leaves itself open to such
damning interpretations as that offered by Pérez regarding
the 1970 census:

'Perhaps the cross-tabulation of the figures on race and
education did not show the expected elimination of racial
differentials in educational attainment that has been a
major goal of the revolutionary government's redistributive educational program since 1960. This explanation
remains the only apparent reason for the suppression of
the data on race and education.'[58]

Questions might also be raised about whether improvements
in educational levels and qualifications have been translated
into progress by non-whites up the occupational ladder. Mesa-
Lago has suggested that the pattern of under and over representation in certain occupations and income categories has not
been fundamentally changed.[57] Domínguez also observes that
non-whites are not well represented in the country's top
political leadership and no symbolic representation has been
accorded to race as it has been to, say, sex in the Central
Committee of the Communist Party.[60]
As a consequence of factors such as these, one is left
with the feeling that the solution of the race question in
Cuba is partly a 'solution-by-definition' as well as a substantive achievement.

Women and the Democratisation of Cuban Education

To avoid duplicating other analyses, this examination of
women and education since 1959 will focus upon recent developments, especially as they relate to female employment.
Some measure of women's expanded educational opportunities and achievements under the Revolution can be found in the
following data. In 1980, 47.2 per cent of the enrolment in
the entire educational system were women: that is 1,570,000
out of 3,350,000. Though slightly less than women's

proportion of the total population, shown to be 49.4 per cent
in the 1981 census, this share of educational enrolment
represents a great accomplishment.   This is further illustrated by the distribution of female students: in primary
education, the female proportion was the same as that in the
general population;   women constituted 50.1 per cent of enrolment in intermediate education, 42.2 per cent in technical-
vocational education, 38.3 per cent in adult education, and
42.2 per cent in higher education.   Between 1974/75 and
March 1979, over 162,000 housewives graduated from the 'battle
for the sixth grade'.[61]   According to data supplied to
UNESCO, female enrolment in technical-vocational education
rose from 19.8 per cent in 1970 to 46.3 per cent in 1981, a
growth in absolute terms from 5,448 to 91,256 female students.[62]   Female enrolment in higher education rose from 39.4
per cent in 1970 to 48.4 per cent in 1981, an increase from
10,366 to 73,413 female students.[63]   Finally, female literacy
levels have also improved, though slightly more slowly than
those of men.   The 1970 census revealed a male illiteracy
rate of 13.5 per cent and a female rate of 12.4 per cent while
in 1979, in the population aged ten and over, the male illiteracy rate was 4.3 per cent and the female rate was 4.9 per
cent.[64]

On the basis of these educational advances and other
social changes, recent years have witnessed a dramatic penetration of the Cuban labour force by women.   Brundenius has
provided a useful analysis of these trends.   According to his
calculations, the female labour force grew from 13.2 per cent
in 1960 to 18.3 per cent in 1970 and to 31.1 per cent in 1979;
an absolute increase from 482,000 to 1,075,000 between 1970
and 1979.   During the same 1970-79 period, 671,000 jobs were
added to the economy and women took up 470,000 of these, that
is 70 per cent.   Consequently, women's share of the employed
labour force grew from 18.3 per cent in 1970 to 28.9 per cent
in 1979, an absolute growth from 476,000 to 946,000.[65]   For
Brundenius, this 'spectacular growth' derived from 'the expansion of educational opportunities for both sexes without
discrimination' and from greater motivation for women to work:

> 'With greater material incentives (in terms of both money
> and supply of durable consumer goods) and increased
> childcare facilities, the young Cuban women leaving the
> educational system in the 1970's have found stronger
> motivation to go out and work.'[66]

Brundenius shows, furthermore, that 'female workers are
substantially better educated than males', as is illustrated
in Fig. 5.   He explains this finding in the following way:

> '... if we recall that the female labour force is much
> younger, the rapid inflow of females graduating from the

Fig. 5: Educational Level of the Population and Labour Force: 1953 and 1979 (in percentages)

Educational Profile	Percentage of the Population having achieved Level of Education		Percentage of Employed Labour Force having achieved Level of Education		
	1953	1979	1979		
	Both Sexes (Pop. over 15)	Both Sexes (Pop. over 14)	Both Sexes	Males	Females
University Education	1.4	3.3	4.5	4.0	5.7
At least 12 years	3.6	18.7	21.6	17.7	31.3
At least 9 years	6.0	41.4	48.4	43.4	60.7
At least 6 years	25.4	65.3	71.8	68.1	80.9
Less than 6 years	74.6	34.7	28.2	31.9	19.1
Illiterates	23.9	5.6	4.0	3.7	4.2

Sources: Censo de Población, Viviendras y Electoral (1953). Encuesta Demográfica Nacional (1979)

educational system makes it quite natural that the average level of education is higher among women.'[67]

Various issues and problems, however, have arisen at the
interface between women's education, work, social participation and leadership.   For example, though some diversification of women's employment patterns has undoubtedly occurred
and this is in no small measure due to expanded educational
opportunities, women still seem to be gravitating towards
occupations with which they have been traditionally associated.   Thus, about two-thirds of all educational workers are
women.   The 1953 census showed that about 80 per cent of all
teachers were women; while that proportion has declined today,
72 per cent of primary school teachers in 1975/76 were female
and this proportion rose to 77 per cent in 1981/82.[68]
Brundenius notes that nearly two-thirds of the new female
workers appearing between 1970 and 1979 were absorbed by the
service sector and many of these new service sector jobs were
in education and health.[69]   However, despite these tendencies
and despite the fact that some occupational categories have
been barred to women, the net expansion of employment opportunities for women is significant as is the limited occupational diversification which has occurred.   In both cases, the
democratisation of education has played a vital role.

Discriminatory practices and outcomes, however, are not
difficult to find in Cuba today.   For example, young women
may have to outperform males academically in order to gain
access to the same courses of study or professions.   This
clearly emerged during the recruitment process for the initial
entry to the Carlos J. Finlay Medical Sciences Detachment.
As the selection process unfolded, it was found that if
academic performance was the deciding factor, then 67 per cent
of the successful applicants would be female.   Such an outcome, however, was unacceptable.   On the basis of pragmatic
and sexist arguments, a ratio of 55-45 in favour of female
applicants was decided upon; later revised to 52-48.   The
effect of this, however, was to make the academic average of
the successful female applicants 92.51 per cent and that of
the successful male applicants 91.05 per cent.[70]

Another disparity is that the occupations and economic
sectors tending to attract large numbers of female workers do
not enjoy high wage rates.[71]   Also, female members of the
labour force have had to suffer higher rates of unemployment
than men.   In 1979, for example, the female share of the unemployed section of the total labour force was 68.6 per cent,
an average national unemployment rate of 5.4 per cent divided
into a 2.5 per cent rate for men and a 12 per cent rate for
women.[72]   Such disparities reinforce the view that 'women
in Cuba are used as a labour reserve' and that female employment is more insecure, being largely dependent on the needs of
national economic development.   Male employment, being

guaranteed, is not so vulnerable.[73]   In addition, women are
under represented in leadership positions at work, in the
political and mass organisations, and in the political system
of Poder Popular.[74]   The government has recognised the disparity and has committed itself to improving women's acces-
sion to leadership roles, but progress has been slow.

Thus, despite many advances, full female equality has not
been achieved in Cuba.   Part of the explanation lies in the
durability of sexist attitudes amongst many Cuban men and
women, notwithstanding the adoption of the 'Family Code'.
Moreover, Cuba has not been able to develop the material base
which would free women for greater social participation.   In
educational terms, this material base would include the provision of day-care centres, scholarships and boarding and
semi-boarding schools.   But in all these areas the government has been unable to satisfy demand;   for example, the
projected construction of day-care centres in the 1975/76-
1979/80 Economic Plan was under achieved by 21.4 per cent.[75]
In recent years, government performance has been handicapped
by severe economic problems, mushrooming enrolments and
other investment needs.   Finally, women's continued inequality partly derives from the choice of development strategy
and certain policy decisions which, in effect if not in
intent, have limited female opportunities.   The adoption of
the socialist principle of distribution, for example, may
have made many women more dependent on their husbands' income whereas implementation of the communist principle of
distribution, based on need rather than ability to pay, might
have reduced this dependence by socialising the provision of
childcare.[76]

In, sum, Cuba's educational revolution and the democratisation of education have prepared many women for more advanced
social participation and responsibilities than the society
can, or will, deliver.   How women respond to this situation
in coming years will be one of the key trends within the
revolutionary process.

Spatial Policy and the Democratisation of Cuban Education

Educational policy, especially the democratisation of
education, has been closely involved with serious attempts to
reduce territorial inequalities in social, economic and
cultural conditions and to break down the separation of town
and country in Cuba.   The main type of territorial inequality, of course, was the huge urban-rural disparity, which was
reflected in the great educational disadvantages suffered by
rural areas before 1959.

With the Revolution came a many-pronged attack on rural
inequalities, spearheaded by the agrarian reforms of 1959 and
1963 which transformed the pattern of land ownership.   A
series of redistributive and developmental policies extended

and deepened the process of rural transformation. Efforts
were made to modernise Cuban agriculture and to increase and
diversify agricultural production; agricultural rents were
abolished; year-round employment was guaranteed to rural
workers; differentials between urban and rural wages were
reduced; rationing helped to raise rural living standards;
and free social services became more widely available.

From the start, educational policy was a vital instrument
for securing rural change. Rural public primary enrolment
grew from 218,850 in 1958/59 to 460,383 a year later. The
number of rural schools rapidly increased, from 4,889 in 1958/
59 to 8,355 in 1959/60, to 10,134 in 1961/62. The number of
rural teachers showed a dramatic improvement, growing from
5,336 in 1958/59 to over 10,000 a year later and to 14,644 in
1961/62.[77] In addition, special teacher-training schemes
were devised to equip new teachers with skills and orientations needed for rural teaching placements. Little growth of
rural secondary schooling occurred in the 1960's but rural
fifth and sixth grade graduates were provided with opportunities to continue their schooling by transferring to schools in
urban areas or other provinces. Finally, the Literacy
Campaign was very much a rural affair and, despite many
obstacles, follow-up programmes were set up in rural zones.

None the less, the quality of rural schooling left much
to be desired. Many of the new schools were crudely built,
multi-grade, and lacking in basic facilities. Many new rural
teachers were inexperienced and under-prepared: in 1968/69,
the rural sector received only 16 per cent of Cuba's professional teachers but had 65.3 per cent of the barely trained
maestros populares (popular teachers).[78] Student-teacher
ratios were higher in rural schools, as were drop-out and
repetition rates, and less hours of instruction were offered
during the rural school year. Nevertheless, despite such
weaknesses, going to school became part of the pattern of
rural children's lives; the reduction in rural illiteracy,
furthermore, was considerable.

In the 1970's, progress in rural schooling saw the near
total enrolment of rural school-age children in primary
schools, whose internal efficiency improved noticeably.
Primary enrolments and the number of schools and teachers
eventually declined during this decade in response largely to
demographic changes and migration. Rural primary schools
continued to be small and under-equipped, with a smaller staff
of teachers on average compared with urban primary schools;
however, from 1970/71 onwards, student-teacher ratios were
consistently lower in the rural establishments.[79] Rural
secondary education grew considerably in the 1970's, largely
but not wholly through the 'schools in the countryside' programme which did much to guarantee continuity of schooling to
rural sixth grade graduates. A number of agricultural
schools were built and enrolments increased, especially after

Education and Revolution in Socialist Cuba:
The Promise of Democratisation

Castro's speech to the Young Communists in 1972. An important development in higher education has been the decentralisation of university centres, there are now 42, making higher
studies more accessible to people living in rural areas.

All these changes have undoubtedly improved the provision
and availability of education in rural Cuba. In addition,
changes in the curriculum have tried to make rural schooling
more relevant to agricultural production and rural life.
Urban-rural disparities do remain, however, being partly
revealed through another aspect of Cuba's pattern of territorial inequality, regional differences. In the 1960's, for
example, urban provinces received disproportionate amounts of
certain educational investments in relation to their share of
the population. With 27 per cent of the total population,
the province of Havana accounted for 49 per cent of the value
of finished school construction while Oriente, with 34 per
cent of the population accounted for only 29 per cent.[80]
More recently, regional as well as urban-rural differences
are evident in the proportion of primary school children enjoying morning and afternoon sessions in their schools. This
proportion is notably higher in more urbanised provinces.[81]

In sum, territorial inequalities remain, though they have
been much reduced. The quality of rural schooling still has
much scope for improvement, but the universalisation of
primary education and the guarantee of schooling beyond the
sixth grade are major achievements.

Attacks on the separation of town and country have taken
many forms in modern Cuba; their educational aspects will be
examined in relation to Castro's demand for 'a minimum of
urbanism and a maximum of ruralism'. The 'ruralisation' of
Cuban education, for example, has been evident in reforms of
the urban-biased curriculum to make its content and orientation more appropriate to a country whose national wealth rests
mainly on agricultural production. The universalisation of
the combination of study and productive labour and the efforts
to overcome the division between intellectual and manual work
have typically involved agricultural labour of some kind.

If schooling throughout Cuba has in some sense been
ruralised, it is also the case that, as part of a policy of
urbanising the countryside, schools have served as injections
of modernity into rural zones. The involvement of urban
students and teachers in the Literacy Campaign, the 'school to
the countryside' scheme, and the 'school in the countryside'
scheme represents a device for reducing the gap between town
and country. The importance of this objective to Cuba's
leaders is shown in the retention of the al campo programme
for urban students, in spite of earlier criticisms when the
universalisation of the en campo scheme did not materialise
for various reasons.[82]

One feature of the 'urbanisation of the countryside' process has been the construction of new rural communities with

a basic set of services which include a primary school. Over
335 of these communities had been built by the mid-1970's,
with over 135,000 residents.[83]   Linked closely with co-operative farms, these communities serve as foci for agricultural
diversification programmes and for the extension of basic
services such as education, in the hope that the flight from
the land can be halted and that young skilled and professional people can be enticed into agricultural careers.   Incidentally, the rural communities may provide some employment
opportunities for rural women as teachers and community
organisers.[84]

In these diverse ways, education has been involved closely in the conception and implementation of spatial policy in
post-1959 Cuba.   The democratisation of education has played
a central role by furnishing concrete benefits of greater integration in the Revolution and in the national community.

Income Redistribution and the Democratisation of Cuban Education

The reduction of social inequalities based on social
class and income level has been a fundamental aim and commitment of the Revolution.   The urban and rural poor were the
primary focus of concern.   To secure an improvement in their
living standards and to win their active support, the new
revolutionary government adopted a number of strongly egalitarian policies in the 1960's which helped to bring about a
substantial redistribution of wealth and income, and a transformation of Cuba's social structure.   The agrarian reforms,
nationalisation of property, the reduction or abolition of
rents, general wage increases and price reductions, in conjunction with rationing, commodity shortages and the stress
on voluntarism and moral incentives, helped to create one of
the world's most egalitarian, even though austere, societies.
The democratisation of education through the expansion of
free educational provision and opportunities was a vital
expression of Cuba's egalitarianism.   However, this educational expansion did not lead directly to income equalisation,
which derived more from other revolutionary policies.   Instead, as Carnoy argues:

'In the Cuban Revolution, increased schooling and more
equally distributed schooling and training were ... a
necessary complement to equalised income and wealth, not
only as a service which itself has to be redistributed,
but also as an important ingredient in socialising Cubans
into the new order and preparing them for roles in the
new organisation of production.'[85]

However, the educational system has not been insulated
from changes in economic development strategy and distribution

policy which have seen inequalities in Cuba grow in recent
years.   Since 1970, there has been a clear retreat from
policies based upon egalitarian distribution, moral incentives
and improvements in worker consciousness as the best ways to
generate economic growth and higher levels of output and productivity in an underdeveloped country.   In association with
the application of the socialist principle of distribution -
from each according to his ability, to each according to his
work - various measures have been adopted which are designed
to reduce the purchasing power of Cubans in order to stimulate
greater productive efforts.   These measures include more
material incentives; closer links between wages and the quantity and quality of output; larger wage differentials; price
increases at higher rates than wage increases; greater availability of commodities and services to exemplary workers and
young professionals, but through two-tier price structures
and parallel markets; and the abolition of certain free
services.

Educational provision has been affected through changes
such as the re-imposition in August 1977 of charges for day-
care centres, fees being based on a sliding scale according
to family income;[86] the end of the free provision of school
uniforms;[87] and the sale of medical textbooks to university
students.[88] Other factors of relevance to this question are
the non-universalisation of boarding and semi-boarding
schools and reductions in the supply of scholarships.   Such
eliminations of free services and restrictions in the availability of educational facilities involving free meals,
accommodation, transport, and so forth are more likely to hurt
lower income families.   However, the communist principle of
distribution - to each according to his needs - has not been
totally abandoned in relation to the free provision of basic
social services.   In fact, these serve to 'attenuate wage
inequalities and take care of some of the workers' needs'.[89]
In comparison with some aspects of social distribution, educational provision has not suffered high levels of damage.
Thus, it is safe to say that the government's commitment to
the democratisation of education remains fundamentally intact.
It is still the case that, in Cuba, 'no person is prevented
from studying due to the lack of economic resources'.[90]   The
implications of Cuba's free education policy clearly emerge
from data furnished by the country's head planner in 1978: if
education had to be paid for, it would cost parents, in pesos
per child per month, 25 for primary school, 52 for secondary
school, 70 for technical school and 100 for university.[91]   In
the early 1980's, Mesa-Lago informs us, the median wage in
Cuba was 150 pesos per month.[92]

If the democratisation of education is basically 'a
necessary complement to equalised income and wealth' as
Carnoy contends, then does it fulfil the same function when
income distribution becomes more unequal?   There is no simple

answer, for if it is argued that a democratised education can
help to 'attenuate wage inequalities', it must also be recognised that those inequalities may be partly, even largely,
based upon credentials obtained through schooling.   In addition, MacEwan's rather casual, unsupported statement that
'there is a tendency for the sons and daughters of the highly
educated to advance most in the (educational) system'[93] does
raise further questions about the future of Cuba's educational
revolution.

CONCLUSION

The democratisation of Cuban education, in all the dimensions considered, is ultimately geared towards the creation of
a more democratic society.   Before the Revolution, many Cubans were barely integrated into national life;   they were
marginalised, powerless and alienated, and their illiteracy
and low educational levels severely restricted their participation in a wide range of social, economic and political processes.   However, through the Revolution in general and
through the democratic aspects of the educational revolution
in particular, a basic level of social mobilisation was
achieved:

'Cubans have... become available for new kinds of organisation and behaviour on a national scale: every citizen
can participate in the society, however modestly, and
every citizen can absorb some minimal level of information from the revolutionary government.'[94]

This basic level of social mobilisation, however, has
been considered inadequate for securing various objectives or
changes thought desirable.   In view of the centralisation and
complete politicisation of decision-making in socialist Cuba,
the implications of higher educational levels in the population for increases in the quality of political mobilisation
and participation demand examination.
During the 1960's, the style of 'direct democracy' in
operation in Cuba was at once a recognition of the people's
low educational standard and limited political awareness and
also an attempt to stimulate an improvement in both.   This
version of democracy had three main strands:

'the essence of democracy is the pursuit of policies that
serve the interests of the people... democracy requires
the active support of the people through their direct
participation in the implementation of public policy...
a direct, non-institutional relationship between the
people and their leaders is sufficient to ensure governmental responsiveness to popular needs and demands.'[95]

Education and Revolution in Socialist Cuba:
The Promise of Democratisation

Apart from an unsuccessful experiment called 'Local Power' (1966-68),[96] direct democracy was dominant in Cuba until the failure of the 1970 sugar harvest alerted the leadership of its misjudgement of popular opinion and of the people's readiness and capacity to engage in the revolutionary process. While not discarded, the style of implementative participation was recognised as inadequate and a more consultative form of participation was devised according to which 'the citizenry discuss and make recommendations on issues selected by the leadership'.[97] Such consultation, however, would demand improvements in the educational level of the people. Indeed, the reform and expansion of the educational system in the 1970's should be seen partly in the light of this need for information from below. This consultation, moreover required suitable channels for the upward and downward communication between the people and its leaders. The process known as the institutionalisation of the Revolution was thus set in motion.

Existing institutions such as the Party, the trade unions, and the mass organisations were revitalised, and a new political structure, <u>Poder Popular</u>, was created. The main aims of the process of institutionalisation were to obtain higher levels of élite accountability and greater popular input in the decision-making process. For example, through elections, the 'rendering of accounts' by elected delegates to their electors could be effected; likewise the popular scrutiny of the work of appointed officials and their bureaucracies. This consultative participation was clearly in evidence during the discussion of the new constitution and the Family Code, but it was also intended to function on a regular basis at municipal and provincial levels and within Cuba's organisations and enterprises. This kind of participation represented a more highly developed form of social mobilisation than existed in the 1960's. It required higher levels of educational attainment as well as a more developed consciousness of the meaning of 'building socialism'. As we have seen, the policy of democratising education began to bear fruit during the 1970's. However, according to Domínguez:

'Higher levels of educational training do not automatically produce a challenge to political authority... Education is a necessary, but not a sufficient requirement for autonomous political participation.'[98]

As Domínguez well knows, 'autonomous political participation' linked with 'a challenge to political authority' is unlikely to appear in Cuba in any form similar to Western, oppositional types of democracy. This consideration, added to his dismissal of the high levels of political consciousness in Cuba as 'highly biased in the government's favour', leads him to the conclusion that 'although there are some democratic

tendencies in Cuba, they remain constrained within a predominantly authoritarian framework'.[99]

Here, however, we must ask whether Domínguez is under-
estimating the capacity of Cuba's revolutionary process to
evolve and change within its own terms in directions which
will permit more popular control over certain areas of public
policy-making within an overall context of continued Communist
Party leadership. Might it be possible for a more educated
Cuban population to seek and obtain more substantive participation in Cuban public life? Does the potential exist, for
example, within Poder Popular, or at the level of the work-
place, for more meaningful participation to occur and will
this potential increase as the people's educational level
improves? Above all, will the country's leaders tolerate and
accept the upward communication not only of information but
also of decisions and policy initiatives?

On one level, questions such as these are premature, for
the implementation of even consultative participation has been
patchy and often disappointing. The upward flow of information, in the quantity and of the quality needed for the making
of effective decisions, has not occurred in ways which satisfy
the leadership. This is the case, for example, in factory-
level discussions of planning targets and production problems,
and it is also evident in the 'rendering of accounts' procedures within Poder Popular, which have become a sterile
formality in many instances. Many Cubans it would seem, are
content with a form of 'popular paternalism' as their system
of government. Such complacency, however, is fraught with
danger in view of the bureaucratic and technocratic tendencies
within a modernising society. As a result, while the general
educational improvement of the people may hold out some long-
term potential for democratisation, the revolutionary leadership is anxious that the rising generation of leaders is
thoroughly imbued with the spirit and values of the Revolution. If the people are to become genuine socialists, then
their leaders must be genuine communists. If the creation of
élites cannot be avoided, then they must be dedicated to
egalitarian values and policies.

There are no signs as yet that the rising educational
levels of the population will persuade the revolutionary leadership to share more of its substantive powers. However, it
seems that improvements will continue to be sought in terms of
consultative participation on the grounds of efficiency as
well as 'democracy'. Educational democratisation will play
an important role in this process for its task will be to
universalise a socialist education which will prepare Cubans
for active roles as citizens and producers. Thus, the social
impact and significance of the policy of democratising Cuban
education remain dependent on the outlook and responsiveness
of the Party and of the revolutionary leadership at its head.
All participation must take place 'within', not 'outside', the

Revolution, and it is the leadership which defines those
critical boundaries.

REFERENCES AND NOTES

1. For further analysis, see Eckstein, S. (1982), Structural
    and Ideological Bases of Cuba's Overseas Programs.
    Politics and Society, Vol. 11, No. 1, pp. 95-121.
2. On Cuba's Isle of Youth, 12,300 out of about 30,000
    children and young people are foreign; see Brittain,
    V. (1983), Cuba's island in a class of its own,
    Guardian, September 30, p. 19.
3. The vulnerability of Cuba's overseas civilian programmes
    to international events is clearly revealed in the case
    of the invasion of Grenada by the United States and by
    the constraints and pressures placed on Nicaragua,again
    by the United States, to have all Cuban personnel, in-
    cluding literacy teachers, sent home. Some indeed, did
    return to Cuba but were later replaced by more volun-
    teers, though their numbers are not known to the writer.
4. This is the basic theme of a recent article, written by
    Cuba's Minister of Education; see Fernández, J. R.
    (1983/84), La calidad de la ensenanza: tarea de
    todos, Cuba Socialista, 9, pp. 32-55.
5. Recent comparative surveys of democratisation of educa-
    tion include: International Institute of Economic
    Planning (1981), Inequalities in educational develop-
    ment: papers presented at an IIEP seminar, Paris:
    IIEP; International Bureau of Education, International
    Yearbook of Education (prepared by Robert Cowen) (1981),
    UNESCO; International Bureau of Education (1979),
    Educational documentation and information: Democratis-
    ation of higher education (prepared by George Z. F.
    Bereday), Year 53, No. 210, UNESCO.
6. Carnoy, M. and Werthein, J. (1983), Cuba: Training and
    Mobilisation, in Simmons, J. (ed.), Better Schools:
    International Lessons for Reform, Praeger, p. 197.
7. As a sign of the regime's substantive intent, Article 50
    of the 1976 Constitution actually specifies the means
    (institutions, facilities, policies) which serve to
    guarantee in practice the right to education.
8. According to Paulston, 'students are taught that new know-
    ledge and skills must be used as social capital to ad-
    vance social reform and development and not be viewed -
    as in the old days - as private capital to be accumu-
    lated for individual or family gains of status and con-
    sumption', see Paulston, R. (1980), Problems of Educa-
    tional Reform and Rural Development in Latin America:
    some Lessons from Cuba, in Avery, W. P. et al (eds.),
    Rural Change and Public Policy: Eastern Europe, Latin
    America and Australia, Pergamon Press, p. 172.

9. Gillette, A. (1972), Cuba's educational revolution,
    Fabian Research Series No. 302, p. 7.
10. Lehmann, D. (1982), Agrarian Structure, Migration and
    the State in Cuba, in Peek, P. and Standing, G. (eds.),
    State Policies and Migration. Studies in Latin
    America and the Caribbean, Croom Helm, p. 374.
11. See, for example, Bowles, S. (1971), Cuban Education and
    the Revolutionary Ideology, Harvard Educational Review,
    vol. 41, No. 4, pp. 477-482, 496-497.
12. Casas, J. (1981), Education et Développement a Cuba,
    Revue Tiers-Monde, Tome xxii, No. 85.
13. Martuza, V. (1981), Introduction - Education in Cuba:
    1961-1981. A special issue commemorating the 20th
    anniversary of Cuba's National Literacy Campaign,
    Journal of Reading, Vol. 25, No. 3, p. 198.
14. See, for example, Jolly, R. (1975), Education, in Seers
    D. (ed.), Cuba: The Economic and Social Revolution,
    Greenwood Press, esp. pp. 190-219; and Morales A. P.
    (1981), The Literacy Campaign in Cuba, Harvard Educa-
    tional Review, Vol. 51, pp. 31-39.
15. Mesa-Lago, C. (1981), The Economy of Socialist Cuba. A
    Two-Decade Appraisal, University of New Mexico Press,
    p. 164.
16. Ibid., pp. 164-65.
17. Hart, A. (1982), Speech to the ceremony marking the 20th
    anniversary of the Literacy Campaign, December 22,
    1981, Granma Weekly Review, p. 5.
18. Valdés, N. P. (1972), The Radical Transformation of Cuban
    Education, in Bonachea, R. E., and Valdés, N. P. (eds.)
    Cuba in Revolution, Doubleday, p. 431.
19. These data are taken from Paulston, R. (1971), Education,
    in Mesa-Lago, C. (ed.), Revolutionary Change in Cuba,
    University of Pittsburgh Press, p. 380.
20. In the early 1960's, Jolly found the type of primary
    teacher preparation based on 'tough romanticism',
    guerrilla-like training, familiarisation with rural
    conditions to be 'the most distinctive, almost dramatic,
    feature of formal education in Cuba'; see Jolly. R.
    (1975), op. cit., p. 237.
21. About 50 per cent of the entire teaching population in
    Cuba left for the United States during the early 1960's:
    'As willing or unwilling representatives of the pre-
    revolutionary society, many teachers found themselves
    confronted with the necessity of either radically chang-
    ing their attitudes, values and approaches to their
    profession, or of no longer being part of the school
    system and the larger society of which it was a part';
    see Provenzo, E. F. Jr., and García, C. (1983),
    Exiled Teachers and the Cuban Revolution, Cuban Studies,
    Vol. 13, No. 1, p. 2.
22. Dahlman, C. J. (1973), The Nation-Wide Learning System in

Cuba, Princeton University, p. 69.
23. Nelson, L. (1971), The School Dropout Problem in Cuba, School and Society, Vol. 99, p. 234.
24. Domínguez, J. I. (1973), Cuba. Order and Revolution, The Belknap Press of Harvard University Press, p. 171, based on Castro, F. (1972), Speech to the closing session of the Second Congress of the Young Communist League, April 4, 1972, Granma Weekly Review, April 11, pp. 1-8.
25. Paulston, R. (1980), op. cit., p. 167.
26. On the 1960's baby boom and its implications for education, see Pérez, L. (1977), The Demographic Dimension of the Education Problem in Socialist Cuba, Cuban Studies, Vol. 7, No. 1, pp. 33-57.
27. Castro, F. (1972), Speech given at the auditorium of the Central Organisation of Cuban Trade Unions on the occasion of the graduation of 2,095 students of the University of Havana on December 8, 1972, Granma Weekly Review, December 17, p. 10, quoted in Dahlman (1973), op. cit., p. 115.
28. Fernández, J. R. (1981), Speech giving a synopsis of the report to the National Assembly of People's Power, Granma Weekly Review, July 5, p. 3.
29. For a description of the principles underlying the Plan and of the new structure and content which it created, see Araujo, M. F. (1979), Políticas de Educación, Empleo y Trabajo Productivo en Cuba, UNESCO, Division of Educational Policy and Planning, pp. 13-22. For a useful, though uncritical, description of its application and results, see Chávez Rodríguez, J. A. (1982). The democratization of education in present-day Cuba, UNESCO.
30. Casas, J. (1981), op. cit., pp. 106ff.
31. Fernández, J. R. (1983-84), op. cit., p. 36.
32. Fernández J. R. (1981), op. cit., p. 3.
33. By 1980 most teachers had a professional qualification, and standards of entry to schools training primary teachers were raised to completion of the ninth grade while entry to institutes training intermediate-level teachers demanded completion of the twelth grade.
34. During the 1970's, over 1,500 new schools were built, including 533 'schools in the countryside' for basic secondary and pre-university students.
35. This summary is based mainly on Fernández, J. R. (1980), Interview, Granma Weekly Review, pp. 2-4; Fernández, J. R. (1981), op. cit., pp. 3-4; Chávez, J. A. (1982), op. cit., pp. 3-18. See also Leiner, M. (1981), Two decades of educational change in Cuba, Journal of Reading, Vol. 25, No. 3, pp. 202-214.
36. Fernández, J. R. (1980), op. cit., p. 2.
37. Comité Estatal de Estadística (República de Cuba), (1980),

Anuario Estadístico de Cuba, 1980, Cuadro 7, p. 216.

38. Jiménez, G. (1983), Education for All, Granma Weekly Review, p. 6.

39. See Casas, J. (1981), op. cit., pp. 107-113, for a useful discussion of the difficulties faced by, and arising out of, the schools in the countryside programme.

40. The reduction in the proportion of basic secondary, pre-university, and technical-vocational students receiving scholarships is brought out clearly in Briquets, S. D. (1983), Demographic and Related Determinants of Recent Cuban Emigration, International Migration Review, Vol. 17, pp. 108-111.

41. Castro, F. (1981), Speech at the graduation ceremony of 10,658 students of the Manuel Ascunce Domenech Student-Teacher Detachment, July 7, 1981, Granma Weekly Review, July 19, p. 2.

42. Jiménez, G. (1984), Current total enrolment: 3 times greater than 1959, Granma Weekly Review, p. 3.

43. Ibid.

44. Brundenius, C. (1983), Some Notes on the Development of the Cuban Labor Force 1970-1980, Cuban Studies, Vol. 13, No. 2, p. 75.

45. See Fernández, J. R. (1983-84), op. cit., passim, for an elaboration of these ideas.

46. This will not prove easy, as Fernández recognises: 'Improving the national education system represents a whole driving force of new ideas that have, of necessity, come up against traditional teaching ideas'. He refers to 'difficulties of a subjective nature, such as breaking with the ingrained mentality of some teachers'; see Fernández, J. R. (1980), op. cit., p.2.

47. See Fernández, J. R. (1981), op. cit., pp. 3-4, and Fernández, J. R. (1983-84), op. cit., pp. 44-47, for further analysis.

48. The sweeping statement of Beauvais, that 'the massive development of education has had little effect on labour productivity', requires close inspection; see Beauvais, J. P. (1983), Achievements and Contradictions of the Cuban Workers' State, in Ambursley, F. and Cohen, R. (eds.), Crisis in the Caribbean, Heinemann, p. 53.

49. Fernández, J. R. (1981), op. cit., p. 4, cites early marriage as one such socio-cultural problem.

50. Castro, F. (1973), in a speech made in Havana on February 10, 1959, quoted by Fox, G. E., Honor, Shame, and Women's Liberation in Cuba: Views of Working-Class Emigré Men, in Pescatello, A. (ed.), Female and Male in Latin America. Essays, University of Pittsburgh Press, p. 279.

51. The impact or significance of that commitment, of course, is predicated upon the continuity of the leadership

itself, which the educational systems of many other
countries do not enjoy (or suffer?).

52. Masferrer, M. and Mesa-Lago, C. (1974), The Gradual Integration of the Black in Cuba: Under the Colony, the Republic, and the Revolution, in Toplin, R. B. (ed.), Slavery and Race Relations in Latin America, Greenwood Press, p. 366.

53. Mesa-Lago, C. (1972), The Labor Force, Employment, Un-Employment and Underemployment in Cuba: 1899-1970, Sage Publications, p. 18.

54. Paulston, R. (1980), op. cit., p. 157.

55. Masferrer, M. and Mesa-Lago, C. (1974), op. cit., p. 375.

56. As reported in Granma Weekly Review, September 4, 1983.

57. Pérez, L. (1984), The Political Contexts of Cuban Population Censuses, 1899-1981, Latin American Research Review, Vol. XIX, No. 2, pp. 156-57.

58. Ibid., p. 157.

59. Mesa-Lago, C. (1981), op. cit., p. 197.

60. Domínguez, J. I. (ed.) (1982), Cuba. Internal and International Affairs, Sage Publications, p. 33.

61. Fernández, J. R. (1980), op. cit., p. 3.

62. UNESCO (1983), Statistical Yearbook, 1983, UNESCO, Table 3.7. However, Fernández J. R. (1981), op. cit., p. 3, provides different figures regarding female enrolment in technical-vocational education in 1980-81, namely, over 104,000 (45.7 per cent).

63. UNESCO, (1983), op. cit., Table 3.11.

64. Ibid., Table 1.3.

65. Brundenius, C. (1983), op. cit., pp. 70-72. A slightly different version of the growth of the female labour force shows that the female share was 14.2 per cent in 1958, 15.6 per cent in 1968, 17.7 per cent in 1969, and 25.3 per cent in 1975, rising to 30 per cent in 1979 and to 39.9 per cent in 1983; see Lewis, O. et al (1977), Four Women. Living the Revolution: An Oral History of Contemporary Cuba, University of Illinois Press, p. XIX; Castro, F. (1980), Speech to the closing session of the Third Congress of the Federation of Cuban Women, March 8, 1980, Granma Weekly Review, March 16, p. 2; and Castro, F. (1984), Speech to the closing session of the Fifteenth Congress of the Confederation of Cuban Workers (CTC), February 24, 1984, Granma Weekly Review, March 11, p. 4.

66. Brundenius, C. (1983), op. cit., p. 64.

67. Ibid., p. 70.

68. Purcell, S. K. (1973), Modernising Women for a Modern Society: The Cuban Case, in Pescatello, A. (ed.), op. cit., p. 261; UNESCO, (1983), op. cit., Table 3.4.

69. Brundenius, C. (1983), op. cit., p. 73.

70. Castro, F. (1982), Speech at the ceremony to found the Carlos J. Finlay Medical Sciences Detachment, March 12,

1982, Granma Weekly Review, March 28, p. 3.

71. See Nazzari, M. (1983), The 'Woman Question' in Cuba:
An Analysis of Material Constraints on its Solution,
Signs: Journal of Women in Culture and Society, Vol.
9, No. 2, p. 259. However, Nazzari does suggest that
the existence of many female professionals in the
female share of the labour force may mean that 'there
may not be a gap between the national average wages of
men and women', p. 259.

72. Brundenius, C. (1983), op. cit., p. 72 and Table 4, p.71.

73. Nazzari, M. (1983), op. cit., p. 260.

74. On women's symbolic political representation, see
Domínguez, J. I. (1982), op. cit., pp. 32-33; on
women's leadership underrepresentation, see Bengels-
dorf, C. and Hageman, A. (1978), Emerging from underdevelopment: women and work in Cuba, Race and Class,
Vol. XIX, No. 4, pp. 368-71.

75. Mesa-Lago, C. (1982), The Economy: Caution, Frugality,
and Resilient Ideology, in Domínguez, J. I., op. cit.,
Table 3.1, p. 114.

76. See Nazzari, M. (1983), op. cit., passim, for a useful
discussion of these complex issues.

77. Paulston, R. (1973), Cuban Rural Education: A Strategy
for Revolutionary Development, in Foster, P. and
Sheffield, J. R. (eds.), Education and Rural Development. The World Year-Book of Education, 1974, Evans
Bros., Table 2, p. 241.

78. Calculated from: Bowles, S. (1971), Cuban Education and
the Revolutionary Ideology, Harvard Educational Review,
Vol. 41, No. 4, Table 5, p. 496.

79. See Comité Estatal de Estadísticas (1980), op. cit.,
Cuadro 10, p. 219.

80. Roca, S. (1982), Distributional effects of the Cuban
revolution: urban versus rural allocation 1975 (mimeo),
cited in Slater, D., State and territory in post-
revolutionary Cuba: some critical reflections on the
development of spatial policy, International Journal of
Urban and Regional Research, Vol. 6, No. 1, p. 15.

81. Contrast the proportion of such children in three urbanised provinces, (City of Havana Province 91.1 per cent;
Matanzas Province 86.5 per cent; Havana Province 71.5
per cent), with four rural provinces (Holguín 18.2 per
cent; Granma 16.7 per cent; Guantánamo 11.7 per cent;
Las Tunas 10.9 per cent).

82. For example, the high constructional and operational
costs, the inability of student output to repay these
costs, and a growing shift from agriculture to
industry.

83. Slater, D. (1982), op. cit., p. 21, fn. 37. Casas, J.
(1981), op. cit., p. 111, fn. 12, makes the point that
these communities which, though often containing less

than 2,000 people, are counted as urban for census
purposes by virtue of their amenities, may serve to
partly explain the rapid decline in the share of the
rural population, from 39.5 per cent in 1970 to 31
per cent in 1981.

84. Lehmann, D. (1982), op. cit., p. 350, states that 'the
educational expansion not only opened up opportunities
for the younger generation but must have enabled many
rural people, especially women, to become teachers'.

85. Carnoy, M. (1979), Can educational policy equalise income distribution in Latin America?, International
Labour Office, p. 32.

86. Valdés, N. P. (1979), The Cuban Revolution: Economic
Organization and Bureaucracy, Latin American Perspectives, Vol. 6, No. 1, p. 26.

87. Mesa-Lago, C. (1982), op. cit., p. 158.

88. See Smith, P. (1983), Too few books give Castro a head-
ache, Times Higher Educational Supplement, February 11.

89. Mesa-Lago, C. (1981), op. cit., p. 141.

90. Valdés, N. P. (1972), op. cit., p. 440. Valdés adds,
however, that 'some people are sometimes prevented from
education due to their political viewpoints'.

91. See Mesa-Lago, C. (1981), op. cit., p. 166.

92. Mesa-Lago, C. (1982), op. cit., p. 155.

93. MacEwan, A. (1981), Revolution and Economic Development
in Cuba, MacMillan, pp. 89-90.

94. Domínguez, J. I. (1978), op. cit., p. 172.

95. LeoGrande, W. M. (1979), The Theory and Practice of
Socialist Democracy in Cuba: Mechanisms of Elite
Accountability, Studies in Comparative Communism, Vol.
XII, No. 1, p. 40.

96. Ibid., pp. 46-49.

97. Gonzalez, E. (1979), Reply: Forum on Institutionalisation, Cuban Studies, Vol. 9, No. 2, p. 81. Gonzalez
suggests a third type of participation, substantive:
'whereby citizen participation in politics can affect
the outcome of significant issues at the national and
provincial levels, particularly those issues involving
the distribution of political power and the allocation
of scarce resources'.

98. Domínguez, J. I. (1978), op. cit., p. 172.

99. Domínguez, J. I. (1982), Introduction, in Domínguez, J.
I., (1982), op. cit., p. 10.

Chapter Three

NATIONAL CONSCIOUSNESS AND EDUCATION IN MEXICO

Erwin E. Epstein

Not all people are conscious of nationality. Indigenous populations living in remote areas of a large country may have no sense of being part of a nation. Even when remoteness does not characterise a group, particular religious or linguistic orientations may eclipse a sense of nationality. Yet national consciousness is the glue that binds a nation together. Without it countries would be simply territories containing loose conglomerations of people. Citizenship would have no meaning beyond designation of residence within specified borders. Governments would have no compelling means to gain citizens voluntary compliance with laws and secure the social order. One reason that countries tend to devote much energy and expense to education is that it can be used as a powerful promoter of national consciousness.

So it is in Mexico, a country of more than 75 million people whose character has been shaped by a confluence of Spanish and indigenous traditions. To be sure, the idea of a Mexican national character simplifies the complexities of life, personality and behaviour in that country. For one thing, to have a strong collective sense of nationality does not necessarily mean that people are united on goals. Mexicans may consider themselves culturally unique and have displayed an energetic nationalism throughout much of their history. Yet observers have noted that manifestations of national fervour - as well as such behavioural peculiarities as machismo, involving exhibitions of exaggerated virility - tend to mask feelings of inferiority and isolation and widespread political instability. Ramos, for example, contends that machismo is a form of national identification; male aggressiveness is elevated to compensate for shortcomings in other areas of social life.[1] By displaying virility the Mexican shows his manly superiority over the European, who is more accomplished in science, art and technical knowledge. Paz claims that because Mexico is the product of highly differentiated traditions, Mexicans are ambivalent about their culture and look elsewhere for guidance in constructing social institutions.[2]

Hence, they slavishly imitate European forms and are obsessed with ritual at the expense of substance in politics, art and literature.[3,4]

Fuentes claims that Mexico suffers serious identity problems because of a schizoid separation between written rights and daily practice. He shows that in colonial times Spain passed enlightened laws to protect Indians and the humbler classes in the new world. But these laws were rarely implemented, and the injustices of daily practice have continued anomolously ever since to weigh against the idealism of formal statutes. A sense of nationality must reside in feelings of national legitimacy, feelings that are eroded when citizens believe that the behaviour of public officials and bureaucrats is inconsistent with national ideals embodied in laws:

'From where does legitimacy come in a country that denies its father, the rapacious Spaniard, and condemns its mother, the traitorous Indian? The feeling of being totally orphaned has been sublimated by attributing paternity to sterile and objective legal text, almost as if to profess a genesis that was pristine. Whoever possesses the text also exercises sovereign dominion. And since text liberates us from the degraded condition of illegitimacy (just as the image of the Black Virgin liberates us from the fear of being children of a prostitute, so we now view our pure and adored Mother on the altar...), we ought willingly to renounce our unbridled liberty as children of the left hand in exchange for the privileged, though submissive, condition as subjects of the right.

Legitimation of the bastard and identification of the orphan are achieved by authority of the text: there is no more basic moral foundation for the vertical society, governed from top to bottom, sustained and nurtured from bottom to top.   Horizontility means renouncing name and place, however humble these may be, within the rigid pyramid. It means losing one's identity repeatedly in the deserts of numerous illegitimacies. Civil record, party identification card, Federal Constitution: Mexicans need a piece of solid paper, appealable, demonstrable, that identifies them by reference to paternal authority, the source of all investiture; it is at any given time, a repository of the juridical texts and representative of the mythical continuity of the social movements that wrote them with blood: the war of independence, the wars of reform and the revolution of 1910.'[5]

Yet the quest for unity and identity is nevertheless strong.   The Mexican Revolution (1910-1920), which exacted a

terrible toll in lives and destruction, is a prime symbol of
Mexican nationality; it represents both a break from the ruling class oppression of the past and independence from foreign
political and cultural forms. So sweeping was its impact
that not a single major bank or newspaper that pre-dated the
Revolution survived. It ruined much of the economy,
especially the agrarian, ranching and mining sectors,[6] but for
Mexicans it was the social culmination of independence from
Spain achieved politically 100 years earlier. And it was the
source of the first significant social and political movement
in Latin America to have elevated the status of Indians and
mestizos, the Revolution's principal beneficiaries. The
Revolution unleashed creative energies that took form in a
renaissance of music, literature and art - largely celebrating
the nation's indigenous roots and people of humble origins -
that reached levels of greatness in the murals of Orozco,
Rivera, Alforo-Siqueiros and Guerrero Galvan. So important
is the Revolution to Mexico's continuing identity that its
symbols and heroes are featured prominently in public institutions, and it is celebrated in the very name of the party
that has dominated politics for over half a century, the PRI,
Institutional Revolutionary Party.

A society is fortunate if its cultural roots are unambiguous, extend deep into history, and nurture an unequivocal
sense of national purpose. Schools then have the relatively
uncomplicated task of transmitting the society's life ways
and world view to the young, thus helping to preserve the
cultural heritage. Mexico does not enjoy that advantage.
Notwithstanding the unifying influence of the Revolution and
pervasive revolutionary rhetoric to keep that influence alive,
ambivalence exists about the national culture, complicating
strategies for promoting unity and compromising the school's
role in seeking to achieve it. In this chapter I will examine
the amgibuities of Mexican life as they affect the relationship between education and national consciousness. In
particular, I will consider how the effort to build a collective sense of nationality is affected by a structure of inequality, the identity of élites, and the difficulties of
identifying cultural uniqueness. First, however, it will be
necessary to review briefly the development of Mexico's
educational system.

THE DEVELOPMENT OF MEXICAN EDUCATION

The Spanish conquest brought together two not entirely
dissimilar educational traditions: indigenous and hispanic.
Both were hierarchical and emphasised particularly the preparation of élites. In Aztec society formal schooling was
limited largely to the warrior nobility, priests, merchants
and a large common class of free peasants; the slave and
serf populations were prohibited. Schools for the higher

classes stressed self-sacrifice, penance, intellectual reading, arts, calendar reading, astronomical calculations and
religion.   Education for commoners included manual skills,
martial arts, dancing, music co-operation, self-defence and
religion.[7,8,9]   Keen observes that the Aztecs generally were
far better educated than the Spanish soldiers who conquered
them.[10]

Spanish education too was class based and emphasised
religion and intellectual pursuits for the nobility, and was
largely entrusted to the clergy.   In the colonies, however,
its primary purpose was to initiate the indigenous populations
into subserviency and impose Catholicism and the Spanish
language.   It was part of a larger effort to eradicate all
vestiges of indigenous culture.   Education for the Indians
generally included religious indoctrination, literacy in
Spanish, and vocational training; but it was available to
very few.   By the end of the colonial period (1821) less
than one per cent of the population was literate.[11]

Upon independence the Church was challenged by liberals
for control of education.   Mexican liberalism stood for
political modernisation, stability and economic growth.   José
María Luis Mora, an early influential liberal theorist,
pleaded for a national public school system that would be in
step with an enlightened political system and improve the
'moral' condition of the people.   His ideas saw fruition,
however briefly, in the reforms of 1833, which wrested control
of higher education from the clergy and sought to establish a
national system of public schools.   Members of the clergy
were prohibited from teaching in government schools, and
private schools were subject to government regulations and
inspection.   These reforms were short-lived, however, because
clerical and conservative groups were able to mobilise effective opposition.[12,13]   Nevertheless, early liberal legislation
laid the foundation for a series of laws enacted in the 1860's
that made elementary education free and compulsory.   The
curriculum included a variety of basic subjects and instruction in morality, but not religion, which was formally excluded in 1874.   The new laws also provided for professional
schools of law, medicine, pharmacy, agriculture, engineering,
commerce, architecture and the fine arts.

Mexican education was shaped in its formative years by
the determined positivism of Gabino Barreda, Joaquin Barranda
and Justo Sierra.   Barreda, as head of a commission
established by President Benito Juarez to propose legislation
on education, was largely responsible for the reforms of the
1860's.   Barranda and Sierra were in charge of education
under President Porfirio Diaz; Barranda served from 1882 to
1901, and Sierra succeeded him until the end of the Porfiriato
(1876-1910), the rule of dictator Porfirio Diaz.   To Barranda
and Sierra fell the task of creating a primary school system
that was obligatory, uniform in content, and extended to the

entire nation.[14,15]

Sierra's administration in particular was remarkable for two reasons: his efforts were opposed by many conservatives and liberals alike, and he worked on behalf of the infamous Porfiriato. Conservatives opposed Sierra's efforts to achieve universal state primary education, because they believed most Mexicans were incapable of being educated and, in any case, education was too expensive to implement and enforce. Classical liberals regarded obligatory education as a tyrannical attack on parents' rights. Sierra was unmoved by these arguments; he consistently defended obligatory public instruction as necessary to national survival and growth. The State, he believed, must intervene by using schools to improve society. Thus, he rejected the notion that the poor, and particularly Indians, were congenitally inferior.[16]

To Sierra, Porfirio Diaz was the patron of Mexican progress, the creator of peace and order whose principal purpose was to bring Mexico within the orbit of 'los paises cultos'. Unlike in advanced societies, where natural laws permitted a policy of laissez-faire, Sierra contended that the central government in Mexico - because of the country's backwardness and susceptibility to internal anarchy and foreign invasion - had to pursue actively a programme of national integration. Schools were to be assigned the task of moulding a homogeneous people equipped with values, attitudes and skills appropriate to modernisation. In pursuing that objective the rights of all children to the fullness of life and of society to survive and prosper were to supercede the freedom of parents to decide whether their children would be educated.[17]

Yet how can the progressiveness of Sierra's views be reconciled with the ruthlessness of the Diaz regime which, after all, precipitated the Mexican Revolution? For one thing, Sierra was part of the positivist movement that regarded intellectual development as the necessary and most natural path to national progress and security. With 'progressive' Europe as their model, positivists were not vigorous advocates of egalitarian and humanitarian ideals. Rather, they believed that the whole of society would benefit materially and politically as people's ignorance was eliminated, even if the central state grew powerful in pursuit of that goal. In this respect, positivism was a philosophy congenial to the Porfiriato, which disdained liberty and equality in favour of order and growth. In fact, Diaz achieved unprecedented stability and economic development, but with resort to considerable repression.

For another thing, Sierra's programme recognised the importance of cultivating allegiances. The school curriculum to be sure, placed a heavy emphasis on the learning of skills, but it also stressed official knowledge, history, values and the promotion of patriotism. Nationalism was instilled to encourage obedience to official authority, and to inspire a collective desire to overcome Mexico's inferior economic and political position vis-a-vis the metropolitan powers. Thus, a passive but enlightened citizenry was viewed as congenial to political stability.

With the end of the Porfiriato came a move to change the base of authority over education. The Constitution of 1917, which grew out of the Revolution, called for theological dogma to give way to scientific explanation, and reduced the Church's hold over schools. Equally important, however, it eliminated the Secretariat of Public Instruction as a reaction against the strong centralised power exercised under Diaz, and placed education under the control of municipality councils. Nevertheless, it soon became clear that the municipalities lacked the resources to provide schools, and there was widespread belief that chaos might ensue without a strong federal government to control the insurgent peasantry. By the end of the Revolution illiteracy exceeded 78.5 per cent, the rate that prevailed under the Diaz regime. In 1921, a constitutional revision provided that a new Secretariat of Public Education (SEP) be established, one that would enjoy a jurisdiction beyond that exercised by Justo Sierra under the Porfiriato.[18]

The eminent lawyer and philospher, José Vasconcelos, was appointed Secretary of the new Secretariat of Public Education. Within three years the government established more than 1,000 rural schools, opened public libraries and widely distributed vocationally and academically-orientated books.[19]

Yet given the turmoil of the Revolution and the thrust for change, the content of education remained surprisingly similar to what it had been under the Porfiriato. Textbooks continued to reflect an ideology of cultural amelioration: Mexico was in need of civilisation to be accepted among the progressive nations of the world. Indeed, the only history text published during the period was Justo Sierra's Historia Patria, which has been written for Porfirian schools. Generally the textbooks viewed the Revolution solely as a political struggle for the restoration of democratic liberties, ignoring social and economic reforms. Eschewing emphasis on the primordial uniqueness of Mexican culture, they stressed European literature and such values as order and progress. Vaughan notes that in 1925 a new publishing company complained that 'although the SEP had asked for texts which were not more than five years old, not exclusively reading-orientated, not discouraging spontaneity, without reference to religion, and not lacking in national orientation, the texts chosen had precisely these defects.'[20]

This is not to say that education was oblivious to the importance of inculcating a sense of nationality. One leading textbook, for example, viewed Mexico as a cauldron for uniting the industriousness of Anglo-Saxon and the artistic

sensitivity of Latin American cultures, and by so doing would
achieve a nationality that displayed the undesirable traits -
Anglo-Saxon egoism and insensitivity and Latin-American
lethargy - of neither.[21]   But emphasis on external values
was self-effacing and a constant reminder of the benefits of
foreign ways and habits.   Implicitly, Mexican children were
urged to believe that to gain the desired national identity
they had to become culturally something they were not already.
        This negative self-concept was mitigated somewhat by the
cultural nationalist movement that flourished under Vasconcelos.   This movement, which began in 1920, conveyed a new
legitimacy to the Mexican Revolution through an emerging
creativity in art, literature and music.   Schools in particular played a key role in spreading the movement beyond the
privileged classes.   It was an effort to use art forms to
create a folk nationalism that would be shared by all sectors
of the population.   By using the Revolution as its central
theme the movement had a focal point with which all Mexicans
could identify.   In particular, the radical muralists Diego
Rivera, José Clemente Orozco, and David Alfaro Siqueiros
received international recognition even though their works
initially provoked outrage in Mexican intellectual circles.
Here were new art forms that promoted powerful images of
Mexican nationality and near-universal acclaim for the
artists who produced them.   The art as well as the artists
became sources of pride to a country striving to achieve a
stable identity.
        In 1934, under President Lázaro Cárdenas the Constitution
was revised in a way that produced an important change in the
image of the State that was to be conveyed to school children.
Education was henceforth to be 'socialist' and to exclude all
religious doctrine even in private schools.   The ideology of
the Revolution became manifestly class-conscious; the
Mexican nation was portrayed in schools as the beneficiary of
revolutionary social reform, which affirmed the legitimacy of
Indian culture, promoted the agrarian ideals of Emiliano
Zapata, unified the worker and peasant as agents of history,
and opposed U.S. and European imperialism.   National and
educational goals were made inseparable, and education became
more centralised and bureaucratised.[22]   Under the succeeding
administration of Avila Camacho (1940-46), the stress on
socialist education was somewhat muted, but not the promotion
of national solidarity and the emphasis on centralisation.
Rural education became more similar to urban education, a
massive national campaign against illiteracy was launched,
and the federal budget for schools increased from 74 million
pesos in 1940 to 208 million in 1946.   From 1946 to the
present, education expanded steadily, although nine states
contain populations with illiteracy rates over 20 per cent,
and the average adult male has less than a 5th grade education.[23,24]

The most noteworthy development under the current administration of Miguel de la Madrid Hurtado is a move toward decentralisation. The effort to reallocate some administrative
authority over education to the states comes after decades
of increasing federalisation, whose explicit justification has
been the consolidation of national consciousness.
Perissinotto contends that the new policy is largely politically motivated; it is an effort to weaken the National
Education Workers Union (Sindicato Nacional de Trabajadores
de la Educación), which has exercised considerable influence
in national politics.[25]   Yet de la Madrid seems genuinely to
want democratic participation in educational planning. It is
important to observe also that educational decentralisation
comes hard on the heels of perhaps Mexico's severest economic
crisis since the Revolution and that de la Madrid plausibly
wishes to defuse some of the widespread antipathy and distrust toward the national government generated by the controversial conduct of his predecessor, José Lopez Portillo. In
any case, decentralisation is to proceed cautiously, negotia-
ted through a committee composed of the governor of the state
being affected at a given time and officials from the
Secretariat of Education, the Secretariat of the Budget, and
the Social Security System for Civil Service.
    The history of Mexican education displays a persistent
ebb and flow in the emphasis given to particular countervailing motives and tendencies: centralisation versus decentralisation, primordial versus foreign cultural orientations,
ethnic pluralism versus assimilation, revolutionary ideals
versus domestic tranquility, Anglo-Saxon industriousness
versus Latin American artistic sensitivity, socialist versus
capitalist explanation, mass education versus education for
the preparation of leaders, science versus the humanities.
Yet a central concern in all of these issues has been the
development of a national consciousness. Mexico's leaders
have always viewed education as the key institution in producing a collective sense of Mexican nationality. But they
have differed considerably on how precisely schools should be
used to gain that objective. In the following sections I
will discuss more specifically how these tendencies have come
to influence the school's role in shaping Mexico's national
identity.

NATIONALITY AND THE STRUCTURE OF INEQUALITY

    Consciousness of class may have an important impact on
people's sense of nationality. People who believe that their
country's social and economic system deprives them of just
rewards for their work and allegiance may display low political identification as nationals. This is not to say that an
inverse relationship will exist between socio-economic cleav-
ages and national identity; people may not be conscious of

existing class differences, and may simply attribute their status to destiny or some defect, intellectual or otherwise, that they themselves - rather than the socio-economic system - embody. This is, incidentally, the condition Marxists refer to as 'false consciousness'. Even if false consciousness prevails, and people display strong national, rather than class consciousness, the presence of large socio-economic distinctions makes fragile their national identity. Perceptions of injustice may be more likely in systems where class differences are palpable.

Mexican educational authorities are keenly aware of the linkage between socio-economic disparities and national consciousness. In 1981, on the 60th anniversary of the establishment of the Secretariat of Public Education, the Secretary, Fernando Solana Morales, declared that the national programme of Mexican education would have four major commitments: improve quality, provide Mexicans with equal educational opportunities, promote efforts to strengthen the country's national culture and cultural identity, and ensure a nationalistic orientation for education.[26] As reflected in the following official statement, educational policy is dictated by a belief that social equality, civic participation and national solidarity are closely linked:

'Displacement of individualism - through dialogue, interaction and, when unavoidable, struggle - is indispensable if we are to overcome social polarisation and construct a democratic society.

Our view is grounded in a well-understood nationalism. Political consensus originates in participatory processes. National unity, the affirmation of sovereignty and the preservation of cultural identity are the fruit of an education that incorporates civic participation. For this reason, Mexico, characterised by a vigorous cultural personality and exposed by its geographical location to efforts at domination from the outside, must employ education to assert and fortify its sense of nationality.'[27]

Given a relationship between national consciousness and socio-economic differences - and the supposed influence of education on both - it is important to consider how socio-economic disparities are displayed in the school system. These disparities are most notable in the distinctions between urban and rural populations and among urban social classes.

An analysis of the polarities between urban and rural sectors is made difficult by a considerable growth in the population overall, and in countryside to city migration. It is estimated that two-thirds of the Mexican adult population (aged 15 and over) inhabit cities, and the growth of urban adults reached 62 per cent during the 1970-80 period. Although the illiteracy rate in the Mexican adult population declined from 26 per cent in 1970 to 18 per cent in 1980 - representing an increase in the literate population of 64 per cent - the absolute number of illiterates changed only negligibly.[28]

In developing countries, illiteracy tends to be regarded as a largely rural problem. In Mexico, however, the large migration of illiterates from rural to urban areas has enlarged the problem to the nation as a whole. Whereas urban illiterates constituted 39 per cent of the overall illiterate adult population in 1970, they represented 45 per cent in 1980.[29] Hence, although the overall rate of illiteracy is declining, a large population growth rate, which matches or even outpaces the decline in the illiteracy rate, and a vast movement of rural to urban illiterates, complicate efforts to reduce illiteracy and provide equivalent educational opportunities for all. Furthermore, the illiterate population of adult females actually increased from 1960 to 1980, a fact that has ominous implications for the future. Literate women can have a powerful impact on economic growth and social equity even if they never enter the labour force. Most girls become mothers, and a variety of studies have shown that their influence on their children's health and fertility is crucial.[30]

Nevertheless, there are signs that female illiteracy may soon decline. Female enrolment has reached almost half of total enrolment in Mexican primary schools, well above the world level and the level for the developing countries, and equal to that for the developed countries. Although the percentage of female enrolment in Mexican secondary schools is still below the level of the developed countries, dramatic gains have been made in recent years and the percentage of female enrolment is now above the overall world level and that for the developing countries. If females reach parity with males in educational levels, the impact on social equity should be significant.

The issue of equity must take into account considerations of efficacy to achieve social mobility. If people believe that their station in life is fixed by external forces, or that schools are ineffective agents of mobility, education will have little impact on social equality. A variety of studies, mainly in the US, have shown that children from higher social classes tend to have higher educational aspirations and do better in school.[31,32,33,34] It is important also, however, to consider whether perceptions of educational efficacy coincide with reality. Misperceptions of the school's effectiveness to promote individuals' socio-economic status may be experienced by both government and the individuals being educated. If schools are really not capable of effecting change, then public funds invested to achieve equity may be wasted, and students' aspirations may be frustrated. Alternatively, governments may experience no gains from such investments if lower class students are unconvinced of schools' efficacy.

School effects have been extensively researched since the 1960's. The findings have consistently shown negligible effects of school and teacher quality and organisational patterns on academic achievement when socio-economic status is controlled.[35-42] Although these studies have concentrated on effects in industrialised countries, several investigations in Mexico, have shown similar findings.[43,44,45]

Nevertheless, it is interesting that these studies have focused generally on urban areas; it is plausible that the findings would display favourable significant effects of schooling if population samples were drawn more evenly throughout a country. Indeed, some findings suggest that in low-income countries the power of educational attainment and, in particular, school achievement to determine occupational success is substantially higher than the power of socio-economic status.[46,47,48] Heyneman and Loxley show that for Mexico school and teacher quality account for 55 per cent of the total variance in academic achievement, considerably higher than that of the earlier studies which concentrated on effects in large cities. They contend that their cross-national findings - which show that in low-income countries the effect of school and teacher quality on academic achievement in primary school is greater than in high-income countries - reflect the fact that as a commodity education is more scarce and in higher demand in the developing countries, and occupational mobility due to education is more demonstrable.[49]

Alternatively, findings by Epstein for Peru[50,51] and Puerto Rico[52] suggest that pupils in geographically and culturally more isolated schools tend to display a stronger sense of nationality, due plausibly to their being more receptive to the patriotic myths learned in classrooms; the larger school effects on achievement observed by Heyneman and Loxley for low-income countries like Mexico may be due as much or more to these schools' plausibly greater impact on aspirations than to their actual direct impact on mobility by virtue of learned skills. Just as schools have a larger influence on national identity in more remote areas, so might they have a stronger overall impact on aspirations in low-income countries, where the value content of education may be more removed - and therefore more easily accepted by pupils - from the realities of national life than in high-income countries. In other words, the larger effects in low-income countries may be attributed to those pupils' relative lack of intellectual sophistication when they come to school, making them more susceptible to the school's value orientation. In high-income countries, by contrast, pupils generally -

including those in rural and lower class urban areas -
because of more developed communication networks, may have
greater extra-school access to knowledge about national
realities, and therefore may be less likely to accept as
readily schools' favourable images of the nation and the
socio-economic opportunities it provides.   More favourable
images of the nation may give rise to high aspirations and
greater striving.   This proposition has yet to be tested -
by focusing particularly on differential school effects in
urban and rural areas of low and high-income countries - but
it does make plausible the linkage between national identity
and educational success that Mexican authorities profess.
The school may indeed play a critical role in shaping national
consciousness and promoting high aspirations, with the effects
on each interacting with and compounding the effect on the
other, in countries like Mexico.
    Perceived socioeconomic disparities may diminish
people's sense of nationality.   But a structure of inequality
may give rise to differential identities; élites may vary
from the masses in their political commitment to and psychological association with the nation.   Hence we turn now to
élite identity, and then will consider the identity of
Mexico's most economically disadvantaged population, the
Indians.

NATIONALITY AND ÉLITE IDENTITY

    There is often a palpable association between political
leadership and national consciousness.   For one thing, a
political élite may set the stage for a nation's identity.
Leaders may appeal to nationalistic sensibilities to induce
solidarity in the face of political turmoil or to encourage
people to work together for economic progress.   The capacity
of an élite to inspire solidarity may be related to its own
sense of nationality.   People who lead by promoting nationalism may be ineffective if they themselves do not embody a
strong national identity which they wish others to emulate.
    There is reason to believe that despite the almost
routine use of extreme nationalistic rhetoric in public pronouncements, national allegiance among Mexican élites is low.
Mexican politics is dominated by personalism - a system of
patronage and personal contacts through which political
mobility is achieved - rather than ideology.   Public office
holders characteristically have few associates on whom they
can rely for help; rather, they place great trust in a very
select group of relatives, long-time friends and compadres
with whom personal loyalty counts politically above all else.
This condition applies throughout the political system, from
the President - whose dominance is authoritarian - to the
lowliest public official.[53,54,55,56,57]
    The prevalence of personalism in Mexican politics raises

the issue of dual loyalty. If leaders commit their allegiance to a tightly-knit group of friends, can they conduct
themselves in the best interests of the nation? Can the
public have confidence in and be inspired nationalistically
by an élite whose conduct is guided primarily by personal
loyalties? Do qualified people lack motivation to achieve
high position because they view the selection process as controlled by powerful cliques? Does authoritarian control of
politics induce resentment and unfavourable images of the
nation among those who are outside the political mainstream?
Although precise answers to these questions are beyond the
scope of this chapter, I wish to consider how they might relate
to education.

It is important first to observe the role of the
camarilla, or political clique, in the Mexican political process. It is a grouping of individuals who interact frequently and are associated through personal loyalties and career
connections. It is the primary unit that drives the engine
of Mexican politics. A set of camarillas forms a pyramidal
structure within the larger pyramid of the official system.
As Camp describes it, 'the camarilla becomes a small pyramidal
group of men which in turn is engulfed by a larger and then
still larger pyramidal structure, until the official system
or pyramid itself emerges'.[58] Generally, a camarilla will
consist of a coterie of followers indebted to and closely
identified with a successful politician who is their jefe, or
chief.[59]

If one requires camarilla connections to gain high
position, how does one gain admission to a camarilla? It is
here that we find schools in a vital role. Higher education
in Mexico is the privilege of a small minority, and it is
from this minority that Mexico's leaders generally emerge.
Although the proportion of eligible school-age population
attending institutions of higher learning is increasing, only
about 11 per cent attended as of 1976.[60] The mean number of
years of education for all Mexicans is less than three, but
is 15 for members of the political élite studied by Camp, and
92 per cent of the élite had a university degree in contrast
to less than 2 per cent for the general population.[61]

To be sure, a university education tends to be a pre-
requisite to high political office in most countries. Yet in
Mexico the camarilla system rewards not simply advanced
education but attendance at particular institutions, and
especially the Universidad Autónoma Nacional de México (UNAM).
Indeed, 75 per cent of the country's political leadership is
educated in Mexico City, and almost two-thirds at UNAM.[62]
The close tie between national politics and the university,
especially UNAM, is reflected by the fact that influential
professors themselves tend to be important political figures
and therefore jefes around which camarillas, consisting
largely of favoured students, are formed. The system is one

of career sponsorship in which the poor and most of the middle class are largely excluded from the pool of eligible recruits by exclusion from favoured institutions, and the process as a whole is controlled by persons already in power.[63]

Students who move high in the political system feel compelled to choose as collaborators, individuals who were socialised at the same level and in the same environment, because they lack the time to develop the deep sense of trust in associates required by office holders. According to Camp, 'all candidates for high political office, whether they are in the executive, legislative, or judicial branch are appointed by the president or his collaborators already in such positions; no office holders, therefore, are selected by a competitive primary electoral process.'[64] And, further, 'those in power serve as gatekeepers for the new political élite, thus extending over a long period of time the leadership of a previous government. In fact, the system has worked so well that many of the original recruiters, out of political office for some time, are reselected for high public office by men who they themselves brought into the public sector.'[65]

The political importance of favoured institutions can be seen in enrolment patterns and the investment of public resources. On the one hand, higher education generally has been the principal beneficiary of educational growth. Enrolment in higher education during 1970-75 increased about 32 per cent, well above the 10 per cent level for the educational system overall. Moreover, higher education absorbs 20 per cent of the education budget while serving only about 4 per cent of the total population in school.[66] On the other hand, this support has not been spread evenly. Expenditures for higher education disproportionately favour the institutions where élite recruitment is important. Whereas institutions in the Federal District (largely Mexico City) enroll less than one-third of all students in higher education, they receive two-thirds of the higher education budget.[67] Clearly, university education is being made increasingly available, but in such a way as not to disfavour those already in élite positions.

What are the implications of this system of élite recruitment on national identity? To be sure, it provides considerable continuity, efficiency and stability. Mexico has experienced little political violence since 1929. Interlocking friendship networks, work effectively to moderate potentially dislocative ideological conflicts. Yet, although inferences can be made only speculatively, there is evidence to suggest that the system has an unfavourable impact on national consciousness.

For one thing, corruption and influence peddling are pervasive throughout the system and erode public confidence. Incoming administrations typically pledge to rid government of dishonest people, but only recently have high officials -

especially those associated with the National Petroleum Company (PEMEX), the Oil Workers Union, and the Department of Police and Traffic in the Federal District - been prosecuted. President Miguel de la Madrid's first State of the Nation address called for a 'moral revolution and a modification of the constitution to specify clearly public servants' norms of conduct and political and administrative responsibilities'.[68] Yet, the tightly controlled system of élite recruitment inspires general scepticism about the government's willingness to clean house, and recurrent appeals for national solidarity by leaders within that system give rise to widespread public cynicism over the government's commitment to the national interest.

Furthermore, by emphasising personal loyalty and contacts at the expense of merit, the system locks out the poor and 'underprivileged' middle classes, setting a condition of constant tension.[69]   I have already touched on the issue of disproportionate resources allocated to institutions such as UNAM; it is also important to observe that despite growing school enrolments, Mexico spends less than 4 per cent of its GNP on education. Its proportionate allotment for education is typically below that for Latin America and the developing countries overall; only briefly during the late 1970's did it rise above the average level for other areas.[70]

The results can be seen on various levels. First, relatively few people complete a secondary school education; the ratio of students in secondary schools to those in primary schools remained static at 1 to 4 during the period 1976-77 to 1982-83.[71] Thus, although more Mexicans are being schooled, a larger proportion of them are not acquiring enough education to make them socially mobile.[72] More education without increased mobility is a formula for turmoil and diminished national allegiance. Those who make it through the secondary level and wish to advance further are faced with rejection or deplorable academic conditions if they are accepted. In 1983 UNAM turned away 26,000 applicants and the National Polytechnic Institute - second in importance only to UNAM as an élite recruitment institution - rejected more than 31,000. At UNAM only slightly more than 10 per cent of the faculty have full-time positions; the part-time people are often public figures who do not meet classes but send poorly trained assistants in their place.[73] As the prestigious universities raise admission standards to keep increasing numbers of applicants out, applications to the lower status institutions, especially teachers' colleges, increase. Consequently, Mexico is experiencing widespread unemployment among school teachers; there are about 23,000 unemployed graduates of teacher-training institutions, and thousands of new applications for admission are now being rejected.[74] Even so, the number of university students pursuing education degrees has fallen short of those in programmes that Camp[75] identifies as being traditionally associated with élite recruitment: law, engineering, medicine and business-economics.[76]

Occasionally the unrest produced by these conditions boils over in the form of student strikes; in 1968 one massive student demonstration in Mexico City resulted in several deaths and hundreds of arrests. For our purposes, however, it is more important to observe effects on general sentiments. Earlier, I noted that studies of Mexican education showed negligible influence on academic achievement at least in cities. Padua contends that the educational system promotes enough social mobility to maintain legitimacy, but that mobility is actually minimal and generally produces no change in the structure of privilege and power. Schools give the illusion of a redistribution of power and wealth, and thus help to reduce tensions experienced by social groups that aspire, but are unable to be mobile. Yet the lack of mobility produces a low level of national consciousness even among many who enter a university.[77] In my recent study of medical students in a culturally mixed environment (57 per cent Mexican, 17 per cent from other Latin American countries, and 26 per cent from the USA) at a Mexican university, pre-liminary findings show that Mexican students have, on the average, a considerably lower sense of nationality than Latin American and North American students. For example, only 57 per cent of the Mexicans displayed strong political identification with Mexican heroes, in contrast to 69 per cent of other Latin Americans who identified strongly with heroes in their own countries and 87 per cent of the US students who identified strongly with North American heroes.[78]

However important is the topic of élite formation in considerations of national consciousness, this discussion would not be complete without reference to the other side of the socio-political spectrum: the indigenous population. It is to that population that I now turn my attention.

NATIONALITY AND INDIAN INTEGRATION

Mexicans' sense of identity is never detached from the Indian presence as symbol and historical reality. Official appeals for national solidarity routinely profess a desire for progress from the backwardness of traditional - implicity indigenous - life ways, or alternatively promote such Indian figures of the past as Cuauhtemoc and Benito Juarez as embodying the kind of courage and dignity that all Mexicans should emulate. Indeed, although the Indian has always had a prominent place in Mexicans' consciousness, rarely has that place been unambiguous.

Ambiguity extends to the very definition of 'Indians'. The only Indians universally recognised as such are the aboriginal populations that existed in pre-conquest days. Otherwise, anthropologists differ considerably over defini-

tional characteristics and even whether ethnically genuine
Indians currently exist. To be sure, more than three million
Mexicans speak an Indian language. But Friedlander, for
example, argues that whatever few pre-hispanic customs survive
lost their original meanings long ago and fail to distinguish
culturally some Mexicans from others.[79] Rather, 'Indianness'
is a primarily negative identity linked to an oppressed
position in the social class structure. Some others, however, contend that Indians are not merely members of underdeveloped peasant communities but culturally distinct ethnic
groups that display strong internal cohesion and vigorous
resistance to assimilation.[80,81,82] Most scholars subscribe
to less extreme views, acknowledging the cultural distinctiveness, especially language, of Indians while emphasising the
structural inferiority of their position relative to the mixed
blood mestizos who constitute the majority. These less
extreme descriptions tend to vary in regard to the nature of
Indians' self-identity. For example, Pozas and Pozas view
Indian identity as an exclusively negative definition of what
Indians lack with respect to the larger society,[83] but Warren
and Hunt and Hunt do not.[84,85] Yet they all agree that
Indian identity represents a source of values contrasting
with those of non-Indian society, while denying that it consists of an indigenous set of beliefs, social forms and
techno-economic adaptations.

There are two transcending issues regarding Indian culture
as it relates to Mexican nationality. First is the question
of the proper link between Indian communities and national
society. In other words, should Indians be assimilated into
the national mainstream or should Mexican society exhibit a
vigorous cultural pluralism? The second issue relates to
whether Mexican identity should be infused by Indian culture.
That is, should Mexican nationality reflect indigenous norms,
values and other cultural characteristics? Until recently
only the first issue, regarding the propriety of assimilationist policy, was seriously contested; rarely had thought been
given to the incorporation of Indian cultural forms, and not
simply symbols of the past, into national life. At the heart
of these issues has been education, because schools have
always been the primary instrument of official policy regarding national identity.

Despite the claims of some scholars that until the
Revolution of 1910 official policy sought to impede the integration of Indians, integrationist efforts, especially with
the use of schools, has been recurrently strong since the
early colonial period.[86,87,88] From that time to the present
there has been an unbroken struggle between those who wished
to integrate the Indians gradually and with due regard for
their culture and those who believed in a more forceful policy
of imposing the Spanish language and hispanic culture. In
the mid-sixteenth century that struggle took the form of a

conflict between Church and Crown. Believing that the
Indian language Nahuatl was the most effective and efficient
language with which to unify and Christianise the Indian
population, Franciscan missionaries defied the decree of
Charles V that Indians learn Spanish. Independence from
Spain brought no relief in the debate; in the 1820's Juan
Rodriguez Puebla, a liberal member of Congress, and Vincente
Guerrero, an Indian who became President briefly in 1829,
urged a system of schools designed by and for the Indians that
would allow the use of their native tongues and maintain an
appreciation of their cultural heritage. But those in control of education insisted that Indians learn the hispanic
traditions inherited from colonial society and accept fusion
with the dominant society. They viewed any special provisions for the Indian as an unacceptable strengthening of
separate Indian societies and a weakening of the nation's
unity.[89]

A century later found policy-makers caught up in the same
debate, only now a national system of education was evolving,
one that had the potential of significantly changing Indians'
lives. In 1910, Francisco Belmar founded the Mexican
Indianist Society, thus giving impetus to an emerging
Indianist movement whose objective was to study Indians in
order to promote their 'progress'. Indianists were most
active in condemning past treatment of the Indian and demanding radical reforms. Educational policy-makers, however,
consistently opposed the preservation of indigenous languages
and cultures alongside the national standard. In particular,
Justo Sierra sought the creation of a national consciousness
through obligatory education in Spanish, and viewed Indian
languages as 'simple archeological documents'. He inveighed
against Indianism (Indianismo) in these terms:

> 'The Polyglot state of our country is an obstacle to the
> extension of our culture and the full formation of the
> conscience of our fatherland. Only by means of compul-
> sory public education throughout our entire nation, will
> we be able to avert disaster... we call Spanish the
> national language. (We do so not only because it is
> the tongue that the actual Mexican society has always
> spoken, and because it is the nation's inheritance, but
> also because, as the only scholastic language, it will
> cause the atrophy and destruction of local idioms. Thus
> it will bring about the unification of national speech,
> the essential force behind social unification.'[90]

As to method, Sierra's ideas were reminiscent of the approach
favoured by those Franciscan Friars who heeded the decree of
Charles V to hispanicise the Indians three and a half centur-
ies earlier.
The intermediate use of Indian languages was to be the

expedient for their own eventual destruction:

> '... to teach the indigenous idioms to the teachers of
> the Indians has for us the prime objective of destroying
> them, of teaching them all the Castilian language, and
> of thus overcoming this formidable barrier to the unifi-
> cation of the Mexican people.'[91]

The succeeding history of Mexican education displays a
continuing conflict between the Indianists - exponents of
specially designed education emphasising indirect bilingual
methods by which Spanish and hispanic culture would be taught
through the intermediate use of Indian languages - and
hispanicists who believed that only direct methods of teaching
Spanish should be used, and eschewed the application of
separate standards for Indian children. José Vasconcelos
was particularly notable within the latter group. As
Secretary of Education in the early 1920's he opposed the
work of Manuel Gamio, an influential anthropologist who proposed the ideal of 'nationalistic integral education', which
aimed at the linguistic unification of Indians after particular Indian regions would be designated for special projects of
education and improvement. Vasconcelos believed that such
special designations served only to accentuate Indians'
separateness; rather, 'incorporation' would be achieved
through a national school system emphasising the literary
classics of Europe, from which all citizens would acquire the
highest standards of morality and be prepared to participate
competently in the Mexican democracy.[92]

It is important to observe that the struggle between
Indianists and hispanicists was generally over means rather
than ends. They did not dispute the aim of Indian integration, and most hispanicists as well as Indianists opposed the
kind of social Darwinism advanced by Francisco Bulnes, who,
at the turn of the century, blamed Mexico's weakness vis-a-vis
the United States on the racial inferiority of the Indians.[93]

Indeed, by advocating an end to exploitation of the
Indian through cultural assimilation, the Indianists in fact
denied a future for indigenous cultures in favour of themselves as middle-class mestizos.[94] But the Indianists
believed that the indirect, bilingual method was more
effective pedagogically than the forceful direct approach
advocated by hispanicists. Ideologically, both groups
sought the eventual absorption of Indians into the hispani-
cised mainstream. Gradually, as evidence seemed to support
the bilingual method, the Indianists came to hold the upper
hand in educational policy.

It was not until the 1970's that a dissenting view within
the Indianist movement emerged. Anthropological research
increasingly revealed a sense of inferiority displayed by
Indian children, and attributed this condition in large measure

to education. The bilingual method is supposed to help suppress feelings of inferiority in its tolerance of biculturation, but the implicit message of hispanic superiority seems unavoidable in the curriculum. National life and history is idealised to break down Indians' resistance to integration.[95] Although an effort is made to depict favourably the Indian population, the emphasis on unity within a mestizo society invites invidious comparisons. In her study of Hueyapan, an indigenous village, Friedlander reports:

'The Hueyapeño children... have just finished learning about how little they do belong. They do not bathe daily or brush their teeth or live in pretty well-furnished homes with gas ranges and refrigerators... And their parents resemble the smiling people dressed in Indian clothes who are frequently depicted in the margins of the pages watching the happy Mestizo school children at play. Thus, since the Hueyapenos are different from the Mestizos, it follows that their history must be different; for if the Indians and the Mestizos have the same history, why are there still two groups today?'[96]

Arizpe observes that Mazahua Indians display resistance to education in comparison to mestizos living in the same areas, and that the contrasting behaviour of these groups can be explained by their differential access to employment and economic opportunities. Mazahua children were unable to gain wage employment in village or town offices. Yet the essentially urban curriculum meant that they could not apply what they learned in school to their agricultural activities. The mestizos, in contrast, could apply this knowledge, since they would be dealing with national institutions and hired in jobs that required skills learned in school. According to Arizpe:

'Schools in the Mazahua region are not instrumental in an absolute sense in bringing about literacy and 'modern' attitudes, that is, behaviour appropriate to industrial work and consumerism. School attendance implies a rejection of the Mazahua identity, and the latter will only be abandoned if economic survival and mobility do not depend on belonging to the ethnic community.'[97]

Pozas and Pozas[98] contend that institutionalised education teaches a set of values that is fundamentally inimical to Indian culture. Traditional Indian life emphasises co-operation and mutual assistance in social relations, and favours egalitarian distribution of economic products. By contrast, the school is orientated toward competitive rivalry, favours inequalities in the distribution of goods, and tolerates economic surplus for some and deprivation for others. These fundamentally different orientations inevitably bring the two cultures into mutual discord. The conflict was made systematic in 1960 when the government decreed that primary school textbooks would be uniform throughout the country.[99]

The results of the integrationist policy have not been favourable. On the one hand, bilingual education has grown enormously to include about 400,000 children. On the other hand, however, there are persistent reports of early attrition and lack of co-operation by children and parents. In an evaluation of the oldest bilingual school system, that of the state of Chiapas, Modiano and Perez[100] found that youngsters who had graduated rather than having dropped out wished overwhelmingly to leave their Indian communities and join the national society. About half became teachers or other government employees serving Indian communities, thus placing themselves with one foot in each world. But most of the others returned to their natal communities with a pervasive sense of failure.

As the unfavourable results of integrationist policy, even with the use of bilingual methods, became clear, the Indianist influence in education took a more pluralistic direction. Indianists tended to adopt the view that Indians could protect themselves effectively from exploitation and externally imposed cultural change while they gain knowledge of the ideas and practices of the national culture in such areas as health, agriculture, medicine, economics, law, electricity, and animal husbandry. With the proper education Indians could choose for themselves the aspects of national culture to adopt and blend with the indigenous culture, as they become equal participants in the social, economic and political life of the nation.[101] To put Indian children in a position to make such choices, they had to become more conscious of the values of their own culture. Therefore, efforts were made to adapt the national social studies programme to local conditions and prepare textbooks on local Indian history.[102]

Such measures have been viewed as mere palliatives by those who contend the inevitability of a clash in cultures with the use of integrationist programmes. Some Indianists argue for the maintenance of Indian ethnicity, and oppose forced cultural integration. In a radical departure from past ideology, they claim that the Indian's loyalties to his own culture - including social organisation, language and religious habits - are not inconsistent with national allegiance. Indeed, they consider sub-national loyalties and cultural divisions as a threat to political integration only when national policy makers promote resentment and incite rebellion by denying cultural and ethnic autonomy to sub-national groups.[103]

In the most recent expression of cultural nationalism, some radical Indianists have gone so far as to call for a reverse in the direction of acculturation, contending that mestizos should be converted into Indians:

'The Mestizo usually is an acculturated Indian who has failed to recognise himself as such. Many of them, despairing of a genuine assimilation that would yield them some benefit, are rediscovering their roots and moving to the front lines in the struggle for our cause, since they have known the pain, humiliation and what it means to lose identity.'[104]

These Indianists believe that Indian languages should be legalised as official national or regional media and taught as primary languages, with Spanish secondary. They accuse organisations such as the Summer Language Institute, a religiously based movement granted official approval to pre- pare textbook translations into Indian lanaguages, of surrep- titiously turning Indians against their own people and thus engaging in 'ethnocide'. Only a genuinely Indian education, they argue, would be non-exploitive:

'We are convinced that the sources of knowledge from which we derive our being, from which we should never have been alienated, are the family and the indigenous community, because in them reside the secret of survival. Traditional Indian education is the only way to extract the knowledge by which we can keep from being objects, become subjects of our own history and succeed as builders of our own destiny.'[105,106]

This radical departure from traditional integrationist Indianist ideology raises the second critical issue regarding Indian culture as it relates to Mexican nationality: to what extent should Mexican identity be infused by the Indian heritage? To be sure, policy makers are unlikely to entertain the radical notion of indianising - or demestizoising - the national population. But they have been slow to consider the potential value of preserving or even enhancing the Indian presence for building national consciousness. The most power- ful instruments of solidarity are the enduring symbols of a nation's uniqueness, and Mexico's distinctiveness lies in its Indian culture, past and present. Yet educational policy in Mexico, even when influenced by Indianist ideology, has con- sistently tilted toward assimilation. That the magnificent National Museum of Anthropology in Mexico City celebrates the ancient civilisations of Mexican Indians, or that some states are allowed to use Indian languages in primary schools, does not negate the government's use of schools to eradicate systematically the Indian cultures. Mexico is a culturally plural state without a pluralistic ideology.

Mexicans seemingly lead a schizophrenic existence. On the one hand, they are besieged by public pronouncements extolling the merits of their national character and calling for solidarity. On the other hand, they read persistently in the literature about their own social and cultural deficiencies. Ramos contends that Mexican history expresses a collective inferiority complex reflected in an obsequious apeing of European culture and giving rise to unhealthy compensations such as aggressive assertions of power that have isolated Mexicans from one another and prevented them from achieving a sense of community.[107] Paz argues that Mexicans have a pervasive sense of loneliness as a result of having renounced their origins. The modern Mexican wishes neither to be Indian nor Spaniard and renounces his descent from them. He thinks of himself not as a mixture but as an abstraction. 'He becomes the son of nothingness. His beginnings are in his own self.'[108] Lewis claims that Mexican society is racked by a deep cleavage between the privileged and members of the working class who are part of a 'culture of poverty' disposing them to violence, authoritarianism, fatalism, and machismo. In this crucible of countervailing messages education is called upon to achieve unity and a coherent sense of nationality.[109]

Effective strategies to build a strong national consciousness can be designed. The cynicism generated by monopolisation of power inherent in the camarilla system could be countered psychologically perhaps by an education that promotes unity by stressing the distinctiveness that Mexicans share by virtue of their Indian heritage. Political favouritism might be ignored within a context of enlightened tolerance for multiple cultures. Yet school authorities - however much they lament intrusions on Mexican culture from the outside, especially the US - eschew the promotion of Indian culture in favour of assimilationist policies.[110] Or, resistance by Indians and other disfavoured groups to embracing a national identity could plausibly be reduced by genuine reform of the political system. It would be easier for disfavoured minorities to relinquish traditional cultural traits if assimilation brought political equality. But political reform cannot be achieved without eliminating the favouritism associated with the camarillas and personalism in the élite schools. Unless appeals for unity are combined with an education that genuinely promotes the unique cultural traits in the Mexican national character or that offers fundamentally equal opportunities for all Mexicans to succeed, they will be heard by only a few. As long as neither strategy is applied, such appeals will hardly be meaningful outside of an even smaller circle: those who are already favoured by the system.

REFERENCES AND NOTES

1. Ramos, S. (1962) Profile of Man and Culture in Mexico. University of Texas Press.
2. Paz, O. (1961) The Labyrinth of Solitude: Life and Thought in Mexico.
3. Hoy, T. (1982) Octavio Paz: The Search for Mexican Identity. The Review of Politics. 44, pp. 370-383.
4. Kinzer, N. S. (1973) Priests, Machos and Babies: or, Latin American Women and the Manichaean Heresy. Journal of Marriage and Family, 33, pp. 300-312.
5. Fuentes, C. (1973) Tiempo Mexicano. Editorial Joaquin. pp. 127-128. Translation by writer.
6. Burns, E. B. (1977) Latin America: A Concise Interpretive History. Prentice Hall. p. 165.
7. Soustelle, J. (1961) Daily Life of the Aztecs. Stanford University Press.
8. Gill, C. C. (1969) Education in a Changing Mexico. US Government Printing Office.
9. Estrada, L. J. and Thomas, J. LaBelle (1980) Mexico in Corsini, R. and Ignas, E. (Eds) Comparative Educational Systems. F. E. Peacock Publishers.
10. Keen, B. (1971) The Aztec Image in Western Thought. Rutgers University Press. p. 456.
11. Weinberg, M. (1977) A Chance to Learn: A History of Race and Education in the United States. Cambridge University Press. p. 141.
12. Alvear Acevedo, C. (1962) La Educación y la Ley: La Legislación en Materia Educativa en el México Independiente. Editorial Jus.
13. Vaughan, M. K. (1982) The State, Education and Social Class in Mexico, 1880-1928. Northern Illinois University Press.
14. Zea, L. (1978) El Positivismo en México: Nacimiento, Apogeo, y Decadencia. Fondo de Cultura Economica.
15. Vaughan, M. K. (1982). op. cit.
16. Ibid.
17. Ibid.
18. Gomez Navas, L. (1968) Política Educativa de México, I. Editorial Patria. pp. 67-105.
19 Gill, C. C. (1969). op. cit.
20. Vaughan, M. K. (1982). op. cit.
21. Cadena, L. (1921) Elementos de Historia General y de Historia Patria, Vol. 2. Herrero Hermanos. pp. 70-81.
22. Raby, D. (1974) Educación y Revolución Social. Sep-Setentas.
23. México, (1983) Plan Programa Presupuesto, 1982. Secretaria de Educación Pública.
24. México (1983) Informe de Labores, 1981-82. Secretaria de Educación Pública.

25. Perissinotto, G. (1983) Educational Reform in Mexico. Current History. 82, pp. 425-428, p. 437.
26. México, (1981) Festejos en el Aniversario 60 de la SEP. Memorandum Técnico de la Secretaría de Educación Pública Año 3, No. 19, p. 1.
27. México (1982) Memoria, 1976-1982: I. Politica Educativa. Dirección General de Publicaciones y Bibliotecas de la Secretaria de Educación Publica, p. 19. Translation by writer.
28. Villaseñor, R. and Fanny, E. de Rosas (1981) Educación para Adultos: Un Problema Complejo. Memorandum Técnico de la Secretaria de Educación Pública. Año 3, No. 19, pp. 5-10.
29. Ibid.
30. Isenman, P. et al. (1980) World Development Report, 1980. The World Bank.
31. Hyman, H. (1953) The Value System of Different Classes: A Social Psychological Contribution to the Analysis of Stratification. pp. 426-442, in Bendix, R. and Lipset, S. M. (Eds) Class, Status and Power. The Free Press.
32. Hollingshead, A. B. (1949) Elmtown's Youth. Wiley.
33. Davis, W. A. and Havighurst, R. J. (1947) Socio-economic Status, Intelligence, and the Attainment of Higher Education. Sociology of Education. 40, pp. 1-23.
34. Sewell, Witt. and Saka, V. P. (1967) Socio-economic Status, Intelligence, and the Attainment of Higher Education. Sociology of Education. 40, pp. 1-23.
35. Coleman, J. S., Campbell, E. Q. et al (1966) Equality of Educational Opportunity. US Department of Health, Education and Welfare.
36. Peaker, G. F. (1971) The Plowden Children Four Years Later. National Foundation for Educational Research in England and Wales.
37. Wiley, D. E. (1976) Another Hour, Another Day: Quantity of Schooling, a Potent Path for Policy. pp. 225-267, in Sewell, W. H., Hauser, R. M. and Featherman D.L. (Eds), Schooling and Achievement in American Society.
38. Bidwell, C. E. and Kasarda, J. D. (1975) School District Organization and Student Achievement. American Sociological Review. 40, pp. 55-70.
39. Harnischfeger, A. and Wiley, D. E. (1980) Determinants of Pupil Opportunity, pp. 223-266, in Dreeben, R. and Thomas, J. A. (Eds) The Analysis of Educational Productivity. Vol. 1, Issues in Microanalysis. Ballinger.
40. Hyman, H. H. and Wright, C. R. (1979) Education's Lasting Influence on Values. University of Chicago Press.
41. Hyman, H. H., Wright, C. R. and Reed, J. S. (1975) The Enduring Effects of Education. University of

Chicago Press.

42. Brown, B. and Sakes, D. (1975) The Production and Distribution of Cognitive Skills within Schools. *Journal of Political Economy*. 83, pp. 571-593.

43. Muñoz, I. C. and Guzman, J. T. (1971) Una Exploración de los Factores Determinantes del Rendimiento Escolar en la Educación Primaria. *Revista del Centro de Estudios Educativos*. 2, pp. 7-27.

44. Ibarrola, M. N. de (1970) *Pobreza y Aspiraciones Escolares*. Centro de Estudios Educativos.

45. Mir, A. A. (1979) Origenes Socioeconomicos, Status de la Escuela y Aspiraciones y Expectativas Educativas y Ocupacionales de Estudiantes de Secundaria. pp. 101-124 in Morales-Gomez, D. A. (Ed) *La Educación y Desarrollo Dependiente en America Latina*. Ediciones Gernika.

46. Currie, J. (1977) Family Background, Academic Achievement, and Occupational Status in Uganda. *Comparative Education Review*. 21, pp. 14-28.

47. Fry, G. W. (1980) Education and Success: A Case Study of Thai Public Service. *Comparative Education Review*. 24, pp. 21-34.

48. Heyneman, S. P. (1980) Differences Between Developed and Developing Countries: Comment on Simmons and Alexander's Determinants of School Achievement. *Economic Development and Cultural Change*. 28, pp. 403-406.

49. Heyneman, S. P. and Loxley, W. A. (1983) The Effect of Primary School Quality on Academic Achievement Across Twenty-Nine High and Low-Income Countries. *American Journal of Sociology*. 83, pp. 1162-1194.

50. Epstein, E. H. (1971) Education and Peruanidad: Internal Colonialism in the Peruvian Highlands. *Comparative Education Review*. 15, pp. 188-201.

51. Epstein, E. H. (1982) Peasant Consciousness under Peruvian Military Rule. *Harvard Educational Review*. 52, pp. 280-300.

52. Epstein, E. H. (1967) National Identity and the Language Issue in Puerto Rico. *Comparative Education Review*. 11, pp. 133-143.

53. Ramos, S. (1962). op. cit.

54. Needleman, C. and Needleman, M. (1969) Who Rules Mexico? A Critique of Some Current Views of the Mexican Political Process. *Journal of Politics*. 31, pp. 1011-1034.

55. Legg, K. R. (1972) Interpersonal Relationships and Comparative Politics: Political Clientism in Industrial Society. *Politics*. 7, pp. 1-10.

56. Tuohy, W. S. (1973) Centralism and Political Elite in Mexico, pp. 260-280 in Thurber, C. E. and Graham, L. S. (Eds) *Development Administration in Latin America*.

Duke University Press.

57. Camp, R. A. (1980) Mexico's Leaders: Their Education and Recruitment. University of Arizona Press.
58. Ibid.
59. Fagen, R. and Tuohy, W. (1972) Politics and Privilege in a Mexican City. Stanford University Press, pp. 25-26.
60. Espinoza, I. (1979) Algunas Reflexiones sobre la Educación Superior en México, pp. 125-142 in Morales-Gomez, D.A. (Ed) La Educación y Desarrolla Dependiente en América Latina. Ediciones Gernika.
61. Camp, R. A. (1980). op. cit.
62. Ibid.
63. Prewitt, K. and Eulan, H. (1971) Social Bias in Leadership Selection, Political Recruitment, and Electoral Context. Journal of Politics. 33, pp. 293-315.
64. Camp, R. A. (1980). op. cit.
65. Ibid.
66. Pescador, J. A. (1981) La Crisis Fiscal y el Financiamiento de la Educación Superior en México. pp. 149-177, in Niebla, G. G. (Ed) La Crisis de la Educación Superior en México. Editorial Nueva Imagen.
67. Espinoza, I. (1979) op. cit.
68. Perissinotto, G. (1983) op. cit.
69. Escudero, R. and Della Rocca, S. M. (1978) Mexico: Generation of '68. North American Congress on Latin America Report on the Americas. 23, pp. 8-19.
70. UNESCO (1974 and 1980-1983) Statistical Yearbooks, 1973, 1978-1979, 1980, 1981, 1982, 1983.
71. Perissinotto, G. (1983) op. cit.
72. Padua, J. A. (1981) Movilidad Social y Universidad. pp. 127-148, in Niebla, G. G. (Ed) La Crisis de la Educación Superior en México. Editorial Nueva Imagen.
73. Beachy, D. (1983) Universities' Plight in Latin America Troubles Scholars. Chronicle of Higher Education. 12, pp. 29-30.
74. Chronicle of Higher Education (1984), May 2, p. 31.
75. Camp, R. A. (1980) op. cit.
76. UNESCO op. cit.
77. Padua, J. A. (1981) op. cit.
78. Epstein, E. H. (1983) La Identidad Nacional y la Capacitación de Técnicos. Memoria del Primer Congreso Latinoamericano de Educación Tecnológica. Instituto Colombiano para el Fomento de la Educación Superior. pp. 123-131.
79. Friedlander, J. (1975) Being Indian in Hueyapan: A Study of Forced Identity in Contemporary Mexico. St. Martin's Press.
80. Aguirre Beltran, G. (1967) Regiones de Refugio. Instituto Nacional Indigenista.

81. Caso, A. (1968) Definición del Indio y lo Indio.
     América Indígena. 8.
82. Fuente, J. de la (1947) Definición, Pase y Desaparición
     del Indio en México. América Indígena. 1.
83. Pozas, R. and Pozas, I. H. de (1978). Los Indios en las
     Clases Sociales de México. Siglo Veintiuno Editores.
84. Warren, K. B. (1978) The Symbolism of Subordination:
     Indian Identity in a Guatemalen Town. University of
     Texas Press.
85. Hunt, R. and Hunt, E. (1967) Education as an Interface
     Institution in Rural Mexico and the American Inner
     City. Midway. 8, pp. 99-109.
86. Stabb, M. S. (1959) Indigenism and Racism in Mexican
     Thought. Journal of Interamerican Studies. 1, pp.
     405-423.
87. Powell, T. G. (1968) Mexican Intellectuals and the
     Indian Question, 1876-1911. Hispanic American
     Historical Review. 48, pp. 19-36.
88. Britton, J. A. (1970) Indian Education, Nationalism and
     Federalism in Mexico, 1910-1911. The Americas. 32,
     pp. 445-458.
89. Brice Heath, S. (1972) Telling Tongues: Language
     Policy in Mexico, Colony to Nation. Teachers
     College, Columbia University.
90. Ibid.
91. Ibid.
92. Ibid.
93. Powell, T. G. (1968) op. cit.
94. Muñoz, B. (1982) Sons of the Wind: The Search for
     Identity in Spanish American Indian Literature.
     Rutgers University Press.
95. Vazquez de Knauth, J. (1975) Nacionalismo y Educación
     en México. El Colegio de México.
96. Friedlander, J. (1975) op. cit.
97. Arzipe, L. (1980) Cultural Change and Ethnicity in
     Rural Mexico, pp. 123-134 in Preston, D. A. (Ed)
     Environment, Society, and Rural Change in Latin
     America. John Wiley.
98. Pozas, R. and Pozas, I. H. de (1978) op. cit.
99. Vazquez de Knauth, J. (1975) op. cit.
100. Modiano, N. and Perez, A. H. (1976) Educación pp. 55-
     73 in Indigenismo en la Acción. Instituto Nacional
     Indigenista.
101. Mack Drake, D. (1978) Bilingual Education Programs for
     Indian Children in Mexico. Modern Language Journal
     62, pp. 239-248.
102. Modiano, N. (1978). Bilingual Education: Research in
     Mexico. International Review of Education. 24, pp.
     410-413.
103. Brice Heath, S. (1972) op. cit.
104. El Dia (July 30, 1979) Declaración de Temoaya.

Translation by writer.

105. Hernandez, F. G. (1979) Declaración de Oaxtepec.
     Speech presented at the First National Seminar on Bi-
     lingual-Bicultural Education Oaxtepec, Morelos,
     Mexico. Mimeo.

106. Bonfil Batalla, G. (1981) Utopía y Revolución: El
     Pensamiento Político Contemporaneo de los Indios en
     América Látina. Editorial Nueva Imagen. The speech
     by Franco Hernandez (1979) is translated by the writer
     and reproduced in this publication.

107. Ramos, S. (1962) op. cit.

108. Paz, O. (1961) op. cit.

109. Lewis, O. (1961). The Children of Sanchez. Random
     House.

110. Solana, F. (1981) Aniversario 60 de la SEP. Memoran-
     dum Técnico de la Secretaria de Educación Pública.
     Año 3, No. 20, pp. 25-29.

Chapter Four

EDUCATIONAL POLICY AND PRACTICE IN PANAMA:
A FOCUS ON ADULT EDUCATION

Pilar Aguilar and Gonzalo Retamal

To a very important extent Panama is the product of
Theodore Roosevelt's 'gunboat diplomacy' in Latin America.
Colombia did not accept the terms of the government of the
USA for the construction of an inter-oceanic canal in the
territory of Panama, up to that time a province of Colombia.
So American agents and some local self-appointed leaders provoked a 'revolutionary' movement of 'independence' in 1903,
which the US promptly recognised and backed with military
intervention. Panama was made dependent upon US political
and military authority. The Canal Zone split the country in
two and became a US enclave from where direct influence was
exerted over the divided Republic. Under these opprobrious
colonial conditions the Republic of Panama began its historical life as an 'independent' nation.
        However, it should be recognised that during the nine-
teenth century the Colombian province of Panama had not been
given sufficient attention by the central government in
Bogota, and a certain regionalist disdain and resentment
towards the central government had been engendered among the
Isthmians. Some attempts to gain Independence had been made
during that period, reinforcing a local regionalist ideology.
As has been pointed out by Ricahurte Soler, the 1903 attempt
had the open backing of a local élite which in fact was looking to promote their own economic interest, thus providing the
classical combination for dependency:

        'The landowners, the commercial bourgeoisie and sectors
        of the petit bourgeoisie were willing to increase the
        value of the Isthmic lands and transform Panama City on
        the Pacific and Colon in the Atlantic coast into big
        world markets under their control. Thus, being in con-
        nivance with US imperialism, they set off forces which in
        the end went out of their hands.'[1]

The educational record in the province during the nineteenth century had been totally inadequate. By 1888 there

79

were only 49 schools with an enrolment of 2,727 students, increasing by 1897 to 4,200.   This poor educational profile continued up to the time of independence from Colombia.

While the 'founding fathers' of the new Republic were committed to the development of education it was still profoundly orientated to the old liberal educational credo of the nineteenth century.   Also, the goals were too high, and the spirit behind the verbatim records of the 1913 First Panamanian Educational Assembly show that the system was basically designed to furnish the manpower needs of the new merchant élite.   This approach proposed that a clear-cut projection of class differentiation within the system should be provided:

> 'The cultural heritage given to the child should be determined by the social position he will or should occupy. For this reason education should be different in accordance with the social class to which the student should be related to.'[2]

None the less, it became evident that as part of the building up of Panama, a US model of 'progressive education' should replace such a conservative ideological pattern.   US assistance became quite active in the educational field after 1920, and the shift to Dewey's concepts of education was clearly evident by 1924.   Was Panama considered to be one of the Latin American countries where pedagogical solutions had been envisaged as the appropriate mechanism for achieving the democratic 'American Dream'? Panamanian pedagogues such as Jephta Duncan and José Crespo became the leading figures of a neo-liberal ideology which relied in an over-optimistic manner on the Panamanian school as the agency for democratisation and the building up of nationalistic self-reliance.   According to Duncan, schools were not to be:

> 'The exclusive patrimony of some political party, nor of any religious sect or social class, but only, part of the Nation, for the Nation.'[3]

The idea of a so-called neutral state was the fiction through which the ideas of Lunarchavsky or Dewey were supposed to develop without conflict.   Furthermore it was precisely this mixture of educational ideologies that gave force to the Pananamian state educational actions of the 1920's and part of the 1930's.

The Secretary of Public Instruction in his address to the nation in 1926 proposed:

> 'It has become increasingly evident that the final goal of our Republic is the need of an education able to help social upward mobility, based on moral, intellectual and

national capacity.'[4]

Some very important developments were produced under this
educational philosophy. Panama became the country with the
highest percentage of its budget devoted to education.   In
1937, for example, 25 per cent of the state budget was dedicated to developing a wide network of primary and secondary
school facilities, and between 1920 to 1934 the primary school
enrolment had already doubled.

However, it should be said that these profound changes in
the educational sphere were not always directly involved with
the education of adults.   According to Madrigales,[5] although
Adult Education was an important issue considered by the
Pedagogical Assembly in 1913, by 1920 there were still only
two adult schools in the country.   By 1923 some steps had
been taken towards such a development.   It is noteworthy
that a special curriculum and programme was laid down for the
Escuelas Nocturnas: five hours weekly of spanish and arithmetic, three hours of civic instruction and two hours of
calligraphy constituted the basic core.   This course was
supposed to function in every provincial capital, and in
Panama City a special course on typing was added with two
hours a week.   The adult programme was scheduled from Monday
to Friday, from 7 to 9 p.m.   There was no special training
for school teachers who took adult classes, but these tutors
received an extra monthly allowance of 10 dollars for their
evening work.[6]   The level of illiteracy, 71.7 per cent in
1923, had been reduced to 50 per cent or less by 1935, by
which time the rapid development of adult education, and
elementary schooling had taken on a different character.
According to de Witt:

> 'The pressures for immediate relief from a depression-
> ridden society were becoming too great to be warded off
> with promises of a better education.'[7]

By 1942, adult education was reconsidered, as part of a
wider reform, with a view to improving its previous low performance within the overall system.   As was pointed out by
senior educational official F. Cespedes:

> 'An educational programme that attempts to develop in the
> young, new attitudes, habits and ways of living, must
> reach the home if it is to be effective.   A programme
> of adult education is therefore indispensable.'[8]

Such a programme, became part of the responsibility attached
to the primary school teacher, who was compelled to devote
part of his or her time to the education of illiterate parents
of day pupils.   However, the initial motivations aroused by
the mid-twenties and thirties were definitely collapsing, and

such provisions fell in a vacuum of increasing bureaucratisa-
tion and apathy. Moreover, most of the early social-liberal
ideology of Duncan and Crespo, although it helped to create
an educational philosophy of the state which is still power-
fully expressed in important educational budgets:

> 'Insensibly degenerated in purely scholastic repetition
> of its motivations and in a sort of inefficient phil-
> osophy aiming to resolve problems through a limitating
> specialised 'technification'.[9]

The political upheavals of the Panamanian state, contributed to the rapid decline of education during the 1940's.
The corruption of the dominant élite in smuggling and illegal
trade, the pervasive cultural US Canal Zone influence in the
everyday life of the Panamanians, and the rising racialist
and prejudiced attitude of 'zonians' towards 'latins' and
'niggers',[10] combined to create a situation of cultural and
political instability which opened the corridors of power to
a corrupt civil dictatorship and to the US trained constabu-
lary officials. Under these circumstances, the State became
not a promoter of education, but rather, as was pointed out
by Escobar, a distributor of jobs, contracts, purchases and
expense accounts which 'maintained the proper atmosphere for
all kinds of shananigans'.[11]

By 1944, although 67 per cent of the population of
Panama lived in rural areas, the existing school systems were
patterned according to a commercial and urban-centred economy.
The school teachers, still influenced by the liberal-social
programme of the 1920's, were somehow involved in the organisation and promotion of adult education in the countryside,
but such projects remained as purely spontaneous and short-
range activities. By the mid-1940's Ofelia Hooper offered
the following critical analysis:

> 'The school as organised today is an isolated phenomenon,
> completely out of touch with the government institutions
> which have been organised to give land to the farmers,
> teach them scientific farming and improve their primitive
> sanitary conditions. It has no connection whatever with
> those groups which labour to improve social and economic
> conditions, although it could be of outstanding import-
> ance if utilised as it should be.'[12]

It should also be added that during nearly fifty years of
educational development, adult education remained as a secondary and erratic factor in the process of bringing down the
illiteracy rates from 71.2 per cent in 1911 to 28.3 per cent
by 1950. The convictions of Duncan and Crespo were not
sufficient to force tangible results in the area of adult
education. Consequently, its contribution was meagre, and by

Educational Policy and Practice in Panama:
A Focus on Adult Education

1950 mostly orientated towards secondary and vocational
education of the urban youth.[13]

By the 1960's, under the pressures of the Alliance for
Progress, some attempts at reform were made under the US hand-
picked Presidents Roberto Chiari and Marco Robles, though
still to very little effect. In the words of Hanke, Panamanian politics was in 1959, still profoundly elitist:

> 'Political decisions in Panama have been made by a few
> powerful families by shifting political combinations, by
> the national police, at times by the clamour of an
> aroused populace, often by American authorities.'[14]

It should also be said that since the beginning of the 1950's,
under the venal and personal leadership of J. A. Remon, the
Guardia Nacional had become the decisive arbiter of Panamanian politics. It ousted Arnulfo Arias, a civilian and
equally venal leader, from the Presidency. However, in the
1970's the Guardia Nacional stepped in for good. Colonel
Omar Torrijos was installed as a dictator, his role legiti-
mised by a new Constitution which granted him extraordinary
powers for a period of six years. However, some populist
measures were taken, some structures of participation were
created at grass-root level, Asambleas de Corregimientos. A
national political body, the Assembly of National Representatives was formed from other state sponsored local organisations. Initial attempts at social and politial mobilisation under the charismatic figure of Torrijos, were generated
with the implementation of an agrarian reform, and other
initiatives of modernisation.

These developments notwithstanding, authoritarianism and
personal paternalism tinted every act of government, and most
decisions were taken by a small but well trained and powerful
military clique. Thus, civilian leaders, or even political
parties across a wide ideological spectrum ranging from
Liberals to Communists, attached themselves to this clique in
order to push forward their personal and social interests.
According to Ropps:

> 'An understanding of the formal machinery of government
> is less important than knowledge of the linkages that
> exist between various high-ranking officers and their
> respective political clientele.'[15]

Apart from this complicated and interpersonal power structure,
it should be recognised that using personal and populist
appeal over rural areas, Torrijos was able to exert, for the
first time in the history of any Panamanian Government, organised leadership against the urban-centred élites. Even more
important, he was in a position to canvass in favour of the
nationalisation of the Canal Zone.

Educational Policy and Practice in Panama:
A Focus on Adult Education

During the first years of the Torrijos government, the military confronted the Catholic orientated organisations working in rural areas.   Repression and the death of priests, allegedly at the hands of the government police, alienated the potential support of the Church for the 'Revolutionary Government' of Torrijos.   Now in the mid-1980's, although not openly against reform, the Church looks with undisguised contempt on the growth and development of state orientated educational and so-called competitive actions among peasants. In practice, however, the co-operation of church and state varies from one part of Panama to another.   For example, in the Northern area of Veraguas, one of the most isolated and poor campesino regions in the country, the Catholic agency CEPAS working in educational actions and community development projects, does not reject totally the social approach of the government agencies in the area. [16]

Agrarian reform has in fact made significant progress, partly because the rural structure of Panama is not heavily concentrated and also because about 90 per cent of the land belongs to the state.   However, little has been done in the urban areas that could be deemed to be equally radical.   The 'Panamanian Revolution' exhibits the same neutrality observed in the slogans of the 'Peruvian Revolution', that is to say towards a third way.   This is illustrated in the slogans of the government, though adding in this case a personalistic touch: 'Neither Communism, nor Capitalism: with Torrijos!'. Certainly, on the 'capitalist' dimension during the 1970's, the government removed most of the limitations on transnational operations.   The Colon Free Zone, the Canal, the dollar-tied monetary system, the systems of tax havens for merchant fleets, and the 'paper' companies and banks have all been given room to operate.   Indeed the existence of the national currency Balboa is nearly nominal.   The domination of the Panamanian economy by the transnational dimension can be illustrated by the fact that in 1976 the internal product was about US$2.2 billions, while the transnational platform operating in the country served 11 billion dollars of foreign deposits, 75 per cent of it in the hands of transnational banks. [17]

On the other hand there have certainly been some socialistic moves.   For example, between 1970 to 1972, some modernising attempts favouring the urban workers and marginal sectors were generated.   Several laws for the control of job stability, social security and housing speculation were promulgated, plus other redistributive measures.   However, under the pressure of the urban and transnational set, such laws were reviewed and eventually rescinded by a new decree, Ley 95.   This measure has generated a sense of discontent and distrust among trade unions and other urban popular sectors which once supported the government. [18]   This episode serves to depict the intrinsic weakness of the government and

especially its dependent bonds with transnational interest.
Although public investment between 1973 to 1975 increased by
about 53 per cent this process has been mostly linked to the
development of a modern infrastructure able to cope with the
requirements of transnational capital.[19]   In fact every action orientated towards social development has only impinged
marginally on the overall structure of the dependency of
Panama.   The process of agrarian reform left untouched the
US Banana enclave in the Northern regions of Bocas del Toro
and Chiriqui.   Actually, the popular basis of support which
is dominated by the governmental system has declined, with
only about 300 agrarian reform settlements involved, occupying 5 per cent of the cultivable land and engaging only 6 per
cent of the total rural working population.   Recent but
erratic action in favour of indigenous tribes, which constitute a small minority of the population, while commendable in
itself contributes very little to resolving the problems of
the mass of the rural population.

In fact, the key element behind the stability of the
regime in terms of 'popular' support should not be seen in the
process of mild internal reformism, but rather in the dynamics
of profoundly rooted nationalism and anti-imperialism emerging
out of the special circumstance of the Canal Zone and US
territorial and military presence in Panama.   Even in the
important agreements reached in 1980, the US succeeded in
introducing a very important clause which gives to that
country the right to intervene not only in the Canal Zone but
also Panama in general, for strategic purposes which are not
only of the military and geopolitical type:

'but also because the American presence in the Canal is
the only guarantee for the important financial operations
in Panama itself.'[20]

The degree to which the Panamanian government can command
popular support on the basis of anti-imperial rhetoric is un-
matched in Latin America, except possibly in the virtual US
colony of Puerto Rico.   So any analysis of the educational
sphere, and particularly of the state system must consider
this context.

The political decay of the 1950's had produced a parallel
collapse of the state educational system, especially at the
primary school level.   By 1955, even official sources recognised that: '... more than 50,000 children went to school[21]
barefoot or sitting down on packing cases or on the floor.'
Most of the budget was allocated to the post-primary sector.
While the rate of illiteracy remained stagnant for nearly two
decades at around 25 per cent, the absolute number of illiterates was rising by at least 15,000 per year.   With the introduction of Alliance for Progress policies during the 1960's,
some provision for reform was made.   However, USAID

educational packages stressed assistance for secondary school
building in the urban areas.[22]   During this time, some provision for vocational education was made and a comprehensive
scheme for adult education was proposed, but as always, the
resources allocated to this provision were woefully inadequate.
Thus, the provisions for combating illiteracy and for basic
adult education needs reached only 8,509 adults in 1964. This
is a miniscule figure if compared with the target illiterate
population of 155,000.[23]   It should perhaps be noted that the
above figures do represent some improvement as compared with
the 1956 to 1957 provision, where only four night schools
existed with an enrolment of not more than 400 adult students.[24]

     By the end of the 1960's, an attempt to reorganise the
administrative and curricula aspects of the educational
system was launched by the government under the total and
direct supervision of a 'University of Pennsylvania - USAID
Agreement'.   The aims and goals of the new Panamanian system
were tailored by these foreign agencies without significant
consultation with the Panamanian counterparts.   Indeed, some
of the US advisers never even took the trouble to learn
Spanish!   The aims of the project were 'purely technical',
that is to say concerned with the achievement of the 'maximum
development of human resources'.[25]   After Torrijos took
over, the leftist and liberal sectors within the Ministry of
Education, pushed forward for different aims.   These were
the reorientation of the project of educational reform towards
a nationalistic and socially orientated perspective, following closely the Peruvian blueprint of reform.   This approach
was rationalised in suitably pompous language, in the 1971
general report of the newly appointed National Commission of
Educational Reform:

> 'The education of the people is encouraged when faced to
> decide the basic dilemma proposed by History: An educa-
> tion which should provoke, give life to an autonomous
> personal consciousness, generate and give rise to the
> transforming energy of the collective consciousness and
> permit a definition of its own values: Popular Educa-
> tion, scientific, Panamanian and Democratic.'[26]

Central to this scheme was the nationalistic bias, an element
considered basic in the task of generating a sense of self-
reliance and to reassert the right of Panama over the Canal
Zone enclave.   It was also considered important to give a
more selective treatment to the diverse cultural models
imported, so as to avoid reproduction of 'dependency, multiple
domination and cultural and social colonialism'.[27]   Finally,
it was decided that state education should be considered as a
redistributive tool of the social product of the Panamanian
society and as such should help to rectify existing

disparities and inequalities in the human condition.

The implementation of these guidelines was enabled by an important allocation of resources in the educational sector. From 30 million dollars in 1969, the educational budget was more than doubled by 1977; a significant increase even when inflation is accounted for.[28]   Investment was channelled mostly into the formal network, Red escolarizada, which followed a pattern similar to the one observed in the basic nine-year provision of the Peruvian educational nuclei. The objectives included not only a basic 3R training and some purely intellectual skills, but also the possible development of a linked practical-theoretical education - an important component on vocational education with an occupationally orientated vocational component well to the fore, especially in the last grades of the system.[29]

While it should be recognised that important efforts have been made to cope with the problems encountered at the rural primary level, where most of the misery and underdevelopment are concentrated, the non-formal scheme of Red no escolarizada is mostly orientated towards two aspects: pre-school education, and adult non-formal education.

Adult education provision has been organised in the same fashion as the Peruvian Educación Básica Laboral, and it is an attempt to integrate the dispersed and overlapping efforts of several Ministries and other autonomous agencies.[30]   This effort of coordination is in the hands of the Adult Education Section of the Ministry of Education.   It comprises the provision of basic adult and literacy education, and the organisation of vocational training in those areas of activity considered by the government as top priority: Agrarian Reform Centres, Co-operatives, Communal Organisations and Special Development Projects.   In general three adult education sub-programmes have been developed at the Ministerial level: literacy and basic adult education; basic labour instruction; special handicrafts.

Between 1970 to 1975 it was claimed that the allocation of resources to literacy and adult basic education was quadrupled.[31]   However, during the years 1979 and 1980 the budgeting of adult education was reduced to something less than 0.8 per cent of the total educational budget.   By considering the figures in the table overleaf it may be suggested that much of the significance of the reduction in the illiteracy rate to 18 per cent in the last decade, is due to a concentration of effort in the primary provision of the Red Escolarizada, rather than to the contribution of the non-formal adult education network.

In attempting to assess the problems involved in adult and non-formal provision it is interesting to note the fact that by 1970 the target population of adult illiterates was 116,363 and growing at a rate of 9.6 per cent in one decade.[32] The actual coverage of the adult education provision in terms

Panama: Enrolment for Non-Formal and Adult Education: 1972-76

Year	Total	Literacy and Basic Adult Education	Basic Training	Special Handicrafts
1972	17,850	14,484	3,206	160
1973	31,221	27,240	3,852	133
1974	20,246	16,480	3,701	65
1975	29,419	24,497	4,810	112
1976*	16,696	11,444	5,162	90

*in 1976 a network of 520 centres existed with a staff of 965 tutors.

Source: Ministry of Education (1977), Panama.

- - - - -

of enrolment during the next decade was 169,267.   However, it
should be noticed that according to recent data only 28,806
adults who attended the basic provision were made literate,
some were enrolled in other provisions, but the majority were
not retained by the sub-system.[33]   Moreover, if such a meagre
output is compared with the enrolment data in the table, it
is clear that the performance of the basic adult education
provision is profoundly inefficient and the final results,
most discouraging.   Given the meagre allocation of resources,
the targets for 1979 and 1980 were reduced to a meaningless
level.   The illiteracy enrolment target for 1979 was as low
as 9,800 illiterates, and for 1980 even worse: 8,700
illiterate adults.[34]   The present provision means a return to
the same absolute figure of 1964.
       Such an appalling record, when analysed within the frame-
work of the general trends of Panamanian literacy and educational attainment, appears to be even more disturbing.   A
fairly recent UNESCO follow-up report of the age cohorts of
Panamanian illiterates which by 1950 had 10, 15, 20 and 25
years of age, suggests that little improvement had occurred in
their situation.   Indeed in some cases, as in the oriental
region of the country, the rate of illiteracy in each age group
had worsened with time.   The most plausible explanation for
the enlargement of the illiterate cohort in recent decades
could be the lack of continuity of the formal or informal
educational action.   Under these conditions, the campesinos
have slipped back into functional illiteracy, which is not
surprising given their marginal and isolated situation.[35]

Educational Policy and Practice in Panama:
A Focus on Adult Education

The examination of such figures and trends is helpful in order
to reinforce the idea that adult education is in Panama a
function of the state, and has a very inefficient structure.
Whatever the rhetoric used by the 'Revolution' to portray its
actual commitments, adult education as a function of the state
system remains in a condition of inertia unable to produce
any significant change.   The potential contribution of the
adult education section of the Ministry is any case restrained
by totally inadequate budgetary allocations.   Moreover, when
important methodological and technical contributions are
developed by the very efficient group of experts working in
the National Directory of Adult Education, those contributions
are reduced or banned.   There ensues a consequent loss of
time, money and perhaps, in the case of the Ministerial
técnicos, patience.
   Behind the governmental rhetoric, there is no doubt an
informal mechanism of political control, that is aware of both
intra-Ministry and external criticism.   The banning of the
Guía del Alfabetizador[36] (Guide for Illiteracy Teachers), very
well devised under the inspiration of Paulo Freire's ideas and
the basic nationalistic principles of the 'Panamanian Revolution' of 1972, is a typical case.   Perhaps one of the most
mature and technically best devised state sponsored projects
of illiteracy in Latin America, albeit based on small budgetary allocations and voluntary action, this scheme was appar-
ently banned without consultation.   Engendering communism
was alleged.   Such a situation shows the weak and unstable
position of the progressive adult educators working within the
state apparatus of the 'Panamanian Revolution'.   In fact,
following a controlled return to 'civil government', and
before his death in 1981, Torrijos was becoming less and less
committed to the development of what had been defined as the
'embryos of popular power' in the jargon of the so-called
revolution.   In other words, a process of demobilisation of
the grass-roots organisations created in 1970 to 1972 was
observed in the early 1980's.   This situation helped to pre-
vent the full implementation of a literacy campaign, which
necessarily had to be based on the voluntary effort of the
grass-roots organisations.   Field interviews[37] with important
decision-makers at the Ministry level emphasised this situation as the basic structural constraint on the development of
a definitive solution to the problem of literacy and adult
education in Panama.   It was also possible to perceive that
the illusions of many well intentioned and progressive
Panamanian adult educators had been let down by the 'middle-of
the-road' Panamanian Revolution.   Thus the phenomenon which
was confirmed in the case of the Peruvian adult education
experiment of the 1970's, was also repeated in the case of
Panama.

Educational Policy and Practice in Panama:
A Focus on Adult Education

REFERENCES AND NOTES

1. Soler, R. (1977), Formas Ideológicas de la nación panemeña. p. 112.
2. Soler, N. J. de (1966), De una educación de clases a una educación Popular. Unpublished dissertation, Universidad de Panama. p. 66.
3. Soler, R. (1977), op. cit., p. 70.
4. Canton, A. (1955), Desenvolvimiento de las ideas pedagógicas en Panama, 1903-1926. Imprenta Nacional. pp. 95-96.
5. Madrigales, Y. (1956), Panama. La Educación. 1,4 pp. 35-36
6. Quintana, I. M. (1957), Educación del adulto en Panama. Unpublished dissertation, Universidad de Panama.
7. Witt, D. L. de (1977), Educational Thoughts in Panama: The Pedagogical Movement of the 1920's. Caribbean Studies. 17, 1-2 p. 144.
8. Cespedes, F. S. (1942), Panama. Educational Yearbook of the International Institute. p. 324.
9. Soler, R. (1977), op. cit., p. 100.
10. Due to the massive influx of labour for the construction of the Panama Canal, notably from Jamaica, the racial composition of the Panamanian population is distinctive within Latin America in being predominantly negro.
11. As quoted by Biesanz, John and Mavis (1977), The People of Panama. Greenwood Press, p. 140.
12. Hooper, O. (1944), The Plight of Education in Rural Panama. Rural Sociology. 9. p. 54.
13. Madrigales, Y. (1956), op. cit., p. 36.
14. Hanke, L. (1959), Mexico and the Caribbean. p. 28.
15. Ropps, S. C. (1979), Panama's Domestic Power Structure and the Canal: History and Future in Wiarda, H. J. and Kline, H. F. (Eds). Latin American Politics and Development. p. 487.
16. CEPAS (1976), Seminario de Reflexión Doctrinaria. Mimeo. p. 6.
17. Gorostiaga, X. (1977), Panama, n'est pas seulement un canal. La Monde Diplomatique. 29,282, pp. 1, 7, 8. Also on the problems of dependency of Panama: Manduley, J. (1980), Panama: Dependent Capitalism and Beyond. Latin American Perspectives. 7, 2-3. pp. 57-74.
18. Diálogo Social (1979), 12, 115. pp. 10-12.
19. Gorostiaga, X. (1977), op. cit. pp. 7-8.
20. Ibid. p. 1.
21. Panamá: Boletín del Ministerio de Educación (1955). 1,2. p. 2.
22. Pan American Union (1964), Yearbook of Educational, Scientific and Cultural Development in Latin America. pp. 119-120.
23. Villareal, A. A. (1971), Situación y Tendencias del

Analfabetismo en Panama, p. 10.
24. Quintana, I. M. (1957), Educación del adulto en Panama.
    Unpublished dissertation, Universidad de Panama, pp.
    23-24.
25. Panama: Comisión Nacional de la Reforma Educativa
    (CNRE) (1971), Informe general, p. 16.
26. Ibid. p. 2.
27. Ibid. p. 34.
28. Panama: MINEDUC (1977), Informe Nacional, p. 15.
29. Ibid. p. 21.
30. Ibid. p. 28.   Also, for a description of the adult educa-
    tion provision see: Espinoza, B. E. and Rivera, L.
    (1978) Alfabetización y educación de adultos en Panama.
    Revista Interamericana de Educación de Adultos 1,2,
    pp. 274-290.
31. Espinoza B. E. et al (1978), op. cit., p. 287.
32. Villareal, A. A. (1971), op. cit., p. 63.
33. Panama MINEDUC. Dirección General de Alfabetización y
    Educación de Adultos (1979). Boletín Informativo 1,
    pp. 12-13.
34. Ibid. p. 12.
35. Meza, F. M. (1978), Análisis de interacciones entre
    variables demográficas, educativas y socio-económicas
    en países Latinoamericanos, 1950-1990.   UNESCO-OREALC,
    pp. 49-67.
36. Panama MINEDUC, Dirección Nacional de Alfabetización y
    Educación de Adultos (1972).   Guía del Alfabetizador.
37. In this respect, special gratitude is due for the candid
    analysis of the problems of illiteracy and basic adult
    education in Panama given by: Mrs. Blanco Espinoza
    and specially to Mrs. Elda Mau de Rodríguez, Sub-
    Director of Planning at the Ministry of Education.

Chapter Five

POPULAR EDUCATION IN ANDEAN AMERICA:
THE CASE OF ECUADOR

Rosemary Preston

INTRODUCTION

Popular education in Andean America has changed, while
the concept retains its essential characteristics. Popular
education has always been compensatory. Initially it provided a service for those unable to pay for it. The idea of
compensation remains embedded in today's concept of popular
education while the characteristics of the target population
have changed and become more sharply defined.

For most of the present century popular education has
implied the formal education of the majority population by
state educational institutions. Excluded from this is the
education provided for fees to predominantly wealthy minority
groups by private institutions. Traditionally, public sector
education has been less prestigious than that provided for the
élite groups, but as the numbers of public sector institutions
and educands have multiplied many have achieved equally high
or superior reputations, affording their graduates the highest
expectations of employment and income. As access to education has become widespread and such prestige has developed, so
what was formerly popular education has become the norm and no
longer perceived to be compensatory.

This expansion of public education, initially at primary
and later at secondary and tertiary levels has taken place in
Andean America in accordance with the development philosophies
espoused by different national governments. In every case
these represent a commitment to modernisation through industrialisation and to an expected resultant increase in GNP.
Following the path mapped out previously by the advanced
capitalist countries of the West, Andean American governments
believe that the education of the people has a major part to
play in achieving these ends. Firstly, education is seen as
an agent through which allegiance to the development culture
may be fostered. Secondly, as a consequence of this, education is an agent through which skills that will enhance the
efficiency of the workforce, by training them for employment

92

in the expanding modern sector.   Andean American governments
are also explicitly committed to the provision of education as
a human right.   Education, and the new prosperity from the
modernisation of the economy, were looked to as major contributors to the alleviation of poverty and to the more equal
distribution of wealth.

The inescapable fact that in spite of steady economic
growth the distribution of wealth in most Andean American
countries is increasingly uneven, is reflected in the uneven
distribution of educational resources and in the demand for
them in areas where they are deficient.   The people have
learned, and accept, that education is a selection process
through which all should be entitled to pass, and from which
those who are successful expect to find opportunities for
highly remunerated and secure employment.   This in turn entails an expected elevation of cultural and social status.
Inevitably, in spite of this, educational discrimination is
widely observed to be strongest against those already in the
weakest social and economic positions.   They include the
urban poor, but principally the rural and, in particular, the
rural indian populations.   The pattern of inequality is
familiar, with matriculation, retention, repetition rates as
well as staff pupil ratios, favouring the advantaged sectors
of the population.[1]

Explanations of these persistent and growing educational
inequalities, couched in terms of social and economic dualism
or in terms of structural underdevelopment,[2] are usually at
national and regional levels.   Analysis frequently compares
educational development between metropolitan centres and the
rural hinterland or explains it in terms of the penetration of
capitalism and its consequences at national levels.   Analysis
at the subregional level, in particular at the microregional
level of the rural parish is rarer, in spite of the fact that
increasing recognition is being given to the social heteorgen-
eity of very small areas.

In this chapter there follows a discussion of the educational disparities that have been observed within the Ecuadorian rural sector and of how they have changed over time with
the expansion of public education.   (See Fig. 1 for Provinces
of Ecuador)   This leads on to an analysis of how these
differences have been affected by more recent programmes of
popular education intended to overcome them.

SPATIAL VARIATION WITHIN THE RURAL SECTOR

Educational provision within the rural sector varies from
place to place both quantitatively and qualitatively and this
inevitably affects patterns of attainment.   Schools are first
established in small towns and then in villages.   Finally
they are opened in the isolated parish hamlets surrounding the
village centre.   This staging of educational expansion

Fig. 1:   The Provinces of Ecuador

according to settlement importance results in a widely recognised spatial hierarchy of educational attainment that is not
overcome when provision is made at the periphery.   This is
because by the time that a single teacher, three or four-
grade school is opened in a parish district, provision at the
village centre has been augmented to complete primary provision or more.   There is no financial assistance, or provision
of boarding schools, so parents wanting their children to
continue their education beyond the levels available locally
have to meet the concomitant costs themselves.   Most are
unable to do so.

The education provided in the outlying districts of rural
parishes is also qualitatively inferior to that provided in
villages.   Regular teacher absence and limited teacher commitment are widespread.   Often alone, without the moral support
of colleagues that can be found in multi-teacher village

schools, espousing values that are more appropriate to towns
than to rural areas and preoccupied with self-image and status,
the district teacher is often alienated from the local community and from the pupils.   There is frequently a latent
conflict between parental expectations that the teacher will
provide their children with a passport to a more secure and
less arduous life, and the teacher's assumptions that the
children have been so disadvantaged from birth in social,
cultural and welfare terms, that they are beyond help.   Closely
linked to the educational variation that is identifiable in
spatial terms is a well defined social variation.

SOCIAL DIFFERENCES IN ACCESS TO EDUCATION WITHIN THE RURAL
SECTOR OF ECUADOR

Although the exact definition of indian and mestizo is
blurred, it is generally the case that educational provision
and attainment in those areas where the rural population
speaks Quechua is considerably below that where Spanish is the
dominant language.   This is immediately apparent when com-
paring literacy rates between rural areas of mestizo and
indian provinces from 1974 census returns (Fig. 2).

Fig. 2: Literacy Rates in Rural Areas of Ecuadorian Highland
         Provinces

Province	Dominant Rural Population	Literacy Rates (per cent population aged 10+)
Carchi	Mestizo	79.6
Loja	Mestizo	76.0
Pichincha	Mestizo	69.3
Canar	Indian	63.4
Bolivar	Indian	60.9
Imbabura	Indian	52.3
Cotopaxi	Indian	54.3
Chimborazo	Indian	44.0

This discrimination is apparent in two dimensions.
Indians at the rural periphery are less educated than the
mestizo populations who dominate the small towns and villages
at the centre of the parishes in which they live.   They are
also less educated than mestizo populations who live in

isolated parish districts, making them the least educated of
the rural populations.

These differences too can be explained both in terms of
differential rates of initial educational provision and of
increases in provision that favour mestizo and not indian
parishes.   The mestizos' greater economic security, better
organised local demand and closer cultural affinity between
petitioners and ministry officials, explains in some measure
these differences in access to education as between areas of
equivalent settlement status, but which are treated unequally
on the grounds of race.   There is no suggestion that indian
populations are not interested in education, although today an
increasing number are questioning the relevance of the contemporary formal system to themselves as indians, to their
cultural heritage and to their social and economic opportunities.

The quality of education provided in indian rural districts is affected by the same problems as those encountered
in mestizo rural districts, but they are exacerbated considerably by an additional clash in cultural and linguistic values.
Few district teachers in indian areas speak Quechua and their
first task is to teach the children to communicate in Spanish.
Single-handed, in a classroom where ages may range from 6-14,
with little or no preparation in how to accomplish this task
as well as to cover the regular curriculum, with the same
motivational and identity problems of district teachers in
mestizo areas, the quality of education imparted by teachers
in indian areas is often very low.   Pupil drop-out rates and
teacher transfer rates are both high.   Both operate to keep
attainment levels down.   They also ensure the continued
cultural alienation of the indian populations from the dominant value system of the developing state.

Within the rural periphery there is also economic differentiation in access to education.   Children in rural parishes
who spend most time in school come from trading families or
from families with above average amounts of land in their
community.   Farming families with little or no land but who
have devised no alternative economic strategy constitute the
poorest sector of the rural population.   Many cannot afford
to buy books or clothes that are necessary to send their
children to school and they require their children's help at
peak planting and harvesting times to ensure the viability of
the family economy.   In the main, the rural poor live on the
rural periphery, in the isolated hamlets and farmsteads of
the rural parishes.   This means that economic differentiation
in education is closely aligned to differentiation in spatial
terms.

In both mestizo and indian areas within the rural sector,
educational attainment is higher among men than among women.
Of the minority of children who do not go to school, the
majority are female and this differentiation is most exagger-

ated in indian areas.   At school it is the male population
that remains longer in the system than the female.   Experience in rural parishes of Ecuador suggests that girls are
withdrawn from school at the onset of puberty, while boys
continue their education.   Observation also makes it clear
that girls rather than boys are called on to take time out of
school to remain at home to perform domestic chores and to
care for siblings.   However, while sexual differentiation is
apparent in both village centres and their surrounding districts, it appears that such practices occur less frequently
among village families.

EDUCATIONAL DIFFERENTIATION OVER TIME

     The philosophy of modernisation assumes that with
increased development and economic growth there will be a
reduction of social and economic inequalities and an overall
improvement in standard of living.   Dependency theory assumes
that social and economic differentiation will increase between
the centre and the periphery as the capitalist classes continue to further their own interests in the pursuit of profit
at the expense of the non-capitalist classes.   The one would
assume that educational differentiation within the rural
periphery diminishes over time while the other would expect
them to increase.
     What can be observed in rural areas is a continuing
superior access to education in rural villages which increases
with time, rather than diminishes.   It has been observed in
mestizo parishes that the gap in attainment is wide between
the oldest villagers and district residents.   In their youth
some initial primary provision was made in the villages but
little, or none at all, in the districts.   The gap then
narrows as single teacher schools appear in the districts in
the late 1950's and early 1960's.   It does not close because
provision in the centre has already been increased to the then
four grades, and later six grades of primary education, while
no more than two or three grades and later four, but very
rarely six, become available in the districts.   Finally, in
those villages where recent secondary or nursery provision has
been introduced, the educational gap between them and their
out-lying districts is wider than it has ever been.   This
means that discrimination increases at the periphery and so is
strongest against the smallest land holder or farming families
who own no land themselves.   (See Fig. 3)
     It seems likely too that discrimination between indian
and mestizo rural districts is also growing and that increases
in the difference in illiteracy rates between Quechua and
Spanish speaking rural areas can be observed over time.   Thus,
in some areas differences of 40 per cent or more between village and district populations aged 59 and over have increased
to between 60 and 70 per cent between those who are nearer to

Fig. 3:   Profile of Educational Differences within the Rural
Parish over Time

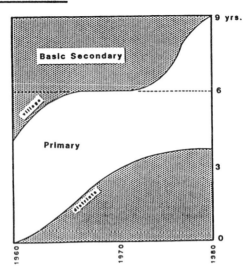

Fig. 4:   Percentage Differences in Literacy Rates between the
Rural Areas of an Indian and Mestizo Parish over Time

Population Age	Per Cent Difference
20-24	71.5
25-29	72.1
30-34	71.7
35-39	66.2
40-44	61.5
45-49	53.0
50-54	52.3
55-59	43.7

school leaving age between 15 and 25 years. (See Fig. 4)

However, there are some exceptions. In the indian parish of Canchagua in Cotopaxi province petty commercial activity has developed through most of this century, with the sale of manufactured clothing in the coastal colonisation areas. This has developed in response to very limited economic opportunities at home, given a lack of fertile land and small opportunity for alternatives to agricultural employment in the area. In the Canchagua area, educational attainment is well above the norm for rural areas of its province and compares with that of some mestizo parishes. It is possible to hypothesise that the existence of economic opportunity, particularly one that would benefit from educational skills, and the probability of taking advantage of it, may have strengthened attitudes and demand for education in the area and increased attendance rates.

In the case of sex differentiation in education the pattern is not consistent. In some villages younger women have higher levels of educational attainment than men, particularly where no more than primary education is available. This may be explained by the fact that women with low levels of education - that is to say with no more than primary educational experience - can find employment away from the community more easily than men, principally as maids in towns. As an indicator of a serious and intelligent employee, town families are demanding educational qualifications and so girls are staying on longer to attain them. Boys with primary education or less and no opportunity to obtain more qualifications have less chance of finding similar low status regular employment, particularly since the numbers of school leavers from towns with secondary qualifications is increasing, devaluing the primary credential. There is therefore, less incentive for them to remain at school without the prospect of being able to continue their education beyond the primary level. At the rural periphery, it is boys in the districts surrounding the villages who stay on longer at school.

It is clear from the above that in spite of the steady expansion of public education into the rural sector the differences in access to education between centre and periphery, between the socially advantaged and disadvantaged, have in general increased even at the microregional level of the rural parish.

Some consequences of this have been discussed elsewhere.[3] They include different levels of occupational aspirations between the more advantaged and less advantaged sectors, differential access to regular non-farm employment, and differential rates of emigration. In addition, migratory patterns observed further increase the gap in educational attainment levels between village and district populations.

However, there is a strong suggestion that individual or local economic opportunity or lack of opportunity is directly

related to subsequent school attendance and retention rates.
Where a direct economic return to education in terms of
employment is perceived by rural people and their children,
their commitment to it will increase.   Where this does not
exist commitment will be lower.
    Thus, there is a mutually reinforcing cyclical process.
Educational attainment increases occupational aspirations and
access to modern sector or off farm employment, but commitment
to education is generated by a realistic expectation of being
able to achieve such ends.

RESPONSE TO EDUCATIONAL DIFFERENTIATION WITHIN THE RURAL
SECTOR

    Successive Ecuadorian governments have been forced to
recognise that in spite of ever increasing investment in
educational provision, major variation in the quality and
quantity of education available in the rural sector persists.
But they have been unable to make the massive investment that
would enable all children to complete the now mandatory nine
years of basic education.   Consequently, they have agreed to
the introduction of experimental schemes in compensatory
education intended to overcome the specific educational deficiencies of specific population groups.   Some such schemes aim
to compensate for a lack of formal education and provide
courses in basic literacy and numeracy for adults who failed
to acquire them when young.   Others are vocational, concerned
to teach new crafts or new agricultural techniques, while
another set are concerned with personal welfare and domestic
hygiene.   Most are consciously but implicitly committed to
the small scale promotion of modernity and to the rejection of
traditional values and customs.   Weaving skills are taught on
modern dutch looms even in communities where highly intricate
weaving is practised on traditional back strap looms.   Sewing
is taught using manufactured materials and machines.   Agricultural innovations include the introduction of hybrid
strains and chemical fertilizers.
    Few such schemes are developed locally.   Most are intro-
duced and financed by foreign development agencies and sponsored by the national government.   These include the bilingual education schemes run by the evangelical Summer Institute
of Linguistics throughout the Andes and the non-formal education project in Ecuador that was developed by the University
of Massachusetts modelled on Paulo Freire's work in Brazil.[4]
Some are modelled on foreign experiments, but are financed
principally from Ecuadorian sources.   These include the
Escuelas Radiofonicas de Riobamba and the current nuclearisation scheme.   None are the result of local initiative and few
have been subjected to substantive evaluation.
    The few comments that follow attempt to identify the
extent to which two of these schemes fulfil some of their

stated objectives.   It is proposed to discuss briefly the
extent to which the nuclearisation scheme reduces the educational differentiation between centre and periphery within the
rural parish, and to what extent the non-formal education project overcomes ethnic disadvantage in access to education and
in attainment in indian areas of the highlands.   It is not
intended to discuss the historical development of the two
schemes or the full details of their implementation.

NUCLEARISATION IN ECUADOR: THE CASE OF QUILANGA

     The nuclearisation programme in Ecuador, inaugurated in
1974, and slowly expanded since then, aims to promote community development through the concentration of educational
resources in the target areas, as part of a multifaceted
development programme.   The educational aim is to develop a
resource centre in the designated area to which all residents
and teachers shall have equal access.   At the same time, the
intention is to increase provision and to democratise education at the local level by encouraging all teachers, parents
and community leaders to participate in the formulation of
educational policy outside the classroom, and to link these to
the development needs of the whole community.   Unlike Peru or
Venezuela, the nuclearisation programme in Ecuador has been
introduced gradually and is not as yet complete.

     In Ecuador, areas chosen as educational nuclei have a
readily identifiable central place, usually a village centre
or occasionally a canton capital, where primary educational
provision at least is already available.   The area has also
to have a series of satellite schools in the outlying rural
areas.   The chosen community has to demonstrate a certain
degree of commitment to development and modernisation.   This
may be manifest in the existence of a development project in
the area, or of a health centre, workshops, a co-operative or
electric light, any of which would have been achieved as the
result of local pressure and organisation.   The reason for
this criterion was to ensure support for the nuclearisation
programme.

     Close observation of an Ecuadorian nucleus (see Fig. 5
for the location of Quilanga) at the time of its inauguration
and after three years makes it apparent that Ministry of
Education Guidelines for the development of nuclei are being
followed very closely indeed.[5]   New schools have been opened
in many of the districts and additional teachers sent to
others where the single teacher was being overwhelmed by the
large number of pupils.   A new secondary school, a kinder-
garten and a night school have been opened in the village
centre.   A nucleus director, to co-ordinate nucleus activities,
has been appointed and is based in the village, as have
specialist teachers in music and carpentry.   These are intended to serve as peripatetic teachers throughout the nucleus.

Popular Education in Andean America:
The Case of Ecuador

Fig. 5: Highland Ecuador - Location of Quilanga

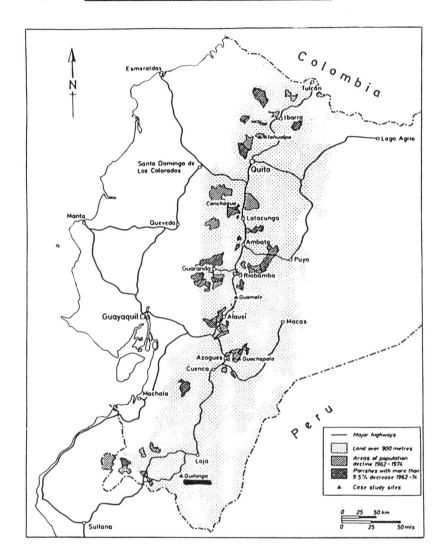

A certain amount of teaching equipment to be available to all, is stored in the village. Monthly meetings are held in one of the village schools to formulate development projects which all teachers, parents representatives and community leaders are expected to attend. Small scale development projects are being carried out.

To what extent has the nucleus reduced educational differentiation within the parish? Without doubt educational provision in the whole areas has increased, but the rate of increase is so much greater at the centre that the gap between provision there and provision in the districts has widened considerably. The doubling of the number of teachers in the village to staff the two new schools means too that the village economy is being boosted considerably by the influx of relatively heavy spenders. There is no such benefit to the economy of the districts.

The nucleus has formally linked the village and district schools, whereas before they were fully independent. Now, village school teachers are recommended to advise and provide examples of innovative and appropriate pedagogy to their district colleagues. This has not resulted in mutual collaboration, but rather in a certain resentment between the two. District teachers are often of similar status and experience to their village colleagues and so do not perceive them to be qualified to give such advice. Furthermore, many feel that the guidance tends to take the form of surveillance and that checks are being made on their absence and punctuality rates. Their resentment is heightened considerably by the position of restricted power that they feel at the monthly meetings. Firstly, they do not like being forced to attend, under a threat of a fine to be deducted at source from their salary. Secondly, they feel that the issues discussed are principally of village concern. Thirdly, on issues that affect the district communities, schools or teachers, they are unable to out-vote the village representatives at the meeting. Even were they able to overcome the tremendous barriers to communication between themselves, to organise a united vote, they would still be in a minority. For, in spite of the fact that district schools out-number those in the village by 7 to 1 and that district teachers are slightly more numerous (32 to 28), the additional village representatives, the priest, community leaders and development workers ensure a village majority at the meetings. Thus, while it appears that a democratic machine has come into being and that teachers and parents are being given a chance to participate in local educational decisions, the voice from the periphery is in practice nearly as powerless as it was before.

Nor can it be said that the new educational resources are distributed equitably. Distance means that district children do not attend the new secondary school, for parents are unwilling for their children to walk the mountain paths alone or after dark and during the wet season they are in any case impassable. Distance too ensures that the new peripatetic staff spend most of their time in village classrooms, of which there are 18, and less in visiting the 30 or so in the outlying districts. The teachers are unwilling to pay the costs of mules, as they cannot claim such expenses back from the Ministry and they are unwilling to walk the precipitous mountain paths to the district schools, Even were their commitment to their job great enough to overcome these deterrents, and equal visits were made to all children in nucleus schools, lessons would at best be very infrequent and continuity would be totally lacking.

Similar factors affect access to the few material resources deposited in the village. District teachers learn quickly that their enthusiasm to use it wanes in the face of the trouble and cost involved. The use of the sewing machines means a return trip to the village to reserve them for a particular time, a return trip with donkeys or mules to collect them and another return trip to return them, all in the teacher's own time and at his or her own expense. Village teachers, not faced with these problems can make use of all equipment much more readily.

Access to the night school is equally biased. Post-primary vocational courses are taught most evenings in the village schools. To compensate for this, dress-making classes are offered three afternoons a week in three of the 30 districts. Their popularity is an indicator of the level of demand for such courses, but more are not provided.

Finally, the small scale development projects, the creation of a library and the organisation of fund raising events, are primarily directed at villagers and not at parishioners living in the districts. This means that district teachers are usually reluctant to participate.

Inevitably, while the educational provision in the nucleus has increased everywhere and attainment levels rise in association with it, it can be seen that within the designated area internal differences remain and in some instances are widened. In every case it is the centre of the nucleus that benefits and the surrounding areas that do not. No wonder then the spatial variation in attitude to the educational changes: villagers feel that the area is taking off and that the new secondary school provides their children with a real chance of finding secure modern sector employment in town. District people are in the main dismissive of these developments and comment that the nucleus has made little difference to themselves, to their way of life or to their expectations.

In addition, the concentration of so many in the main, qualified teaching personnel and other development agents in a tiny village has a strong hidden effect on the values and aspirations of the people there. Villagers witness their sophisticated manners, their smart dress and economic well-

being and attribute them to educational success and to a
commitment to modern culture and society. This reinforcement
of the formal education system does not occur in the districts
where the isolated teachers contrive to battle to maintain
their urban identity and self-esteem.

NON-FORMAL EDUCATION

It has already been observed that in most indian areas of
Ecuador, children first attend school at the age of six and
are directly confronted with the need to communicate in
Spanish. Although the government has piloted research into
bilingual education for these children, at least in the
initial stages of their educational careers, policy has been
inconsistent and often ineffective. The non-formal education
project, set up in the Ecuadorian highlands, under an agreement between the Ministry of Education, USAID and the
University of Massachusetts set out to evaluate the relevance
of rural education to the indian population, to experiment
with alternative strategies and to develop educationally
appropriate teaching materials.[6]

The philosophy of the scheme introduced was that of
conscientisation, the heightening of student awareness of the
reality of his or her own and his or her community's situation
through which participants would be encouraged to develop
their own evaluation of their educational requirements and of
the form in which they should be met. The project did not
aim to provide a body of experts to set fixed guidelines for
the pattern of educational development in each area. It
aimed to provide didactic materials as and when required by
the different participating communities.

These, at the start of the project were invited to nomin-
ate one of their number, who need not necessarily have had
formal educational experience (although this was preferable),
to become the facilitator of the non-formal education scheme
in the community. The facilitator would be given some
limited training in initiating discussion and be introduced to
a range of specially produced materials to stimulate a
structured questioning of and learning process within the
community. These included games, photo strip stories and
pictures.

Enthusiasm for the project was particularly strong among
the facilitators who were given the opportunity to participate
in training sessions in Quechua by committed and skilled communicators. Enthusiasm was also strong, initially, back in
the community, but it tailed off as the limited depth of knowledge and expertise of the facilitator became apparent. Discussion quickly became circuitous and attendance at meetings
waned. Without the possibility of a qualification for
participating in the scheme there was no instrumental reason
to justify continuation. Indeed, since literacy and numeracy

were not the principal objectives of the scheme, many were
disillusioned from the outset.

When the project's agreement with the Ministry of Education ended in 1976, an attempt was made to persuade the
Ministry to convert all adult compensatory education to the
non-formal system.   Indeed, adult literacy was renamed non-
formal education and the materials to be used were those
developed by the project.   However, the idea of community
facilitators was abandoned and, instead, rural teachers were
invited to give literacy classes in the evenings for a 30 per
cent salary supplement.   As far as has been observed, the
methods of teaching have remained conventional and largely
teacher centred.

Various observations can be made about the project and
its effects.   Contrary to stated intentions, the demand for
non-formal education within the participating communities was
not spontaneous.   Both the demand and the form that it took
were carefully manipulated at the outset of the project.   How
else would so many communities ask for particular types of
material which, it so happened, were available?   In addition,
for all the care to employ Ecuadorian communicators and
administrators the dynamic for the project lay with the
Massachusetts research team.

The scheme has not had a significant effect in compensat-
ing for the lack of formal education in the indian areas where
it was realised.   It may have had a limited effect in increasing self-awareness: it did not lead to equivalent educational
qualifications which would enhance employment prospects of
participators.   Those who are most likely to have derived
long-term benefits from it are the facilitators.   They may
well have enhanced their prestige in the community as inter-
mediaries with external agencies and as teachers.   They may
well have become motivated to acquire more education themselves.

Otherwise, the Ministry of Education would appear to be
the principal beneficiary in that it has acquired an attractive package of much needed educational materials, directly
intended for use with adult learners.

REVIEW

In this chapter, two recent examples of popular education
schemes in Ecuador have been discussed, which have very
specific goals aimed at specific target populations.   Although very different in nature, several points in common can
be identified between them.   Both claim to be committed to
the democratisation of education and yet in neither case is
this achieved.   However, disguised, the programmes developed
are externally developed and manipulated, often in the minut-
est detail.

The benefits that derive from the schemes do not neces-

sarily result from fulfilment of their principal objectives.
Nuclearisation enables the Ministry of Education to provide a
package of educational increases in a designated area. Since
government agents and statistics on the whole ignore intra-
parish differences, the greater inequality that this expansion incurs within the nucleus and its complexity is not dis-
closed. The non-formal education scheme was an interesting
educational experiment from which the Ministry rather than
the target population seemed to gain.

Finally, both nuclearisation and non-formal education
originated spontaneously in rural areas of Bolivia and Brazil
respectively. Their institutional appropriation[7] by international agencies such as UNESCO and USAID and their sponsorship by national governments, means that their fundamental
ideologies are necessarily distorted to meet other ends.
Their principal objectives as seen by their target populations
may not have been achieved, but at national or even regional
level their effects may be deemed to be positive.

Andean governments are well aware of the educational
deficiences of their respective countries but they are hamper-
ed in many ways in their efforts to overcome them; that is
assuming that they wish to do so.

They lack the money to make equalising increases in provision and argue that they are confronted by competing demands
of different interest groups for those resources that they do
have. Their political instability means that development
decisions in any domain cannot affront too many of their
supporters. Extensive investment in compensatory education
for minority and marginal groups would do just that.

At the' same time Andean governments are also pressured by
international agencies to increase educational provision for
the disadvantaged. This means that when such groups invite a
local Ministry of Education to host an experiment in compensatory education at the agency's own expense they are likely to
accept. They can be seen to be concerned for the least
advantaged and experience minimal cost.

Too often, the schemes intended to integrate marginal
groups are themselves not wholly appropriate to the needs of
the people in the historical moment in which they are promoted.
This is largely because they only attack the symptoms of that
marginality and not its causes. In particular, it might be
argued that without some economic relevance, however tenuous,
and regardless of all attempts to make them culturally relevant, popular enthusiasm for them will wane. This is not
intended to minimise the symbolic value of educational experience but it is a reality within the rural sector and, for
future projects of popular education, one that should not be
ignored.

Popular Education in Andean America:
The Case of Ecuador

REFERENCES AND NOTES

1. Preston, R. A. (1981), Education and Migration in Highland Ecuador, unpublished PhD thesis, University of Leeds.
2. Long, N. (1977), An Introduction to the Sociology of Rural Development, Tavistock Publications.
3. Preston, R. A. (1981), op. cit.
4. Freire, P. (1970), Cultural Action for Freedom, Penguin.
5. Ministerio de Educación Pública (1972), Convenio Andres Bello de integración educativa, cientifica y cultural de los paises de la region, Quito.
6. Niehoff, R. O. and Neff, K. L. (1976), Nonformal Education and the Rural Poor, University of Michigan.
7. Pearse, A. (1974), Structural Problems of Education Systems in Latin America, in; Brown, R. (ed.) Knowledge, Education and Cultural Change, Tavistock Publications.

Chapter Six

DISPARITIES AND CONSTRAINTS IN PERUVIAN EDUCATION

Roger M. Garrett

INTRODUCTION

Disparity and inequality still characterise the provision and outcomes of most of the educational systems in the South American Republics and Peru is no exception. Although a Peruvian child born today stands a good chance of at least learning to read and write, the advice offered by Gale[1] to Colombian children some 15 years ago can still be given: the wise Peruvian child should choose its parents with care, selecting a couple who live in a city and, if the child is a girl, she should additionally seek parents with non-traditional ideas about the education of females. Although it may well be true that only 17 per cent of the population of Peru are illiterate, a most laudable situation irrespective of the criteria that might be the basis for such calculations, this average figure nevertheless comes from a wide and variable range.[2] Thus the figure for rural males is an almost negligible 3.4 per cent while illiterate rural females run to a disheartening and disturbing 53.4 per cent. (See Fig. 1) Another example of the imbalance of educational provision comes, paradoxically, as the result of an attempt to produce a fairer and more comprehensive system. Under the guise of equality of opportunity, all those students who can complete secondary education and can pass the entrance examinations have the right to university entrance. Consequently, 34 universities have been founded, together with other institutions of higher education. The outcome is that about 11 per cent of males and 8 per cent of females are entering tertiary education. In itself this seems admirable, but becomes tarnished when compared with the 9.2 per cent of 15 year-old boys who in 1981 received no instruction whatsoever. For 15 year-old girls, the equivalent figure was a totally unacceptable 32.2 per cent. (See Fig. 2) Of course it may not be the case that the provision of university education at one end of the scale has directly deprived a large section of the population of even basic instruction. None the less, there

Fig. 1: School Enrolments and Illiteracy Rates by Sex

	Rate of Enrolment		Illiteracy
	6-14 year	15-19 year	
General total	90.3	56.7	17.4
males	91.8	61.3	9.5
females	88.8	52.3	25.1
Total urban	95.7	67.5	7.7
males	96.3	71.3	3.44
females	95.1	63.9	11.8
Total rural	80.6	32.5	38.3
males	84.0	39.7	22.1
females	77.0	25.2	53.4

Source: Montero, C. (1983), Ser Pobre y ser mujer, Auto-educación, Revista de Educación Popular, Año 111, 6, pp. 34-39.

- - - - -

Fig. 2: Educational Profile of the Population - 15 years Upwards: (1981 figures)

Level of Education	Male per cent	Female per cent
Without instruction	9.2	32.2
Incomplete initial and primary	26.5	24.9
Incomplete primary	18.8	16.4
Incomplete secondary	19.6	15.0
Complete secondary	13.8	11.9
Further and higher	3.5	3.5
University education	8.6	5.0
Absolute totals	4 714 149	4 889 001

Source: Montero, C. (1983), op. cit.

would seem to be an imbalance of provision and an undue emphasis in a direction that may not be appropriate in terms of the relationships between education and the economy in Peru.

At the heart of these imbalances and injustices lie a number of complex problems which, given their extraordinary dimensions, would seem to be almost insurmountable. Human inequalities are manifested in the economic, political, social and cultural patterns of Peru, but these in turn are deeply rooted in the historical, geological and ecological dimensions of the country. In particular the geographical patterns are immensely influential. Rich in vast and abundant natural resources, both terrestrial and marine, it is paradoxically the mode of their exploitation that absorbs the readily available and equally abundant resources of energy and manpower. This results in a modern, cash dependent, and foreign dominated culture and economy.

With a population of about 17 million and an area approximately equal to that of France and Britain combined, Peru is on average sparsely populated but in fact the bulk of its people live in a few urban clusters, and in many ways this is typical of Latin American countries. Latitudinally it is tropical but a combination of its high Andean backbone and the strong cold Humbolt current in the adjacent Pacific Ocean help to provide an extraordinary range of possible micro climates. Taking a profile of Peru from West to East one moves from parched and totally lifeless deserts fed irregularly by a few short rivers, through forests and fertile 'alpine' valleys, up to the cold, rarified paramo on an altiplano over 4,000 metres high, before descending to the thick tropical rain forest of the humid Amazon basin.

Away from the arid coastal strip, even North-South communications become difficult by land and cross-Andean travel is only realistic by air. Coping with such a range of ecology and terrain obviously poses immense and daunting problems. The resultant difficulties impinge upon all sectors of life, and drain the resources and imagination of any government charged with providing even the most basic provisions under such conditions. It is to no small extent then that these fundamental characteristics of the country have been influential in the contemporary socio-economic structures, tensions and challenges.

Historically, the indigenous Peruvian people have occupied the highlands. Descendants of the Inca civilisation, and inherently timid, they still cling largely to the high mountain valleys where they retain Quechua and Aymara as mother tongues. This geographical concentration ensures the survival of indigenous languages as major features alongside the official Spanish. Even in large urban centres such as Cuzco and Ayacucho a predominantly bilingual pattern flourishes. Consequently, a major effort is being made to cater adequately for these two indigenous language groups by providing mother tongue texts for the first years of primary education. This in itself is a task of such dimensions that consideration of similar support for the numerous but geographically limited languages of the Amazonian Indians is not a practical proposition, at least as far as any official patronage and support is concerned.

In addition to the indigenous Amerindians, there is a largely European-derived population which is clustered in the coastal areas and in particular around the capital, Lima. Such a general and simplistic division of races no longer holds, in detail there having been considerable mixing and migration. However, the class system of the country ensures that the coastal 'European', and more recently North American, culture dominates which is largely to the detriment of the Indian and Mestizo population, and nowhere is it more clearly seen than in the capital city. In common with many countries in the process of development, a dramatic feature of population distribution is the phenomenal growth of urban areas which shows little sign of abating.[3] This has resulted in large satellite townships springing up around the major cities. It is to these pueblos jovenes that most of the poor rural migrants come and many of them thereby experience an even poorer quality of life than had they remained in the countryside.

The mass migration into the cities in search of social and economic opportunity places further strain upon all the already overstretched public services, which are in any case struggling to keep pace with the natural increase of the population. This additional complication hits education particularly hard, and the influx of peasants to the towns inadvertently sharpens and heightens the urban/rural distinctions in educational provision alluded to above. Ironically it is this very disadvantage from which they seek to escape, but which in turn will help speed the influx of migrants from the country.

To provide an adequate nation-wide education appropriate and relevant for all is, as this introduction has already shown, extremely difficult. The outlying rural regions, if for no other reasons than of the simple logistics of transportation, will inevitably be less well provided for than the major urban areas. Unfortunately, by moving into shanty towns and bringing the urgent demand for social justice, including better education, to the very doorstep of the minister in charge, the peasant exacerbates the rural problem. The clamour of the newly urban poor for better resources can be answered relatively easily as compared with the remote pleas from the country. What few resources are available, are therefore spent increasingly in the towns, thus starving the rural regions still further. The result is an implosion of resources which, if undeterred, will not merely starve the outlying regions but crush the very cities themselves. This problem can only be solved by a massive return to the land and the profound changes in social, political and economical attitudes that this implies. Such a change, would require an education sector prepared and resourced to assist in an imaginative and radical way.

This rural/urban drift can no longer be explained in terms of simple economic desires on the part of individuals. Larger term strategies are now tending to underly internal migration. A recent study by the Ministry of Labour indicates that the recent immigrants are arriving in Lima and other cities with better educational levels than previously.[4] Whereas in the 1960's and 1970's the proportion of the economically active 'immigrants' without any form of education was 55 per cent, the proportion is now reduced to 32 per cent. So despite efforts to produce a better education system in the rural districts, and the evidence does suggest that significant improvements have been made, at least at primary level, this does not seem to be solving the problem and may even be aggravating the situation. Having tasted even a limited form of schooling, together with the informal education derived from the invasion of the countryside with the material products of a consumer society, the appetite for more has been whetted. The lesson of the media, especially television is that the only place to achieve modernity is in the larger cities. Thus a move to the urban centre is regarded as a means of improving the lot of entire families. It is an insurance towards the prosperity of future generations, with the promise of better social services. Not least among these is education, which is perceived as the key to a more prosperous and 'modern' way of life.[5]

The educational system has therefore to cope with the typical problem of a developing country, that of a high birth-rate and a potentially lower death-rate.[6] Not only that, however, for at critical points there is a disproportionate demand upon the limited resources available. At first sight it would seem that the system is coping remarkably well, at least at primary level. Figures 3 and 4 indicate that an exemplary 90 per cent of all pupils between 6-14 years are entering primary education, and that overall teacher/pupil ratios and provision of school building is keeping pace with the increases. The literacy rate is improving and greater absolute numbers of children are being educated than ever before. Thus, while the Ministry of Education is the largest Ministry in the country in terms of personnel (even more than the Ministry of War), it would seem that this massive outlay is helping to win the battle. However, behind the statistics of quantitative expansion lies a picture of educational provision that is quite depressing in terms of quality. An intolerable strain is being placed upon the infrastructure with two and three shifts turnos occupying the same buildings

Fig. 3: Some Basic Data on the Peruvian Educational System

Level and Type	Pupils		Teachers		Schools	
	Total	Urban	Total	Urban	Total	Urban
Peru total	5 926 916	4 193 036	186 674	143 208	30 026	13 359
Public	4 969 458	3 360 620	149 396	110 374	25 793	10 185
Primary	3 343 631	2 040 517	89 370	55 597	21 335	6 036
Public	2 902 934	1 679 754	75 599	44 490	19 281	5 100
Secondary	1 249 293	1 153 468	50 075	45 079	2 789	
Public	1 049 604	971 731	39 898	36 182	2 153	
Lima total	1 809 676	1 643 735	65 940	60 744	4 575	3 820
Public	1 307 271	1 167 462	43 844	40 432	2 708	1 893
Primary	804 407	710 058	23 570	20 691	2 245	1 668
Public	615 301	537 582	16 896	14 751	1 532	1 033
Secondary	482 164	466 585	19 429	18 247	700	671
Public	371 229	358 448	13 305	12 842	379	166

Source: Ministerio de Educación, Dirección de Estadísticas (1983). Peru 1982, Estadísticas de la Educación

114

Fig. 4: Some Basic Data on the Peruvian Educational System

Level and Type	Pupils		Teachers		Schools	
	Total	Urban	Total	Urban	Total	Urban
Peru total	5 713 273	4 022 028	178 826	136 470	29 121	12 023
Public	4 802 113	3 250 999	143 898	106 086	24 735	8 812
Primary	3 215 322	1 940 223	86 249	52 844	20 981	5 121
Public	2 796 320	1 621 266	73 111	42 915	18 757	3 936
Secondary	1 212 499	1 121 032	47 106	42 932	2 617	2 325
Public	1 032 260	954 578	37 476	33 955	1 971	1 698
Lima total	1 735 843	1 578 065	61 631	57 388	4 529	3 782
Public	1 263 046	1 129 282	41 915	38 684	2 662	2 044
Primary	770 948	680 526	22 672	19 832	2 220	1 649
Public	591 194	516 520	16 305	14 172	1 507	1 016

Source: Ministerio de Educación, Dirección de Estadísticas (1982). Estadísticas de la Educación. (Cifras provisionales)

successively each day. Similarly teachers and parents alike are under stress, suffering financially, both though low income or by being asked to provide all the necessary resources, other than the basic infrastructure.

Can anything be done to ease the situation? Is anything being done? Before we can begin to consider these questions it is prudent to look rather more closely at the system, and in particular the teachers and their pupils.

THE EDUCATIONAL SYSTEM

The structure of the system is illustrated in simplified form in Fig. 5 and this will suffice to indicate at this stage that it is typical of a centralised system with most information flowing through the vice-ministerial office. Thus even the simplest of decisions are finally taken at the highest levels and only a vice-ministerial order decreto will suffice. There is hardly any cross-sectional communication and therein lies a fundamental problem when one comes to look at the tasks of curriculum development and general improvement of educational provision. If teachers are to be released from classroom duties to attend courses, even for the smallest further qualification, then a vice-ministerial order is required. However, there is a degree of flexibility provided for teachers at the classroom level that is not so usual in Latin America. They are free to organise and devise their own teaching plans within a general curriculum that is laid down by the ministry. This will be the subject of further comment below.

THE PRIVATE SECTOR

It is opportune at this point to consider the role of private schooling, and in particular to note that, like many other states in Latin America, it is of considerable importance. In Peru approximately 25 per cent of schools are private and they employ 20 per cent of the teaching force of the country.

It would seem therefore that without the private sector the state system would not be able to cope. Numerically this is probably true, but the situation is not as simplistic as that. For many teachers, the private schools represent a second and probably more lucrative salary in addition to the one they receive from the state. Thus, the teacher pupil ratio is improved in these schools to a level infinitely superior to that which the raw figures indicate. From the individual teacher's point of view the presence of these schools represent a source of improved personal well being and life style. A further benefit for both individual teachers and the system as a whole, is that many of the private schools are prestigious foreign supported institutions, and can afford to import and effectively utilise the most up-to-date teaching

Fig. 5: Simplified Structure of the Educational System
         in Peru

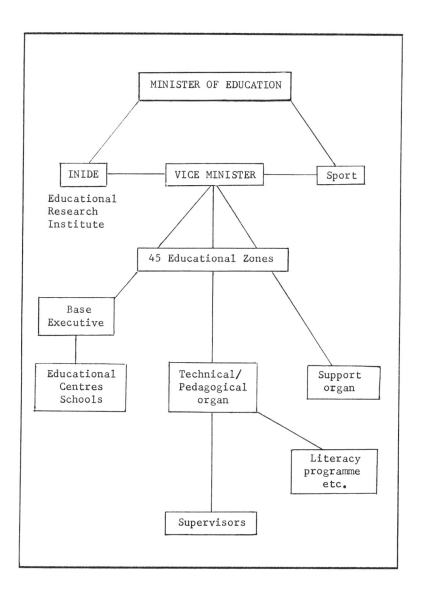

materials.   In this way they may act as a source of ideas and enrichment for the local school milieu.   However this effect is probably slight and almost certainly countered by other factors.   In particular, the private schools will tend to absorb the most able of the local teaching pool; enticing them with attractive salaries.   This effectively drains the state system of a high percentage of the type of teachers it requires to put into practice the more modern methods so desperately required.   The presence of the private school is, therefore, a mixed blessing and perhaps a resource that could be gently, and more efficiently used by the state in some sort of innovatory role.

THE STATE SYSTEM

a)   <u>Initial Education</u> is offered only in the larger cities and is normally private.   From 0-3 years the schools are known as <u>cunas</u> (cots) and for 3-5 year-olds are kindergartens or <u>nidos</u> (nests).   There is a growing movement urging more state provision of these facilities but this must be regarded as totally unrealistic, given the present state of under-funding of the existing school system.

b)   <u>Primary Education</u> is the first officially sponsored and compulsory stage of education and, in common with the secondary phase, it is offered in five modes: for minors;   for adults (fifteen plus);   special education (including provision for the exceptionally gifted as well as for those pupils with physical and/or mental handicaps);   occupational education; distance learning.

Entry into primary level is normally at six years of age after an examination for both physical and mental development. A series of six grades thereafter provides for education up to at least the age of twelve, though many pupils will be considerably older than this before completing the primary cycle. This is due to the need for pupils to pass each year before proceeding to the next.   At this level no continuation fee is charged of those who fail a year and in theory all primary education for both minors and adults is free.   But this refers only to the provision of teaching staff and the basic infrastructure of the buildings and furniture.   There are additional and often high 'hidden' costs in the provision of school uniforms for class and sport, stationery, texts and expendable materials that go to make up the normal child's desk, and for the minimal functioning of laboratories or workshops.

As far as adults are concerned there is a certain degree of flexibility in terms of the grades required to move on from one year to the next.   Providing the gap between periods of instruction is not too large, the simple presentation of an attendance certificate is usually sufficient for entry into the next grade of study.

c) <u>Secondary Education</u> is not obligatory but is free in the same sense as described for primary, and again adults are provided with evening classes in the same school premises as the children. Of the five grades offered 1-2 provide a common curriculum for all pupils, while grades 3-5 offer a diversified curriculum, <u>curriclum diversificado.</u>

Five diversified curricula are offered: agriculture <u>agropecuario</u>; craft/manufacturing <u>artesania</u>; commerce <u>comercio</u>; industrial <u>industria</u>; scientific/humanities. The first four options tend to be offered according to the locality and the likely employment demands. Thus agriculture is offered in rural areas while commerce is a standard offering in large cities. The fifth variant, that of science and humanities, is offered in all areas and is easily the most popular with both students and parents. This is largely a question of status, and of access to higher education.

In theory it is possible to move on to a university programme irrespective of the option followed, and of course certain careers are benefited from having followed a particular route. For example, business studies draws from the commerce option. None the less it is true to say that the most popular careers contemplated by the vast majority of students are those perennial best sellers: medicine, law, letters and fine arts. These are offered by most universities, and the traditional humanities/science curriculum is the best preparation for access. That is to say, these courses prepare students to pass the entrance examinations to the universities which are biased towards that style and content of curriculum.

The cost of maintaining a large family at school is a great burden at any level, but it is at the secondary stage that the costs become particularly difficult to bear. Again, the provision of teachers and basic structures are free but there is a constant demand upon parents to provide funds to finance even basic instruction, as well as through organised events such as raffles and sales to produce even routine resources.[7] As a consequence of financial constraint, and despite often heroic efforts, there is little activity within most classrooms other than an uninspired passing on of information. Practical classes and activities are rare.

The lack of stimulating classes is not necessarily a result of poor facilities. Considerable external aid has in fact been invested in all sectors of education. For example, two recent <u>convenios</u> with Hungary and Spain have provided large quantities of science equipment. Most of the apparatus and associated reagents however remain unused - often even unpacked - on the shelves of the laboratory store-rooms. This is partly because the materials are inappropriate to the demands and level of the curriculum, but also because most teachers have no training and have themselves hardly ever handled equipment.

d) <u>Tertiary Education</u> comprises three main areas of provision: <u>normales</u> for the training of teachers up to primary level, polytechnics and universities. This sector is dominated by the universities, being the most sought after form of higher education. In consequence, they tend also to dominate what is taught in the secondary schools in the humanities/ scientific strand. There has been an explosive provision of universities in the last two decades. From only seven in the 1960's there are now over thirty. For a population of 17 million this would seem to be excessive, especially in view of the disproportionate funding of the university sector as compared with primary schooling. Of course, it must be borne in mind that many of the universities are private, and that even in the state institutions the education provided is not free.

There are a number of factors behind the Peruvian university phenomenon. Politically it is often useful to found a university in a district that lacks any institution of higher education, but there are also sound educational reasons. As there is no provision for student accommodation in universities, then they must choose, as far as possible, the university closest to home. If a district totally lacks a university then the pressure is for the student to move to the city (usually Lima) and this in most cases becomes a permanent move. Thus the local area of origin is deprived of skills and training as well as the clusters of graduate unemployed in the cities being boosted. Furthermore, there is a tendency for whole families to move with students, and recent evidence suggests that, since more universities have been opened outside Lima, this trend has been stopped and even reversed. With competition being extremely fierce for places some Lima residents have even moved to less popular areas where entry into university is that much easier.

The universities are autonomous and variable in the quality of teachers and courses they offer. Ranging from the very best - that are on a par with any European or North American university - to some that are of extremely dubious quality whose teachers do not all possess degrees; they still remain the most sought after prize for anybody completing secondary education. Given the very general education provided at secondary level, the degree courses are long in comparison to British degrees. With initial levels low, large numbers of students have to be sifted during the first two years. The result is that a large proportion of those enrolling never finish their first degrees. This kind of wastage-based process of selection is inevitably extremely expensive.[8] Higher education is tasted by the few, and completed by the very few, and so it is necessary to return to a consideration of schooling, and try to understand what the problems are and how they are being tackled.

THE SCHOOL

a) Physical Provision and Curricula Framework

Most of the basic organisation is laid down by the Ministry of Education, and as with any centralised system this provides for a considerable degree of uniformity. The school year runs from the first working day in April to the 20th December, during which period there must be a minimum of thirty-eight teaching weeks. This is divided into two terms, there being a two-week break in July/August. A certain degree of autonomy exists for the districts to make local adjustments, particularly in the high mountain and tropical rain forest regions where climatic and even seismic conditions often interrupt the normal process. Zonal directorates make decisions to accommodate these hazards as and when necessary.

Despite the centralised nature, some autonomy of action and planning extends down to the teachers. Indeed during the month of March teachers are required to be in the schools to plan their courses, with no prescribed texts and only a general curricula guideline and suggested teaching method provided by the central ministry. So there is, theoretically, considerable scope for the inventiveness of the individual teacher to make itself felt. In reality the story is very different as we shall see below.

Provision of state school buildings vary markedly from region to region. Considerable efforts are being made to produce new or improved facilities and where they exist they compare favourably with the best found in most countries, at least as far as the provision of sound basic classrooms is concerned. The bulk of secondary schools consist of either a single or two-storey building surrounding a paved patio area. This basic pattern may be repeated in the very large schools or 'Great Scholastic Units' Gran Unidades Escolar. While the secondary school will almost invariably be of brick construction a primary school, be it within the same complex as a Gran Unidad Escolar or separate, is much more likely to be of old adobe construction or made of very flimsy, temporary plywood materials. The building will almost invariably be painted in yellow and red ochre, be noisy, and in urban areas especially, dusty and dishevelled.

Once inside a classroom the picture tends to become even more standardised and predictable. Although most primary teachers will attempt to put up a map and one or two pictures on the walls, the typical secondary classroom will be devoid of any such focus of interest. What will occupy most children's attention most of the day will be the dominating figure of the teacher and the overworked blackboard. Only in

121

the comparatively rare classroom will one find an interest corner display table, or the pupils' desks arranged in informal patterns or working group configurations. Some limited storage space will be the only additional furniture in the classroom, one for each turno, and these will contain just a few books. The only visual aids will be one or two display charts, laminas, or models made by the teacher or pupils. As a general rule no audio-visual hardware will be available, thus there will be no television, radio, tape recorder, overhead projector. In the school in general one is even less likely to encounter a computer or a video recorder. Even subject specialist rooms are rare except in the very largest or newest schools. Primary schools have virtually no provision for anything but standard classroom space and even in those secondary schools that are provided with laboratories there will be no more than one for each science, biology, chemistry and physics, irrespective of the number of pupils the school might have. Only about 40 per cent of secondary schools have any laboratory at all. For other specialisms such as home economics, technical subjects and the arts, provision is even worse. Materials in any specialist subject will at best be insufficient and even when provided, will be under-utilised.

b) Teaching Force

Of the total teaching force almost half are unqualified and most of the qualified staff will be found in the secondary sector. Indeed the need to provide in-service training for teachers is one of the major preoccupations of the moment, absorbing a significant proportion of the educational budget. The aforementioned sharp increase in the provision of higher education is luring the more able and better qualified teachers from the schools by offering higher salaries, and improved working conditions; to say nothing of status.

One observation can be made of the Peruvian teacher with total confidence: they are underpaid. So poorly remunerated are they, that even for basic survival of the most humbly living family, a teacher must retain two jobs. This is achieved either by teaching both morning and afternoon shifts within the two-tier system; by working in both the private and public sectors; by teaching additionally in adult classes or institutions of higher and further education; or simply by driving a taxi or operating some other form of private enterprise. With inflation running at very high levels it is difficult to provide any very meaningful indications of the cost of living. Suffice to say that at the time of writing, Peruvian banks are offering between 85 and 111 per cent interest on deposits. Within such a context salaries and costs are difficult to quote. However, on the first of April 1984, teachers were given a rise of approximately US$33.3 (100,000 soles), producing a salary scale of between 222,000 soles per month, (US$74), for a grade I teacher to 360,000 soles, (US$120) per month for a fully qualified grade VIII teacher.[9] The grade 1 teacher would be working 24 hours per week, the grade VIII teacher 40 hours.   At that same time, a kilo of meat cost US$4, a kilo of rice US$0.66, and a monthly water bill would be about US$6.6.

In such circumstances, it is not difficult to understand why the major preoccupation of the average teacher is with the basic survival of the family, and this necessitates working as many hours as is possible.   Consequently, having completed the formal hours of class contact for the day, a teacher will feel no obligation to stay, in effect unpaid, and prepare classes for the next day.   Rather he will leave for the second place of employment.   Identification with, and dedication to one school cannot be expected to figure high on a list of priorities, and lesson planning will be largely confined to the period of non-teaching in March, which is designated for this purpose.

A further, self-sustaining cycle of factors make it difficult to initiate an improvement in the quality of teaching provided.   Even those teachers with training are provided with a poor model upon which to build a personal teaching style.   Indeed the teacher who even attempts anything more than a simple exposition of information and more than choral recitation involvement on the part of the children is very rare indeed.   A lack of materials leads to dull classes, a lack of time and example stultifies the imagination required to employ cheap, throw-away substitute materials.   It is somewhat surprising, given such an environment, to find that many teachers do care, are concerned to improve their performance in the classroom, and do make great efforts to produce materials for themselves.

The stamp of bureaucracy is the final blow to any creative energies that might be present.   Any spare time that a teacher may have is fully absorbed in complying with a string of demands only marginally concerned with classroom activities.   A brief description of the assessment procedures will perhaps serve to illustrate the sort of demands made upon the teacher in Peru.   Bi-monthly tests are required in each subject.   Training in the design of assessment materials is not of a standard that permits teachers to produce anything other than simple tests of recall.   The value of such tests, either as valid assessment instruments or as teaching extensions is doubtful.   None the less, since assessment, as opposed to teaching, provides a visible outcome, these tests are vested with great symbolic importance by teachers, pupils, parents and educational officials alike.   Great store is set by them and much time spent in their production and analysis. All tests and assessed work is marked on a scale 0-20, and these are then averaged at the end of the year to produce a final mark for each subject.   To pass the year and move on to

the next stage of education each pupil must obtain an overall
average of at least eleven. This being the average of the
average marks for each subject. At the same time they must
not get below eleven (the failing level) in more than three
subjects, excluding maths and spanish which must be passed.
Thus with four or more subjects failed a pupil fails the year,
three or less and he revises these subjects in special classes
and tests during the month of March; thus taking up a large
proportion of teachers' time in a period when they are supposedly freed to make their preparations for the next school
year.

Subject specialisation is normal at the secondary level,
all teachers concentrating upon one subject and often on just
one year of that subject. Figure 6 provides an illustration
of the range of subjects in the secondary school curriculum
in Peru.

c) Pupils

Any pupil in any school in the country will be wearing
the nationally standardised grey uniform, with the only distinguishing signs being a plastic clip-on badge to indicate
the particular school to which they belong. This is one of
the few visible remaining signs of the Educational Reform
produced by the Revolutionary Government of General Velasco,
(Ministerio de Educación 1970).[10] The other significant
remnant of that reform is the large number of co-educational
schools, but this is in process of change.

The Peruvian child, depending upon whether they belong to
the morning or afternoon shift, will turn up at 8.00 a.m. or
1.00 p.m. and will spend seven periods sitting in the bleak
classroom with up to fifty or so fellow pupils. Seated in
rows at double desks (primary schools) or individual chair/
desks, they will spend most of the 45 minutes of each lesson
in a passive role, listening or copying from the board or
book. Scope for the emergence of any individuality or
creativity, even within the so-called creative subjects is
very limited. For it is these creative and craft subjects
where insufficient provision for the training of teachers is
most noticeable. Classes are often left in the hands of
local craftsmen who do their best to learn themselves, while
passing on a few basic skills to the pupils.

And yet, as with the physical setting, the curricula
situation has not dominated the pupils. A few minutes in
conversation with a class is all that is required to discover
many lively minds ready and able to cope with the demands that
might be made of them by the most skilful and inventive of
teachers. Such potential sadly remains largely untapped.

Fig. 6: <u>Secondary School Curriculum</u>

ASIGNATURAS	7o EBR 1 Secundaria	8o EBR 2 Secundaria	MODELO A 9o EBR			MODELO B 9o EBR		
			3 Sec.	4 Sec.	5 Sec.	3 Sec.	4 Sec.	5 Sec.
Lenguaje y Literatura	5	5	5	4	2	3	3	2
Idioma Extranjero	2	2	2	2	2	2	2	2
Historia del Perú	3	3	3	3	5a	3	3	4a
Geografia del Perú y Mun.	2	2	2	-	5b	2	-	4b
Historia Universal	2	2	2	2	-	2	2	-
Educación Religiosa	1	1	1	1	2	1	1	1
Educación Civica	1	1	1	2	2	1	2	2
Educación Artistica	2	2	2	1	1	2	1	1
Educación Fisica	2	2	2	2	2	2	2	2
Educ. para la Form. Militar	-	-	-	*	*	-	*	*
Filosofia y Logica	-	-	-	-	2	-	-	2
Psicologia	-	-	-	2	-	-	2	-
Economia Politica	-	-	-	-	2	-	-	2
Matematica	5	5	5	5	5	4	4	4
Ciencias Naturales	4	4	-	-	-	-	-	-
Quimica	-	-	4	6a	-	3	4a	-

Continued/...

Fig. 6: Secondary School Curriculum (Continuation)

ASIGNATURAS	7o EBR y Secundaria	8o EBR y Secundaria	MODELO A 9o EBR			MODELO B 9o EBR		
			3 Sec.	4 Sec.	5 Sec.	3 Sec.	4 Sec.	5 Sec.
Biologia	-	-	-	6b	-	-	4b	-
Fisica	-	-	-	-	6	-	-	5
Formación Laboral	3	3	3	3	3	8	8	8
Orient. y Bienest. del Educ.	1	1	1	1	1	-	-	-
TOTALES	33	33	33	34	35	33	34	35

Source: Ministry regulation No. 100-82-ED.

CONCLUSION

What can be said in conclusion? The description given so far would seem to amount to that of a system barely keeping pace with its most obvious needs of providing for an increasing population. Providing schooling in quantitative terms, and in respect of basic provisions[11] still lacks the quality that distinguishes effective schooling from informal education. Is there any realistic hope for improvement in the foreseeable future; until the population growth slows dramatically and/or the economy flourishes? Massive efforts are being made and, as has already been noted, it would seem as if the limit has been reached for expansion of provision, particularly as the ageing facilities place a further burden upon the system. One of the most intractable problems to be faced by the Peruvian educational system is the rapidly decaying state of the infrastructure. It is estimated that 85 per cent of schools in 1982 required fundamental repairs and re-equipping, merely to keep them functioning at the current absolute minimum level.[12]

So what is the root cause of the problems; is it merely the lack of money in a low income country? Undoubtedly, funds with which to provide sufficient materials is an essential component of any plan to improve the quality of educational provision. But the most important single factor by far is teacher quality. The provision of sufficient cash to permit the average teacher to concentrate wholly upon his task and to remove the constant need to search for alternative sources of income is fundamental. However, to demand a professional salary one must offer a professional service, and professionalism is not merely having command of the relevant information nor is it just the application of the associated skills; as it happens, both of these vital attributes are largely absent among Peruvian teachers. Professionalism is primarily an attitude of commitment to the task and to the continual improvement of the quality of performance. So while union activity within Peru has been largely, and understandably, concerned with the improvement of financial conditions of members, there is room for at least equal activity in presenting a case for improved teacher training, both initial, and in-service. This coupled with a relaxing of the system to allow for differences in styles of teaching to emerge and flourish, is one of the greatest needs. It would allow teachers of vision to experiment and explore alternative approaches thus developing a rich context and environment within which each teacher can find his or her own preferred approach.

While, theoretically at least, the right balance has been struck between a prescribed curricula foundation and individual teacher freedom to work within this framework, Peru lacks one essential element which would enable teachers to

take advantage of the system. For whatever reason there is
no tradition of experiment within the classroom. Individuality is not a characteristic of the Peruvian school; neither
among teachers nor to be encouraged in children. Thus alternative models for young teachers to choose between do not
exist. Lack of experimentation and differentiation has reinforced and fossilised sterility and mediocrity.

As Polanyi has observed,[13] connoisseurship is not something that can be taught in a classroom or laboratory in any
conscious, focused manner. Such awareness is subsidiary and
can only be gained by working through a long period of
apprenticeship with a skilled practitioner as a model. Such
ineffable knowledge is absorbed only by watching and practis-
ing. The conditions for such an environment can of course
only be built up slowly, and swift solutions to this problem
are not to be found - indeed one would be suspicious if any
were proposed.

What then can be done? Concentration upon improvement of
the training of teachers is vital. The nurturing of the most
skilled teachers, concentrating them in a few schools, rather
than dissipating them and losing them might be a way to begin.
If a few expert teachers can be gathered into a number of
experimental schools which in turn are used as teaching
practice schools, (much like teaching hospitals) then slowly
such apprenticeship may be provided. Similarly in-service
training might, at least in part be better offered on a small
scale at the individual school level.[14] Such improvements in
the teaching profession have no chance of realisation unless
the stifling bureaucracy is tackled and the system unblocked
of the choking tasks it imposes at all levels. At the same
time there should be moves to facilitate consultation within
and between the various sectors of the education system.
Inspectors, curriculum writers, research teams, universities,
schools and teachers should all be working together and not at
cross-purposes. As it stands, most Peruvian teachers are
starved of creative contact with those concerned with operating the system and developing the curriculum.

REFERENCES AND NOTES

1. Gale, L. (1969), Education and Development in Latin
   America. Routledge and Kegan Paul.
2. Montero, C. (1983), Ser pobre y ser mujer. Autoeduca-
   ción, Revista de Educación Popular. Año 111, 6.
3. In a recent newspaper article, (Anon (1984) Lima destino
   de los migrantes, El Comercio, Junio 29, p. A10), it
   was shown that from 1940 to 1981 Lima had grown 7.3
   times compared to an increase of 2.7 times for the
   whole country. While the decade 1972-1981 showed a
   marked decrease in the rate of growth for Lima, this
   can be attributed to new urban poles of attraction for

the migrant rural worker.

4. Anon (1984), Mejor nivel educativo de los 'recién bajados'. El Comercio, Junio 29, p. A10.

5. Another recent newspaper article (Anon (1984), El Comercio, Junio 14, p. A-G), reported that the estimated life expectancy of the urban child was 64 years as opposed to 49 years for the rural child. (An average life expectancy of 58 for Peru in general as compared with 62 for Latin America in general). The article also reports the recent guide published by the Censejo Nacional de Poblacción, which indicates that in the 1981 census the population of Peru was about seventeen million of which eleven million lived in urban areas and six in rural districts. An average population increase in urban areas was 3.5 per cent while only 1.0 per cent was recorded for rural areas.

6. The same article (in No. 5) reports the birth-rate to be difficult to calculate, but that it is around 2 per cent. If infant mortality drops from its present 11.1 per cent to 5.2 per cent then, by the year 2,000 the population will have risen to 31.5 million.

7. Only in the frontier schools is all education and associated materials totally free. In the jungle schools, and with the army's help, teachers move in with all their materials for several months at a time. These are interesting responses to the geographical and ecological problems outlined in the introduction.

8. In 1982 an estimated 266,000 students entered university, of a total university population of 300,000. The number of graduates in 1981, however, was 13,000 (See Galvani, V. (1982 a.) La educación en el Peru: algunas cifras significativas (2). Plana. Servicio Informativo de la Oficina de Educación Iberoamericana. Julio/Agosto, No. 249-250).

9. Supreme decree (1984), in El Comercio, 7 May.

10. Ministerio de Educación (1970). Reforma de la Educación: Informe General. Editorial Universo, S.A. 200 pp.

11. Galvani, V. (1982 b.), La educación en el Peru: algunas cifras significativas (1). Plana. Servicio Informativo de la Oficina de Educación Iberoamericana. Mayo/Junio, No. 247-248.

12. Galvani, V. (1982 b.), op. cit.

13. Polyani, M. (1962), Personal Knowledge: Towards a Post-Critical Philosophy. Routledge and Kegan Paul.

14. A project in the in-service training of primary school teachers to teach science is currently experimenting with such a school-focused approach.

Chapter Seven

EDUCATION AND NATIONAL DEVELOPMENT IN BRAZIL

Hugh Lawlor

Brazil has long been referred to as the 'Country of
Tomorrow'. Her size, geographic position and enormous pool
of human and natural resources attest to her potential as an
independent, developed nation. However, many factors including geographic conditions: demographic expansion; regional
jealousies; rigid social structures; economic policies;
political organisation all interact to militate against the
achievement of this ultimate goal. In particular, political
structures and conditions have determined the limited contribution made by education to the social and economic development of a substantial proportion of the population. Social,
welfare and public education programmes have a low priority in
the Government's national development plans. Indeed, in
1984 Brazil is suffering its worst economic recession, with
dramatic reductions in real wages and consequent reductions by
local authorities in health and education spending.[1]

THE POLITICAL CONTEXT OF EDUCATIONAL PROVISION IN BRAZIL

Since its 'discovery' by Pedro Alvares Cabral in 1500,
Brazil has been governed by Colonial, Imperial and Republican
systems. At the proclamation of the Republic in 1889 only
3 per cent of the total population were receiving any formal
education.[2] Between 1890 and 1920 school enrolments increased steadily, but most of this expansion was taking place in
the wealthier Southern and South Eastern states, with the
impoverished North and North East almost unchanged from
Imperial times. As the economic emphasis changed from agriculture to industry in the late 1920's the economically and
socially dominant land-owners were joined by the new indust-
rialists from São Paulo and Rio de Janeiro and by the urban
professional groups. It was against this background that a
group of junior army officers tenentes seized power in 1930
and installed Getúlio Vargas as President, believing him to be
a force for social and economic change. In the event, Vargas
proved to be a highly authoritarian figure and his regime

marked the beginning of an extreme centralisation of executive power. He established a Ministry of Education and Health which began to centralise the education system, and also set out to reduce the very high illiteracy rates. Paradoxically he succeeded only in reducing the already low level of quality within the system. Primary courses in rural areas lasted for three years instead of the original four, and teaching was limited to lessons in reading, writing and arithmetic. In 1937, out of 29,406 primary schools, 90 per cent were one-room rural schools, with scarce funds being used to fight illiteracy at the expense of investment in the school system itself.[3] Vargas no doubt underestimated the enormity of the task in attempting to reduce illiteracy rates, and perhaps more significantly received no support from the wealthier and influential groups in Brazilian society.

Democratic government was restored in 1945 and states and municipalities (local administrative units) assumed responsibility for some government functions, for example, primary schools. Overall control of policies and priorities remained at the federal level. The 1946 Constitution stated that free, compulsory primary education was to be provided with access to other levels of education, and without charge for those unable to pay. Although the 1971 Education Law eventually established a free, compulsory first cycle of eight years education, many areas still do not have the financial resources to comply fully with this law more than a decade later.

In the 1950 elections Vargas was surprisingly returned to power, but powerful military opposition led to his suicide in 1954. Under President Juscelino Kubitschek, Brazil entered a period of rapid industrial and economic development, with an influx of transnational corporations encouraged by tax incentives and easy profit remission. The federal capital was relocated in the new city of Brasilia, and regional development boards were established. Unfortunately, Kubitschek's development strategy totally neglected the agricultural sector, probably in order not to upset his land-owning allies. Brazil's urban population rose by 60 per cent during the 1960's and yet little provision was made for the necessary expansion of food supplies, transportation, education, health, housing and social services.[4] By 1961 and the end of the Kubitschek presidency, inflation had risen sharply. Brazil had a massive deficit, and had still not embarked on any noticeable programme of social or educational development.

Historically, politics at the centre in Brazil has been based on compromise, and parties were not founded on specific interests. Thus, in the early 1960's when the left-wing President João Goulart attempted to introduce drastic reforms, the right began to conspire for his downfall.[5] In the resulting economic and social chaos, the military took power on the 31st March, 1964 to end Brazil's brief flirtation with parliamentary democracy.   Castello Branco, Marshall of the Army, was appointed President, and the entire political system modified.   Traditional political parties were dissolved and the former Senate and Congress members were grouped into the Government sponsored ARENA Aliança Renovadora Nacional, and a moderate opposition party MDB Movimento Democrático Brasileiro. The return to military rule had been supported by moderate middle-class groups, but by 1969 disenchantment had led to a dramatic decline in civilian support, and this led to a situation of military dictatorship.   By 1970, under the presidency of General Emilio Médici the military regime was in total control and worked only with a technocratic élite whose primary function was the formulation of economic development plans.   The political system in the 1970's and early 1980's was characterised by extreme centralisation, repression, a vast and ineffectual bureaucracy, limited or nonexistent participation by the majority of the population in political life, and an obsessive preoccupation with national security and nationalism.   Despite the holding of free elections for the Senate in November 1982, President Figueiredo encouraged Congress in 1984 not to support free presidential elections until 1988 at the earliest.   It seems that only limited democratisation will be permitted, but not moves that might diminish the considerable executive powers of the President and thereby the key influence of the military and its supporting social groups.

The forceful capitalistic policies of the successive military regimes transformed the national economy so that by 1972 Brazil was achieving an economic growth rate of over 11 per cent.   Whilst the real value of wages declined during this period of rapid economic growth, the new middle classes prospered as the multinational companies employed more managers and the demand for engineers, civil servants and doctors grew.   In fact it was the demand for these professionals that resulted in the considerable expansion of private secondary and higher education, with the number of university students increasing from 278,000 in 1968 to almost 800,000 in 1974.[6]   However, a sharp and continuing decline in economic growth since 1974 has not prompted any noticeable deviation from the economic development model which is essentially export orientated.   This policy has reinforced the unequal distribution of income, so that in 1976, 11 per cent of the total income was shared by the bottom 50 per cent of the population whilst the top 5 per cent received 39 per cent of the total income.[7]   The economic model relies heavily on foreign capital and on capital-intensive industrial projects which require increased numbers of skilled manpower.   The role of education in the development plan is to contribute to the 'modernisation' of society, and specifically to provide the disciplined and skilled manpower for industrial development.   Education is also expected to encourage changes in

spending and saving patterns, and thus contribute to the
narrowly based economic model. The educational contributions
in the overall development plan are framed to maintain the
'status quo' in society and are motivated more by politico-
economic than social considerations. Educational reforms
outlined below may satisfy the short-term objectives of the
present economic development plan, but they fail to lay the
foundations for any long-term sustainable development, especially in social terms.

Education has long been recognised as a priority area in
plans for the modernisation of Brazilian society. The first
ten-year plan for education was formulated in 1967 and brought
about a massive expansion of enrolments, especially of private
secondary and higher education. Investment in education rose
considerably up to 1973, but in real terms has been steadily
declining since that period. The reduction in spending
occurred in spite of the fact that the 1971 Education Law extended the length of compulsory schooling from four to eight
years. However, any discussion of economic growth and educational expansion has to be viewed against the background of
enormous regional and social disparities. There are marked
and striking differences between urban and rural areas and
between regions of the country. In 1959 Lambert spoke of
'Two Brazils' and this distinction is still largely relevant
today; one is the traditional agricultural-aristocratic
society that has changed only minimally since the late nineteenth century and still exists in many parts of the North
and North-East, the other is the modern, industrial, 'progressive' South.[8]

With a total population of 119 million in 1980, an annual
growth rate of 2.8 per cent and 53 per cent of the population
under the age of nineteen, considerable strains are placed on
the country's resources.[9] Health and education facilities
must double in thirty years if even the present inadequate
provisions are to be maintained, while at the same time the
non-productive sector of the population is inexorably rising.
Rapid urbanisation (approximately 68 per cent of the population lived in urban areas by 1980), particularly to coastal
cities has created serious social and economic problems.
Cities cannot adequately assimilate the rural migrants, many
of whom still choose to remain in the cities, often living in
shanty towns favelas. Education services are unable to cope
with the extra demand, and the administrative pressures to
provide additional urban facilities has made many rural areas
even more deprived and isolated. In the industrial areas
employment protects many families from the more obvious
characteristics of poverty, but the income earned by more than
one-third of the urban labour force is still, and has long
been, below the minimum wage.[10] For the millions of unemployed there is often no alternative but to beg or steal. Education in rural areas, particularly in the sparsely populated

Fig. 1: Regions and States of Brazil

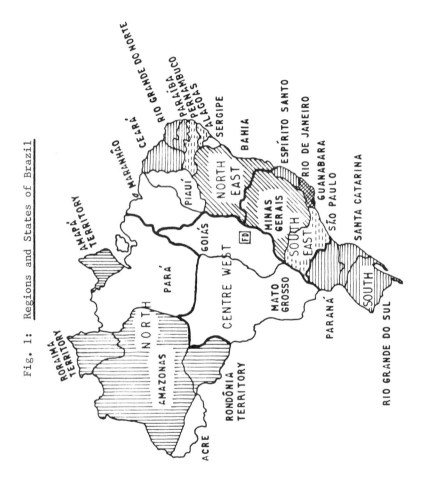

interior, is expensive to provide and attendance difficult to enforce. It has proved almost impossible to attract qualified teachers to leave relatively comfortable urban posts for areas where the standard of living is invariably low. Inadequate communications, economic backwardness, extreme poverty and the difficult physical environment make attendance at school extremely difficult in much of the North and North-East of Brazil. In contrast, the South and South Eastern regions have developed a relatively efficient education system helped by considerable private investment, good communications and an accommodating environment. However, in these regions of Brazil many rural areas are isolated from administrative centres and the educational facilities compare unfavourably with those in the state capitals.

In the 1980's Brazil remains a highly socially stratified society, with a large and still growing middle class that has begun to blur the earlier two-class system. For the vast majority of the population, educational achievements represent the only means of obtaining upward social mobility. However, there is a close correlation between membership of the middle and upper classes and access to the higher levels of provision (notably upper secondary and university sectors). In the 1940's and 1950's successful completion of primary schooling gained entry to skilled and semi-skilled occupations and by the 1960's completion of lower secondary schooling was serving as a means of upward social mobility. In the late 1970's and early 1980's higher education was the major path towards increased income and social status, but access to this level is dominated by the middle classes. In his investigation of higher education in Brazil, Jerry Haar found that candidates from the higher income families had the highest passing rate in the college entrance examinations and that for children of the poor, selection for higher education began long before the entrance examination competitions due mainly to the shortage of places in public secondary schools and the high cost of attending private pre-university crammer courses.[11]

In the review of any education system it is the political, social, economic and regional conditions that determine the extent to which education can play a positive and co-ordinated role in any national development plans, but it is particularly clear in Brazil that political considerations dominate present strategies. President Geisel's speech at the first meeting of his new cabinet in March, 1974 recognised the enormous disparities in Brazilian society:

'the disparities of individual incomes were more pronounced among us than in most countries of the Western world; that the benefits arising from development in the decade of the sixties were reaped mainly by the richest sectors of the economically active population and that the differentials between the wages of skilled and nonskilled labour were excessively high by international standards. At the same time acute economic disparities persist as between regions, with a relatively developed Centre-South and, in contrast, a North and a North-East still suffering from stark underdevelopment.'[12]

A decade later these disparities remain and must be fundamental to any analysis of national development strategy and the part played therein by educational provision.

AN ANALYSIS OF THE FORMAL EDUCATION SYSTEM

The 1961 Education Law attempted to establish a decentralised system of educational administration. However, federal control over curriculum structures, teachers' qualifications and types of schools has resulted in a combination of local organisational responsibility, with but limited scope to exercise initiative or real autonomy. Devolution from the federal to the state level has taken place, but with the Federal Council of Education retaining considerative directive powers. Each of the twenty-two states is divided into municípios varying in size from small towns and rural localities to the industrial city of São Paulo. The Federal Government regulates overall educational policy and determines the legislative norms for all levels of education, with a Federal Council of Education - a consultative committee composed of prominent educationalists - determining basic curriculum requirements, validating teachers' qualifications and advising on the distribution of federal funds. Primary schooling (7 - 14 years) is the responsibility of the município and the state, with increasing município responsibility. States differ considerably in their administrative organisation and their willingness to devolve responsibility to the municípios. The more developed southern states operate a highly decentralised system, delegating power to the well organised and well staffed município departments of education, but these powers are still largely administrative. Each state has a Council of Education which has some administrative responsibility for secondary and higher education, but within carefully defined federal directives. At the higher education level the Federal Government has a dominating influence with federal approval needed for course content. All university teaching appointments are made either with the approval of the Federal Council of Education, or the State Council of Education in the case of state universities. Throughout the system federal, state and município regulations abound, so much so that even an outside observer would be surprised by the extent to which the bureaucracy dominates the system. Administrative personnel are constantly being replaced, particularly at the state level, with a resultant lack of continuity of policies, and frequent reinterpretation of regulations.

According to the 1961 and 1971 Education Laws the states and municípios must spend at least 20 per cent of their budgets on education.   It is clear that since primary and secondary education is the responsibility of the individual states, the resources of the individual states determine the level of investment and amount of educational provision. São Paulo, the major industrial centre, is able to spend almost as much on education as all the other states combined and has committed itself to the restructuring of the school system as decreed in the 1971 Education Law.   Less developed states have serious difficulties in even maintaining their present inadequate facilities, and cannot extend the length of compulsory schooling without federal aid.   If a truly national system is to emerge, then the federal authorities will not only have to give priority funds to the less developed states but also actively consider means to redress the present imbalance by redistributing individual state revenues.   Viewed in the light of traditional regional loyalties this could prove extremely difficult.

The 1971 Education Law combined the four-year primary course with the four-year lower secondary course (formerly the ginásio school) into an eight-year compulsory period of schooling, (see Fig. 2).   In many urban areas, particularly in the South and South-East, this restructuring process has taken place, but in a significant number of rural areas the old system still operates.   The removal of the examination barrier at the age of eleven years has improved attendance figures, but high repetition rates remain.   In any case since repetition and wastage take their heaviest toll in the first few years of primary schooling, the removal of this examination is a purely academic, almost theoretical improvement in opportunity as far as the mass of the population is concerned. None the less, increased attendances have resulted in larger classes and increased teacher work loads.

One important consequence of these changed conditions has been an increase in the number of middle-class parents transferring their children to private schools.   Prior to 1971 many state primary schools, particularly in the large cities, had good reputations and mixed social intakes.   State schools at the new First level are now predominantly attended by pupils from the lower socio-economic groups, and the socially divisive nature of the private school sector has been reinforced.   Any increase in private school enrolments must reduce the pressure on the education authorities to improve the public sector, for those groups in society with the most influence to bring about changes are increasingly opting out of the public sector.   Private education continues to expand in the 1980's, and with increased revenues is more able to provide improved resources and attract the better qualified teachers.   Such developments are not only socially divisive,

Fig. 2: Brazilian Education System: Post 1971 Reforms

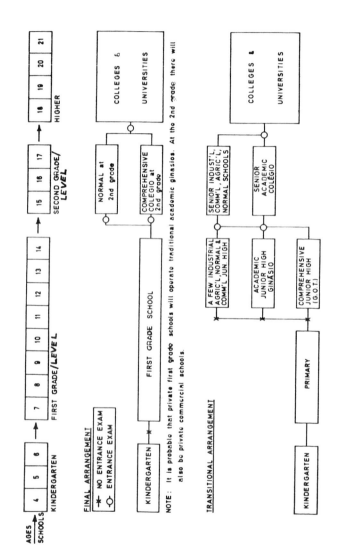

NOTE: It is probable that private first grade schools will operate traditional academic ginasios. At the 2nd grade there will also be private commercial schools.

but could be deliberately designed to limit the contribution of the public education sector to national development plans.

Education at the First level seeks to develop the child's individual talents, provide some qualifications or preparation for work and introduce the child to the concept of citizenship.[13] The curriculum should contain a part of 'general education' and another of 'special formation'. General education forms the basis of all teaching in the first four years and must still be the dominant part in the last four years. The complete reorientation of aims and curriculum is seen as an attempt to eliminate past preoccupations at the ginásio level, (junior high school), with preparation for upper secondary and university courses. By concentrating on general education it is hoped students will be prepared to continue their formal schooling or have a sufficient basic education to enable them to enter the labour market for training or immediate employment. The schools must teach basic vocational subjects, but in many schools the approach is highly theoretical, comprising mere descriptions of occupations found in industry, rural communities and business. In rural areas the vocational component tends to be treated as a more integral part of the curriculum, but many urban schools tend to omit it, thus invalidating one of the major aims of the educational reform, namely that First level schooling should be a basic preparation for work and life in the community.

The 1971 Education Law established Second level schools, (the former colégios), which officially cater for the ages fifteen to seventeen on a selective basis. Due to the high incidence of repeaters in the compulsory stage, the Second level age range is more often from sixteen or seventeen to nineteen or twenty or above. Since 1971 the separate teacher-training schools have been phased out, with teacher-training at the secondary school level as part of the so-called 'professional component' in the Second level schools. Enrolments at this level have steadily increased from 910,000 in 1969 to 3,143,800 in 1979, with the majority of students opting for the prestigious academic Second level schools and with less than one per cent enrolled in agricultural courses.[14] The Government has declared that all types of Second level schools are to be considered equivalent and to provide access routes to the university, and other forms of higher education. It is difficult to see how this can be achieved when nearly 60 per cent of these schools are private and most are highly academic in orientation.

Academic Second level schools are divided into two branches, classical and scientific. The curriculum of both branches is composed of a 'general education' and a 'special formation' component. As at the First level a 'common core' curriculum is determined by the Federal Council of Education, but at the Second level the 'special formation' component predominates.[15] In such schools this means that emphasis is

given to the traditional arts and science subjects necessary
for university entry.   Although the 1971 Education Law made
the inclusion of 'professional courses' compulsory, very few
academic schools in fact offer professional subjects.   In
part this is due to resistance by parents and students, who
still consider the main purpose of Second level schooling to
be preparation for university entry, but also due to the
shortage of finance for the practical equipment, and the
chronic shortage of qualified teachers in professional subjects.   As in the upper stages of the First level schools,
the Second level schools have very high repetition rates,
with many students engaged in paid employment during the day
and attending fee-paying schools in the evenings and at week-
ends.
    Students who successfully complete the Second level
course and want to enter university must pass a highly competitive examination vestibular.   The average success rate is
around 40 per cent (ranging from 12 per cent in medicine to 68
per cent in philosophy), but the number of candidates for
entry continues to increase at an alarming rate.   The highly
competitive nature of the entrance examination means that many
students attend a refresher cursinho course for a year on
leaving the Second level schools.   Evidence exists that the
private Second level schools tend to produce the best examination results, and that many students cannot afford the costs
of the private refresher courses, the result is a predomina-
tion of upper and middle-class students at the university
level.
    The restructuring of primary and secondary education has
resulted in a larger proportion of pupils benefiting from the
extended period of compulsory schooling, but financial and
examination barriers at the Second level of schooling serve to
limit access to higher education to many students from the
lower income groups.   The legislation to provide 'general
education' combined with some 'professional courses' at the
Second level appears to have had minimal impact on the academic schools, where the courses remain implicitly aimed at
university preparation.   The technical or vocational sector
at the Second level is divided into three branches: industrial, commercial and agricultural.   Due to the high prestige
of the academic branch, most technical courses have failed to
attract the more able students and this partly explains the
shortage of middle-level manpower and professional support
staff.   All the Second level technical schools have a curriculum consisting of the federally defined 'common core' of
subjects and a series of vocational courses appropriate for
the particular branch.   In these schools the vocational
element in the curriculum is supposed to predominate, with
professional qualifications awarded on completion.
    Skilled and semi-skilled personnel are trained at
apprenticeship schools operated by the National Service for

Industrial Training (SENAI). The service is organised and
directed by the National Confederation of Industries and is
financed entirely by industry in the form of a one per cent
annual payroll tax. Although enormous strides have been
made in the industrial training field, the supply from Second
level industrial schools and the trade schools does not provide Brazilian industry with sufficient skilled and semi-
skilled manpower. This is partly due to the fact that
technical courses have a low status and fail to attract a)
sufficient students and b) students of the necessary quality.
It is also partly due to the policy of many industralists
employing men with practical rather than technical experience,
and thus saving on labour costs. Commercial training is
provided by public and private agencies, but the majority of
students attend private schools. Most of the Second level
Commercial schools are in the southern states, with most
students attending on a part-time basis in the evenings. By
contrast the Second level Agricultural schools are publicly
supported, but considerably undersubscribed. This is due in
part to the low salaries and status attached to agricultural
occupations, and partly to the fact that agricultural training provisions have changed very little over the last three
decades.

The demand for higher education continues to grow and far
exceeds the available places.[16] Although a university qualification still bestows status on the holder, in 1984 it no
longer guarantees employment. Plans for the reform of higher
education were introduced in 1968,[17] and aimed to make this
sector more efficient and productive. The Government was
particularly concerned to standardise the organisation and
curriculum of the institutions of higher education and in
particular to focus courses in universities and reduce the
number of private institutions. Some reforms, such as unified entrance examinations and the removal of life-professor-
ships, were introduced, but the private institutions of higher
education continued to flourish. Unfortunately, these
private tertiary institutions are catering for the able students from lower income groups, while students from the private
Second level schools obtain the majority of the free places
in the public (state and federal) universities: this paradox
serves neatly to epitomise the character of Brazilian educational provision.

EDUCATION AND NATIONAL DEVELOPMENT

The nature and provisions of the Brazilian education
system represent a situation common to many developing
countries, with problems of reduced investment in education,
the search for curriculum relevance, an overcrowded curriculum, and the disproportionate representation of upper and
middle-class students in influential schools and sectors.

It is, however, the strength and seemingly immutable nature of influences outside the education system, in particular the political, social and economic forces, that are preventing any significant improvements in the public school system and thus limiting the potential contribution of this sector to national development.   Pressures to modify the impact of these influences and reform conditions and provisions in public education have had minimal effect.   This is because the powerful interest groups in society such as the military, landowners and business groups do not generally subscribe to the public school system.   More significantly, the role of education in national development plans is determined by these powerful and élite groups, and is perceived within a narrow economically-biased model that appears to consider individual development and self-awareness secondary to the maintenance of political and social structures.

Development strategies in the 1960's and 1970's produced considerable economic growth, but without any real redistribution of income or reduction in the enormous social, economic and educational disparities between and within regions.   In education the outcome of investment has been a network of education systems across the country, theoretically united by common federal legislation, but with levels of provisions and conditions dependent on the financial and political power of the region and community.   In the 1980's, as Brazil attempts to cope with mounting external debts and a deepening recession, the underdevelopment in many regions is seriously inhibiting developments in the formal education system and in adult literacy programmes.   From the study of an adult literacy programme Campos concluded that:

'The solutions then to literacy programmes do not simply lie on a more adequate type of programme, methodology, training or follow-up studies for the illiterate population, but on more radical changes in terms of redistribution and benefits accruing to the poor groups.'[18]

In the last two decades there has been an undeniable expansion in school enrolments, with a sharp increase following the extension of compulsory schooling in 1971.   In common with the vast majority of developing countries this quantitative expansion has not been matched by qualitative reform. Public schools in many urban areas are attempting to cater for a rapidly increasing enrolment with insufficient, often inadequate, resources and diminishing financial support.   Many of the public schools have between forty and fifty-five pupils in each class and some schools have few textbooks.   In rural areas most schools only operate at the First level and these are usually one class/one teacher institutions offering schooling for less than the compulsory eight-year period.   The 1971 Education Law, outlined ambitious plans for the extension of compulsory schooling and for the provision of more relevant courses for the majority of pupils, but legislative planning appears to have taken place without regard for the actual conditions in schools, availability of specialised vocational teachers and resources, and sufficient funds to implement the reforms. The reduction in education expenditure from 1975 has meant the shelving of many proposals contained in the Law, and with increased enrolments a subsequent decline in the quality of education in the public sector.

The low government priority given to educational spending in the public sector, particularly noticeable since 1968, has resulted in a widening gap between those pupils attending public schools and those from the higher socio-economic groups able to afford private education. Divisions between public and private education have widened and as private schools continue to provide better facilities and staffing ratios, the socially divisive nature of private education has become more apparent. Public schools in urban areas normally operate a three-shift teaching day with a maximum of four or five hours teaching per day. With such limited teaching time, the combination of obligatory federal curriculum subjects and state curriculum control, has resulted in overcrowded curricula at the First and Second levels of schooling. Most teachers are compelled to adopt an encyclopaedic approach, and although the authorities have attempted to introduce more relevant courses, shortage of funds and of specialised teachers has prevented the implementation of these 'professional' courses in most areas. In addition, at the Second level there has been strong opposition from those parents who have traditionally benefited from the purely academic courses, and saw their advantageous positions being threatened by a widening of both access and content.

The 1961 and 1971 Education Laws devolved certain powers to state and municipal authorities, but with overall control resting at the federal level. The political and administrative centralisation of the education system has meant that many educational reforms, whilst theoretically impressive, are divorced from the reality of school and higher education conditions. In addition, the oppressive bureaucracy at the state level has been a major inhibitor of educational change, not least because of the rapid turnover of officers.

National development plans have emphasised efficiency and economic expansion, with little obvious concern for individual human dignity, social and regional equity or personal self-awareness and fulfilment. In fact earlier development models have deliberately reinforced the social structures, strengthened the position of the private education sector and encouraged urbanisation at the expense of rural development. Educational reforms have been formulated to satisfy specific manpower and economic goals within those development plans, but as economic expansion is replaced by recession and

uncertainty it is important that education becomes involved in
the social and political development of the population.
Narrowly defined educational objectives limited the potential
contribution to both individual and national development, and
particularly affect those in the public education sector,
namely the mass of the population.   Thus they fail to
establish a firm base for future long-term development.   However, such a modified role for education will not be possible
without a radical reassessment of government priorities, the
support of the dominant social groups and a redistribution of
funds to improve both quality and access in the public sector.
It is probable that the size of the foreign debt, high inflation, rapidly rising unemployment and underemployment, and
conditions imposed by the international money agencies and
markets will largely determine social and economic policies in
the short-term.   It is predictable that there will be massive
curbs on public spending, with education being one of the
major victims.   It is also highly likely that the present
growing inequalities between public and private education, the
North, North-East and South, South-East regions and rural and
urban areas will continue for the foreseeable future, and that
the contribution of education to individual and national
development will be restricted by internal political conditions and external economic constraints.[19]   If Brazil is to
become the 'Country of Tomorrow', then these constraints will
have to be overcome.

REFERENCES AND NOTES

1.   Rocha, J., Guardian, 5 June, 1984.   Inflation is run-
      ning at 235 per cent per year, three million are un-
      employed and nine million underemployed.   Education
      cuts have closed some university laboratories and
      reduced lecturers' salaries.
2.   Havighurst, R. J. and Moreira, J. R. (1965).   Society
      and Education in Brazil.   University of Pittsburgh
      Press, p. 76.
3.   Ibid., p. 92.
4.   Latin America Bureau (1982), Brazil: State and Struggle.
      Latin America Bureau, p. 32.
5.   In particular the military, the landowners association,
      bankers and several conservative press barons vigor-
      ously opposed suggested land reforms.
6.   Latin America Bureau (1982), op. cit., p. 49. Of the 65
      Universities in Brazil, 21 are private.   Of the 887
      Institutions of Higher Education in Brazil, 670 are
      private.   Source: Sinopse Estatística do Brasil
      (1981).
7.   Jornal do Brasil, 22 October, 1978.
8.   Lambert, J. (1959), Os dois Brasis, Ministério de
      Educação e Cultura.

9. Instituto Brasileiro de Geografia e Estatística (1981). _Anuário Estatistico do Brasil._

10. Goodman, D. E. (1976), The Brazilian Economic Miracle and Regional Policy: Some evidence from the Urban North-East in _Journal of Latin American Studies._ Vol. 8, Part 1, May. The minimum wage is a 'subsistence' income and should cover the basic necessities for a family of 4.3 persons. In 1981 the average minimum wage in industralised states was US$96.36 per month.

11. Haar, J. (1977), _Politics of Higher Education in Brazil,_ Praeger, p. 187.

12. Brazilian Embassy, London (1974), _Social Aspects of Brazilian Economic Development,_ p. 3.

13. 1971 Education Law. Article 1. (Law No. 5.692)

14. Instituto Brasileiro de Geografia e Estatística (1981), op. cit. The figure of 3,143,800 enrolled at the Second level represents 24.1 per cent of the age group 15 to 19 years in 1979.

15. The common core curriculum consists of Portuguese, Brazilian Literature, History, Geography, Maths, Physics, Biology and Moral and Civic education and is followed for the first two years.

16. In 1979, 1,375,000 students were enrolled in higher education courses in Brazil. This represents 12.6 per cent of the 20 - 24 years age group, but includes part-time students. It should be noted that the higher education institutions range from private colleges of dubious quality to the prestigious University of São Paulo, which compares favourably with the best universities in Western Europe and the USA. Source: _Instituto Brasileiro de Geografia e Estatística (1981),_ op. cit.

17. 1968 Education Law, No. 5,540.

18. Campos, S. N. (1980), _Adult Literacy in National Development: A Case Study of a Developing Country._ University College of Swansea, Centre for Development Studies. Monograph No. 10, p. 26. The literacy rate in 1980 was 74 per cent. Source: _Latin America Bureau_ (1982), op. cit., p.3.

19. Political forces and conditions are changing so rapidly in 1984 that it now seems likely that elections for a civilian government will be held early in 1985, thus reversing an earlier Senate decision. It is possible that the old MDB opposition party (now the PMDB - Brazilian Democratic Movement Party) might defeat the former dominant ARENA party (now the PDS - Democratic Social Party). Whatever the result of these political changes it will still be some considerable time before any significant social and educational reforms can take place.

Chapter Eight

THE DIVERSIFICATION OF SECONDARY EDUCATION IN LATIN AMERICA: THE CASE OF BRAZIL

Nigel Brooke

INTRODUCTION

In the four-year period between 1969 and 1972 no less than five Latin American countries embarked upon the process of secondary school reform. The declared purposes were those of initiating students in technical-professional studies while placing the various types of secondary school on an equal footing with regard to university entrance. The two essential components of these reforms were the seven to nine-year basic education cycle combining primary and junior secondary, and the diversification of higher secondary schooling. In this way, Venezuela, Peru, Colombia, El Salvador and Brazil[1] proposed to delay occupational choice until the beginning of grade eight to ten at the same time as attempting to reduce the evident social dualism of a secondary school system divided into technical and academic streams. By the creation of new vocational institutions at the higher secondary level, such as the Institutes of Diversified Secondary Education (INEM) in Colombia and the Schools of Higher Professional Education (ESEP) in Peru, or by the expedient of reformulating curriculum priorities, these five countries made it their plan to direct the majority of school-goers into vocationally-oriented studies as part of a general policy of social and economic development.

The purpose of the present study is to look at the theory of these reforms, the way in which they were converted into practice and the effect of this practice on the reformulations to which they were later subjected. Two aspects are presented as being of special interest. First, the perceived relationship between education and work, with the definition of the middle-level technician that this relationship implied second, and with particular reference to Brazil, the question of how the secondary school preserved its selection function in the face of an authoritarian attempt to modify traditional patterns of social discrimination.

146

The Diversification of Secondary Education in Latin America:
The Case of Brazil

THE LATIN AMERICAN MODEL OF DIVERSIFIED SECONDARY SCHOOLING

The high degree of consensus regarding the need to make
vocational education a pre-requisite to University entrance
and, as a consequence to dismantle the differences between the
university-track academic colleges and those technical schools
frequented by a lower middle and working class, suggests that
the roots of the reform movement were not entirely indigenous.
Such technical schools had at most offered access to short
polytechnic courses. So in many respects the reforms
appeared to draw sustenance from the international debate of
the 1950's and early 1960's which had centred on the socially
divisive anachronism of the German gymnasium, the French lycée
and the English grammar school. These schools had been
criticised for their selectivity and for the obvious disadvantage, with regards a continued education, at which they
placed those who failed to enter them. The result, in one
form or another, had been the birth of the unified secondary
school which was to offer both academic and vocational preparation to a wider social intake.

Influenced by international organisations with a variety
of interests in the region,[2] the Latin American version of the
comprehensive school debate emphasised to a much greater
degree the relation between schooling and the labour market in
response to the apparent need for middle-level technical manpower at a time of economic growth. The Venezuelan reform
came as the result of that country's entry into the Andean
Pact and heavy State and US investments in the steel and
petrochemical industries.[3] In El Salvador the hopes of a
sizeable expansion of the secondary labour market, as the
result of the creation of the Central American Common Market,
was an incisive influence on the reform,[4] and in Brazil the
'economic miracle' was still progressing.

To the extent that the labour market became the key
principle in the reorientation of the secondary school in
Latin America, (along with the emphasis on middle-level manpower, 'lateral exits', 'voluntary terminality', labour market
studies and the wide range of technical sounding diplomas), so
did the demand for a homogeneous, unselective pre-university
preparation lose ground. In all but one of the five
countries at least a part of the academic stream was allowed
to survive, with all that it represented as the preferred
channel of access to higher education of the middle class.
In the event, the demand for trained technicians was stronger
than the arguments in favour of a secondary school that made
no distinctions in terms of vocational/academic balance, and
that would therefore not accede to the privilege of any
particular social group. Although the terminal secondary
school was eliminated by the 1969 reform in El Salvador, the
new three-year Diversified Secondary Schools admitted an
academic course as one of the nine vocational areas. In

The Diversification of Secondary Education in Latin America:
The Case of Brazil

Colombia there was a similar situation, with the same
Bachelor's diploma going to graduates of the academic
'Bachillerato Clássico' as well as to those of the commercial,
industrial, agricultural and teacher training courses of the
new Vocational Middle Education cycle.   In Venezuela, despite
the elimination of the entrance exam to the public 'liceo' and
the diversification of its courses in the interior of the
country and on the outskirts of Caracas, the science and
humanities courses of the private colleges remained intact
and in 1979 were responsible still for 68 per cent of enrolments at this level.[5]

THE MEANING OF EDUCATION FOR WORK

The only exception to the Latin American rule of permitting the continuation of an academic stream was the Brazilian
reform.   In its initial version,[6] the 1971 Reform Law made
clear its intention of vocationalising all secondary education
by eliminating the previous distinctions between Secondary
(academic), Commercial, Normal, Agricultural and Industrial
Schools, obliging each school to offer a variety of vocational
courses according to the needs of the pupils and the labour
market.   In a clarifying advisory document emitted by the
Federal Council of Education in 1972 and based on studies by
persons connected with the Division of Industrial Education of
the Ministry, this intention was restated.   A list of 52
technical and 38 auxiliary technical 'habilitações' (vocational courses) were suggested, of which 32 were related to industry.   The document stated that through the process of
'uniting head and hands' no-one should reach the end of
secondary schooling without some sort of training for work.[7]
The possibility of treating certain academic or 'general
studies' as if they were an 'habilitação' was only acceptable
under exceptional circumstances, such as when the student
already had a technical qualification.
The criticism of the new law came from various quarters;
the owners of private schools, state authorities, technical
schools and the teachers.   The complaints varied but centred
on both the immense difficulties of converting all schools to
their vocational training role and also the radical effects
of such a move on the quality of the general or humanities
component of the new courses.   The government reply came in
a further advisory document in 1975.[8]   For the first time the
Federal Council of Education admitted a distinction between
work training and work-related education treinamento profissional and educação profissional.   The second category opened
up the opportunity for a new type of course, the basic
'habilitação' which related to the pupils' interests rather
than to the labour market and would be more an introduction to
a particular field of work than preparation for a particular
type of job.   The obligatory nature of such a preparation was

maintained, however, despite signs that the task of implementation was creating considerable strain.[9],[10]

The modifications introduced reflected the same problem of interpreting the relationship between school and work experienced in Venezuela. Did the demand for the 'productive incorporation' of the student into the labour force mean the teaching of skills for a particular type of occupation or a general grounding for a broad range of occupations? In both countries the narrower, more technical view represented the point of departure. In Venezuela, emphasis in the first moment was laid on the study of occupational profiles, on manpower projections and the analysis of industrial needs in the regions. In Brazil likewise, with the basic education cycle responsible for the discovery of vocational interests and aptitudes, and the diversified secondary school as a supplier of trained middle-level technical personnel in accordance with detected needs. The number of classroom hours spent on the professional-technical component of the courses were to be greater than for the general education component, each with a minimum content established by the Federal Education Council. The justification for this technological approach was clearly stated as the 'explosion of occupations at intermediate levels' and the belief that a more generalist, science-oriented curriculum would become a simple preparation for university entrance.[11]

Only after the first attempts at implementation did the alternative, pro-science argument gain force in the two countries. The policy arrived at in Venezuela was to direct the vocational courses towards an 'ample and polivalent basic formation' in order to reduce the costs of schooling and to permit the occupational mobility of graduates.[12] Although the difficulties of predicting future labour market needs, of equipping schools for technical courses and of training the necessary teachers were never officially admitted in Brazil, the excessive specialisation of such courses as 'Fertilizer Auxiliary Technician' and 'Blood Bank Auxiliary Technician' were implicitly recognised in the 1975 advisory document. The move to 'basic professional formation' for broad families of occupations, such as Agriculture, Health, Commerce, Electricity and Electronics, was justified by the existence of on-the-job training opportunities. At the same time the law number 6297 of 1975, permitting an income tax deduction amounting to the double of that spent on manpower training, up to 10 per cent of company profits, had cut a good part of the ground from under the school reform. The government was now clearly stimulating an alternative policy for the training of middle-level personnel.

The definition of a technician had suffered an important alteration. In their technological phase both the Venezuelan and Brazilian reforms had understood the technician as someone with a technical function who would require a technical pre-

paration in order to perform that function adequately.   In
their second phase it was understood that a person begins to
be a technician when his or her work depends more on knowledge
than on manual ability.   This applies whether the knowledge
was gained either deliberately, through study, or by gradual
accumulation.   This definition would certainly explain why
the 1975 advisory document in Brazil emphasised that job
training was not the exclusive responsibility of the school
and why a general, more humanistic introduction to the various
worlds of work was now a permissable option alongside the
technical courses.

Not that all the contradictions had been resolved.   The
objective still remained that of 'professionalising' all
students by producing a unity between thinking and doing.
However, the work component of the curriculum could now be
somewhat diluted in the general education dimension, and the
world of work given the task of teaching the practical,
functional aspects of a particular occupation.   And there had
been no official discussion of the true worth of vocational as
opposed to general education on the employment, salary and
mobility of graduates.   A number of studies can now show that
in the Latin American context, as elsewhere, vocational training does not necessarily offer the supposed advantages.   In
El Salvador, McGinn and Balart[13] failed to detect higher
employment rates or salaries for those with middle-level
training.   This view is confirmed in Mexico by Muñoz-
Izquierdo and Rodrigues,[14] where general education graduates
receive, on average, 30 per cent more than technical graduates
and gain 70 per cent more per year of experience.   A study
purporting to show some advantage for the technical graduate
in Colombia and Argentina by Franco and Castro[15] is less con-
vincing.

AN EVALUATION OF THE BRAZILIAN REFORM

It was only in 1982 that the pressure for a revaluation
of the 1971 Education Reform Law in Brazil produced the long
desired result of eliminating the compulsory nature of the
work training or work-related courses.[16]   The Brazilian
secondary school had come through an 11-year experience which,
without equal in Latin America, raises two important questions.
The first is: how had the compulsory reform been possible,
given the importance traditionally attached to a general
science or humanities education for university entrance?   The
second is: how had the system maintained its selection
function?   Levin[17] suggests that in the face of comprehensivi-
sation the European university took up the social selection
role of the secondary school.   This would be in line with
other critiques of liberal educational reforms that take the
existence of a social division of labour as an unavoidable
deterrent to any profound modification to the school's role of

promoting one social class to the detriment of another.   If
one level of schooling begins to offer similar opportunities
of access and outcomes to the working class then it is axio-
matic that another level will compensate for this apparent
equalisation of educational opportunity.

This approach understates the degree of selectivity that
can occur within schools or between schools of nominally the
same type and intake.   Although Brazil theoretically
abolished the disadvantage with regard to university entrance
suffered by technical education, by creating a single type of
diversified secondary school, both public and private, it cannot be argued that the move necessarily created a homogeneity
of options, experiences and results at this level.   Indeed,
the study of some general tendencies, using secondary data,
indicates that the new secondary school did little to modify
the type of student reaching the university or indeed the type
of studies pursued by the middle class.

THE CONTEXT OF THE BRAZILIAN REFORM

One approach to the process of educational reform has
been to depict final policy outcomes as the product of negotia-
tion and compromise between conflicting interests.   This
scenario of pluralist politics emphasises the competition for
governmental largesse between groups whose countervailing
pressures generally add up to a fine and zealously guarded
balance.[18,19]   However, the power of an authoritarian
military government is not to be underestimated, especially
when that government has ulterior motives for a particular
organisation of the educational system.   In order to understand how such a radical form of diversification was possible
in Brazil in the face of the same entrenched interests as in
the rest of Latin America, it is necessary to look a little at
this authoritarian background to the reform.

There seems little doubt that the authoritarian military
government, installed by the 1964 coup, was committed to the
reform for other than purely economic reasons.   Cunha
argues,[20,21] that perhaps the principle role of diversification was, in continuation of the 1968 University Reform, to
contain the ever-increasing flow of secondary graduates to a
university overloaded with humanities students and unable to
offer a return to the heavy investments involved.[22]   Increased
pressure on university entrance had been fostered by the expansion of secondary education,[23,24] and by the consolidation
of an economic model that through the concentration of capital
in an increasingly centralised economy, had rapidly reduced
the traditional channels of social mobility via small family
enterprises.   The middle classes had turned to the university
as the provider of the necessary paper qualifications for employment in the new state and multinational bureaucracies.[25]

In order to stem this flow it was not sufficient, nor

The Diversification of Secondary Education in Latin America:
The Case of Brazil

politically desirable, to create further obstacles at the
point of the university entrance exmination, the
'Vestibular'.[26]   What was required was a reduction in the
number of aspirants for university entrance.   In this sense
the reform had a double purpose, first to modify the supposedly archaic attitudes that deprecated manual labour, by interesting the student in a range of middle-level occupations, and
secondly to make this change of attitude productive by offering professional courses related to the needs of a rapidly
expanding economy.[27,28] (See Fig. 1)

Fig. 1:   Enrolment and Growth Indices - Higher Education:
           Brazil 1960-1971

Year	Enrolment (1.000)	Index
1960	93.2	100.0
1961	98.9	106.1
1962	107.3	115.1
1963	124.2	133.3
1964	142.4	152.8
1965	155.8	167.1
1966	180.1	193.2
1967	212.9	228.4
1968	278.3	298.6
1969	346.8	372.1
1970	430.5	461.9
1971	557.0	597.6

Source: Cunha, L. A. (1977) A Profissionalizacão no Ensino
Médio, 2nd ed. Eldorado, p.113.

Note: The 1968 University Reform had taken a variety of
measures and this was an attempt to control the increase in
the number of students and in the costs of higher education.
Such measures included the unification of the entrance examination by region;   the institution of a classification system
according to the number of university places;   the creation
of a one-year basic course;   a new system of credits.
                         - - - - -
           Corvalán Vázquez[29] argues that the new ideology of
technical education also stems from the need to empty the
content of secondary education of its élite characteristics,
it being no longer desirable that a mass clientele should
have access to the cultural and behavioural characteristics of
the ruling class.   In more specifically Brazilian terms,
Saviani[30] shows how the reform law was to support the doctrine
of 'interdependence' of the military who blamed the institu-

tional crisis of 1964 on the lack of correspondence between
the economic model and the dominant ideology. The military
saw a contradiction between an economic system firmly engaged
in the international division of labour and an ideology, reinforced by the school, that was essentially nationalist and
in favour of a greater degree of cultural and economic independence. In this light, the undeniably technological
flavour of the reform was a step in the direction of a new
compatibility between the ideological and economic spheres.
The new social doctrine was to value efficiency, modernity
and productivity with the secondary school playing its part
in this ideological indoctrination by introducing the new
subject of Moral and Civic Education, emphasising professional training and calling for the attainment of national
development goals.

In the euphoria of the Brazilian miracle a call, of
'all hands to work' made sense. Whether this can be attributed to a doctrine that proposed ideological change independ-
ently of economic transformations, or whether it was proposed
that the ideological consequences would flow from the
increased productivity and social mobility that a mass middle-
level training scheme seemed to offer, cannot be neatly
resolved. Be that as it may, the Reform Law was produced and
passed in Congress in less than one-tenth of the time that the
previous Education Act had taken to pass on to the Statute
Books.[31]

SOCIAL SELECTION IN THE BRAZILIAN REFORM

Despite its authoritarian roots, the reform was undoubtedly influenced by liberal intentions. First, by
academicising the traditional technical schools and by vocationalising the academic, no student was to be left without
the necessary preparation, or in a position of advantage, with
regards to the essentially academic university entrance examination. Second, by creating a curriculum and a school
language that gave prestige to the technical, the working
class could potentially compete better than in a school environment dominated entirely by a humanist culture. Third,
the technical-professional training offered seemingly immediate returns, thereby increasing the chances of survival for
those students who needed to work. However, the pressures to
reduce rather than increase the demand for university places
was real, creating a potential contradiction to be resolved
either by the efficient implementation of the job training or
job-related courses in such a way as to motivate students of
all social classes to take up middle-level occupations, or by
the formulation of new mechanisms of selection.

The resolution of this contradiction can be studied in
four aspects of the reform in Brazil: implementation; student
survival; the quality of education; outcomes.

The Diversification of Secondary Education in Latin America:
The Case of Brazil

a) Implementation

Open refusal to implement the reform was not a viable
option.   Despite severe criticism and the serious problems of
equipping and staffing the new courses, the authoritarian
legislation and the lack of any authentic political opposition
to the government did not give margin to defiant responses.
The State Education Secretariats were obliged to accomplish
the impossible in order to guarantee the flow of Federal funds.
The private schools, however, adopted a subterfuge that
virtually amounted to non-implementation.   By choosing technical courses that could easily act as cover for the traditional science curriculum, or by giving such little importance
to the vocational content, many, mostly those with a higher
middle-class clientele, could continue to guarantee some
degree of university entrance examination success.
In the state schools the lack of funds and teachers
ensured that the easiest vocational options, such as accountancy and teacher training, would also flourish, thereby alter-
ing considerably the type of implementation initially envisaged.   In the State of Minas Gerais, for example, the number of
approved vocational courses related to tertiary sector
activities, such as tourism, office work and accountancy,
represented 78.5 per cent of the total in 1979, with courses
related to industry responsible for only 19.3 per cent and the
remaining 2.2 per cent related to agriculture.[32]

b) Survival

The official statistics show that the widening of
secondary school intake was not accompanied by increased survival rates.   While final year enrolments were 90.7 per cent
of first year enrolments in 1972, by 1976 they had fallen to
84.9 per cent.   The evolution of the flux of students tells
the same story.   While the proportion of students who managed
to survive the three-year course shows a relative stability
between 1964 and 1974, from 1975 the tendency is for this proportion to fall.   In other words, two to three years after
the implementation of the reform, when its effects begin to be
felt, the signs are of a continuing reduction in the ability
of the school to retain its students.   (See Fig. 2)
The average of the drop-out rates for the seven-year
periods before and after the reform range from 6.73 per cent
to 16.98 per cent for the first grade; 3.35 per cent to 11.96
per cent for the second grade; 2.09 per cent to 6.87 per cent
for the third grade. (See Fig. 3)
The higher levels of drop-out for the night courses and
the increase in enrolment in the parallel, non-formal secondary school courses for those above age, are both indications
that it is the working class that is disproportionately
affected by the drop-out phenomenon.

The Diversification of Secondary Education in Latin America:
The Case of Brazil

Fig. 2: Student Flux - Secondary Education in Brazil:
1963-1979

Years	Enrolment first grade (A)	No. continuing to second grade the following year	No. continuing to third grade the following year (B)	Survival rate (per cent) $\frac{B}{A}$
1963/65	182.807	135.727	123.645	68
1964/66	199.608	158.563	141.730	71
1965/67	226.900	148.844	164.731	73
1966/68	266.834	210.512	190.347	71
1967/69	309.929	247.577	220.772	71
1968/70	359.216	287.990	248.712	69
1969/71	397.506	304.441	264.658	67
1970/72	445.773	347.435	303.595	68
1971/73	503.132	407.882	352.014	69
1972/74	580.157	464.563	411.270	71
1973/75	639.718	523.000	440.113	69
1974/76	722.636	577.161	483.503	67
1975/77	885.349	687.226	571.746	65
1976/78	1004.013	763.554	610.331	61
1977/79	1065.848	780.336	629.606	59

Source: Ministério de Educação e Cultura (1981). Dados.

The Diversification of Secondary Education in Latin America:
The Case of Brazil

Fig. 3: Same Year* Drop-out Percentages - Secondary
Education in Brazil: 1965-1978

Year	First Grade	Second Grade	Third Grade
1965	4.78	3.46	3.69
1966	7.04	2.98	1.22
1967	6.00	2.06	0.82
1968	11.29	4.19	1.86
1969	5.26	4.30	3.24
1970	5.75	2.70	2.61
1971	7.03	3.77	1.90
Average 1965-71	6.73	3.25	2.09
1972	14.66	10.24	3.87
1973	13.35	8.9	5.41
1974	17.64	10.53	6.11
1975	17.09	13.57	9.45
1976	19.27	14.40	7.89
1977	18.65	13.29	7.71
1978	18.17	12.81	7.68
Average 1972-78	16.98	11.96	6.87

Source: Ministério de Educação e Cultura (1981). Dados.

*As opposed to those who drop out between school years.

156

The Diversification of Secondary Education in Latin America:
The Case of Brazil

The night course became a regular feature in state
schools, particularly after the relative clampdown on public
school expansion as from 1974.   They attract principally
working-class students who during the day are involved in full
or part-time occupations.   There have been sufficient complaints, however, in the press and national educational
encounters, to doubt the official position that these courses
are an exact replica of the day-time courses.   Often with a
reduced timetable, less qualified teachers and little or no
access to sports, workshop or laboratory facilities, there is
reason to suspect that their lower retention rates are, in
part, attributable to their inferior quality.   The increase
in enrolments in the parallel, 'supletivo' courses is a reflex
of the same phenomenon.   The clientele of these courses, exclusively working class, are in large part drop-outs of the
formal secondary system.

c)   The Quality of Education Received

The expansion of secondary schooling from 1970 to 1976,
which increased enrolments from 18.1 per cent to 28.4 per cent
of the 15 to 19 age group, benefited principally those of the
lower income groups.   While in 1970 only 1.8 per cent of
those from families with incomes up to a half the legal minimum salary frequented the secondary school, by 1976 this proportion had increased to 3.4 per cent.   Similar increases
took place for those with family incomes of up to 2 minimum
salaries, with the higher income groups remaining stable.[33]
This expansion in the initial phases of the reform did
not take place without leaving its mark on the yearly pass and
fail rates.   Since 1972 the pass rates for the first and
second grades show a constant decline, accompanied by an
increase in repetition rates for the second and third grades.
The slight improvement in the post-reform repetition rates for
the first grade can only be explained as the result of
increasing drop-out amongst those who fail the year.
The causes of this obvious deterioration in the efficiency of the school are many and generally more difficult to
quantify than the teacher pupil ratio which goes from 1:9 in
1971 to 1:15 in 1980.   However, one factor should be emphasised, that of the uncontrolled form in which private and
municipal education grew in the post-reform period in some
states, absorbing a large part of the new demand for schooling
at this level.   Fig. 4 shows the growth of Federal, State,
Municipal and Private schools in the State of Minas Gerais.
Although there is no exact correspondence between school
ownership and the quality of education offered, there being
high quality public and private schools, there is little doubt
that the worst schools are private.   Created in the absence
of any policy for the increase in public schools, many of
these private schools are installed in completely unsatis-

The Diversification of Secondary Education in Latin America:
The Case of Brazil

Fig. 4: Growth in Number of Secondary School Establishments
Minas Gerais: 1972-1982

	Federal	State	Municipal	Private	Total
No. Schools 1972	18	214	65	544	841
No. Schools 1982	17	216	160	655	1048
Growth 1972-1982 (%)	- 5.6	0.9	146.2	20.4	24.6

Source: CEDINE. Secretaria de Educação. Minas Gerais.

- - - - -

factory buildings with untrained teachers and an absence of
basic equipment. The irony is that these poor quality, fee-
paying schools are generally reserved for the working class
because they have no entry criteria.

d) Outcomes

Even before the reform was introduced, studies had
indicated that the labour market for school-trained middle-
level technicians was narrower than that imagined. In a 1970
study, Pastore and Bianchi[34] had shown that, of 17,625 workers
defined as middle-level by their function in 705 firms in the
State of São Paulo, only a third had received some sort of
secondary level training. The difficulties encountered by
schools in identifying labour market demands, and of orienting
the vocational courses accordingly, were therefore inevitable
and could only grow as the economy began to run into difficulties as it did from 1973.

In the face of employer indifference to the new secondary
school product and the continued importance of a university
degree, the demand for university entrance continued to grow.
But with the drop in school quality and the increasing
severity of the 'vestibular' as from 1976, fewer and fewer
schools could guarantee their graduates a university place.
This situation rapidly led to a generalisation of one-year
post-secondary cramming courses which can now be considered
the true third level of the education system.

The social selectivity inherent in these cramming schools
resides in two of their characteristics. The first is their
cost, their being exclusively privately owned, profit-making
organisations. The second is that studies show a high correlation between secondary school quality and 'vestibular'

results.[35]   Even the best cramming schools cannot act as substitute for an adequate second-level course or make up for
the damage of an inadequate one.   Eight years after the
reform's implementation in Minas Gerais, 90 per cent of new
university students at the Federal University in Belo Hori-
zonte were from just seven of the city's secondary schools,
five private and two public.[36]   In Rio de Janeiro in 1980,
54 per cent of those who passed in the selection examination
were from 10 per cent of the schools.   In the same study it
is calculated that 98 per cent of secondary graduates continue
to aspire to university entrance.

CONCLUSIONS

    The tensions generated by the attempt to pursue two
largely contradictory objectives simultaneously, namely:
professionalising the secondary school curriculum and promoting the homogenisation of results across social groups, appear
to have altered the process of identification and discrimination of the working class student.   While this traditionally
took place between schools of different types, it now occurs
within schools of nominally the same type or between fee-
paying schools and those maintained by the State.   Although
the data only permits a first approximation in the study of
the qualitative stratification process unleashed by the reform,
it would appear that the 'voluntary terminality' of the
secondary school student has been achieved, but not as a
result of the technical-professional training received.   It
seems that most of those students who do not reach university
fail to do so because they have received an education whose
quality prohibits further studies.   Aspirations for middle-
level employment are not a significant factor.
    The effects of the liberalisation of the reform legisla-
tion, removing the compulsory nature of the vocational content,
are yet to appear.   It seems likely, however, that only a
small minority of private schools, mainly those with a pre-
reform tradition in technical education or which have invested
heavily in equipment, will continue to offer a vocationally-
oriented curriculum.   The state schools with technical
courses will probably be obliged to continue to offer these
while the other auxiliary and 'basic habilitacão' courses will
be phased out.   An attempt will be made to maintain a work-
oriented subject area but it is unlikely that this will amount
to more than a few hours per semester for the study of labour
legislation and the like.

REFERENCES AND NOTES

1.   The dates of the reforms are the following: Venezuela
     (1969), Peru (1972), Colombia (1969), El Salvador
     (1969), Brazil (1971).   Interesting sources on these

reforms, not cited in the text, are the following:
for Venezuela, Trocone, Pablo A. (1971) Bases Ideo-
lógicas de la Reforma de la Ley de Universidades,
Revista Pedagógica. No. 1; for Peru, Churchill,
Stacy (1976). The Peruvian Model of Innovation: The
Reform of Basic Education. Experiments and Innovations
in Education No. 22, The UNESCO Press; for Colombia,
Ben-Jumea, Fernando Galvis (1981). El Sistema Educa-
tivo Colombiano, Revista Latinoamericana de Estudos
Educativos. Vol. XI, No. 3, and Ministério de Educa-
ción Nacional (1980). Evaluación de los Institutos
Técnicos Industriales; for El Salvador, Werthein,
Jorge (1978). Los Límites de la Reforma Educativa en
El Salvador, Revista del Centro de Estudios Educativos.
Vol. 8, No. 1, and Mayo. John K. et al (1975).
Aspiraciones Académicas y Profissionales de los Estud-
iantes del Tercer Ciclo en El Salvador, Revista del
Centro de Estudios Educativos. Vol. V, No. 1.

2. Between 1963 and 1971, 72 per cent of World Bank loans
    were channelled into secondary education. Of this
    total 44 per cent went to diversified schools and 29
    per cent to professional training. See Vazquez and
    Llomovatte (1979) Dilemas y Tendencias de la Enseñanza
    de Nivel Médio en America Latina. Revista Latino-
    americana de Estudios Educativos. Vol. IX, No. 1.
    The Ford Foundation, along with the University of
    Wisconsin, were instrumental in creating this conson-
    ance between the objectives of schooling and economic
    development in Venezuela as were the Ministry of
    Education/USAID agreements in Brazil. See Loyo, M.
    and Montiel, M. (1981) Trabajo Social y Educación:
    Alternativa para Educación Média. Cuadernos de
    Educación. No. 89, and Rodrigues, N. (1982) Estado,
    Educação e Desenvolvimento Econômico. Autores
    Associados/Cortez.

3. Calonge, S. (1981) Tendencias de la Orientación en
    Venezuela. Cuadernos de Educación. No. 88.

4. Tedesco, J. C. (1978) Industria y Educación en El
    Salvador UNESCO-CEPAL-PNUD. Proyecto DEALC. No. 9/
    Reimpr. 1.

5. Equipo Cerpe (1981) El Ciclo Diversificado Industrial en
    Venezuela. Revista Latinoamericana de Estudios Educa-
    tivos. Vol. XI, No. 2.

6. Law No. 5692, 11 August, 1971. The Law of Directives
    and Foundations of 1st and 2nd Level Education.

7. Parecer No. 45/72 Conselho Federal de Educação in Schuch,
    V. F. (1979) Educação no Brasil, Legislação Mínima.

8. Parecer No. 76/75 Conselho Federal de Educação (1975).
    Ibid.

9. Cunha, L. A. (1975) Mercado de Trabalho e Profissional-
    ização no Ensino de 2° Grau. in Educação Brasileira:

Questões da Atualidade.

10. Langoni, C. G. (1974) Educação e Tecnologia. Ensaios Econômicos. Expansão e Cultura/Fundação Getúlio Vargas.

11. Much of the underlying philosophy of the reform in Brazil can be found in the Relatório do Grupo de Trabalho (Working Group Report), June-August, 1970, Mimeo, Brasilia, and in a text written by one of the Federal Education Council members: Chagas, V. (1971) Mais do que uma reforma, uma nova concepção de escola. Mimeo.

12. Equipo Cerpe (1981). op.cit.

13. McGinn, N. and Balart, E. T. (1980) Una Evaluación de la Educación Média Técnica en El Salvador. Revista Latinoamericana de Estudios Educativos. Vol. 1, No. 2.

14. Muñoz-Izquierdo, C. and Rodriguez, P. G. (1980). Enseñanza Técnica: Un Canal de Movilidad Social para los Trabajadores? Revista Latinoamericana de Estudios Educativos. Vol. X, No. 3.

15. Franco, M. A. C. and Castro, C. de (1981) La Contribuición de la Educación Técnica a la Movilidad Social. Revista Latinoamericana de Estudios Educativos. Vol. XI, No. 1.

16. Lei No. 7044, October, 1982. This law proposes that schools still include a subject area called 'afeiçoamento', which literally means to inspire affection or devotion to work.

17. Levin, H. (1978) The Dilemma of Comprehensive Secondary School Reforms in W. Europe. Comparative Education Review. Vol. 22, No. 3.

18. McGinn, N., Schiefelbein, E. and Warwick, D. P. (1979). Educational Planning as Political Process: Two Case Studies from Latin America. Comparative Education Review. Vol. 23, No. 2.

19. Shirk, S. L. (1979) Educational Reform and Political Backlash: Recent Changes in Chinese Educational Policy. Comparative Education Review. Vol. 23, No. 2.

20. Cunha, L. A. (1978) Educação e Desenvolvimento Social no Brasil. Third Edition. Livraria Fco. Alves Editora.

21. Cunha, L. A. (1979) Vestibular, a Volta do Pêndulo. Encontros com a Civilização Brasileira. No. 3.

22. The growth in university enrolment between 1960 and 1971 had been 497 per cent, and by 1971 the number of Humanities, Letters and Arts' students represented 63 per cent of the total.

23. Secondary education enrolment increased by 278 per cent between 1964 and 1972, and is an attempt by the military to secure support from the regime's social base, the middle and lower-middle classes.

24. Heimer, F. W. (1975) Education and Politics in Brazil. Comparative Education Review. Vol. 19, No. 1.

25. Cunha, L. A. (1973) O Milagre Brasileiro e a Política

Educacional. Argumento.No. 2.

26. The university entrance examination had been an explosive issue throughout the 1960's, centring on the 'excedentes', those who had achieved the minimum score but were unable to find places. More severe entrance criteria were introduced in 1976, with a change in the political climate. This policy raised the number of aspirants per university place from 2.2:1 in 1975 to 4.5:1 in 1980.

27. Cunha, L. A. (1978). op. cit.

28. Warde, M. (1977) Educação e Estrutura Social: A Profissionalização em Questão. Cortez e Moraes.

29. Vazquez and Llomovatte (1979). op. cit.

30. Saviani, D. (1978) Análise Crítica da Organização Escolar Brasileira Através das Leis 5540/68 e 5692/71, in Garcia, W. E. (Ed) Educação Brasileira Contemporânea: Organização e Funcionamento. McGraw Hill.

31. The previous, 1961, Law of Directives and Foundations of Education had been in debate for almost 15 years prior to its approval.

32. Data from the Secretariat of State Education of Minas Gerais.

33. These and other data in this section are from MEC. Dados (1981) Ministério de Educação e Cultura. A deterioration in income distribution between 1970 and 1980 discounts any alternative explanation in terms of an alteration in the definition of middle income groups.

34. Pastore, J. and Bianchi, A-M.F. (1976) Estrutura Ocupacional da Indústria e Demanda de Mão-de-Obra Especializada. Revista Brasileira de Estudos Pedagógicos. Vol. 1, No. 137.

35. Castro, C. de (1981) Sua Excelência. O Vestibular. Educação e Seleção. No. 3.

36. Mafra, L. (1979) Occupational Status and Aspirations for Higher Education: A Brazilian Case Study. Ph.D. thesis, University of Pittsburgh.

37. Castro, C. de (1981). op. cit.

Chapter Nine

CHANGES IN THE CHILEAN EDUCATIONAL SYSTEM DURING ELEVEN YEARS
OF MILITARY GOVERNMENT: 1973-1984

Ruth Aedo-Richmond, Ines Noguera and Mark Richmond

As a consequence of the military coup d'etat which took
place in Chile in September 1973, the country's economic,
social and political structures were radically transformed.
Within this transformation, education experienced profound
changes which effectively destroyed the logic and coherence of
its historical development since the 1930's.
    During the forty years prior to the military coup, Chil-
ean education had evolved in close association with a model of
socio-economic development characterised by an emphasis on
import - substituting industrialisation and the adoption by
the state of a leading role in the development process.   The
state, in fact, became the nation's principal economic actor
and had the decisive voice in the distribution of the economic
surplus.   Chilean education, stimulated by the active role
assumed by the state, became an effective instrument for
securing some social mobility despite the constraints imposed
by the system of capitalist dependency;   a large proportion of
the population gained access to the educational system, especially during the 1960's.
    The 1965 Educational Reform under Frei's Christian Demo-
crat administration[1] may be seen as the culmination of several
decades of national debate and attempted reforms whose main
aims were to make education more functional and relevant to
the needs of economic, social and political development and to
modernise the educational system by incorporating scientific-
technological advances into the plans and programmes of study.
These earlier reform proposals and actual policies, however,
had failed to dominate or significantly modify the central
structural features of the educational system.   Furthermore,
they left intact the contents of education and traditional
pedagogical principles and methods.   Education continued to
be old-fashioned, intellectual and authoritarian, despite
being exposed to severe criticism both inside and outside
educational circles.   None the less the Frei Reform was
greeted with great optimism, for it appeared to promise a
genuine radical improvement in Chilean education.   A number

of advances were indeed achieved, for example, the problem of
educational access was largely resolved and the possibilities
for participation by various social groups in the formation of
educational policy were considerably enlarged.   However, the
Frei Reform had neither the time nor, more importantly, the
real intention or capacity to fulfil its original promise.
This is reflected in the persistence of certain basic problems,
such as those of drop-out and repetition, which continued to be
severe, especially during the first years of primary education.   By raising and then disappointing the people's expectations, the Frei Reform opened the way for education to become
a more overt means through which the class character and
inequalities of Chilean society became evident to its class
constituents, particularly the urban workers and peasants.

The process of educational democratisation begun under
Frei was carried several stages further under Allende, although it should be noted that radical educational reform was
not the top priority of the <u>Unidad Popular</u> government.[2]   However, between 1970 and 1973, the educational system became an
arena within which the conflicting forces of Chilean society
fought many battles.   Education was thoroughly politicised.
Nevertheless, despite the actual and attempted changes which
mark this short but intense period, there was a recognisable
continuity in the orientation and line of development of the
educational system.[3]

THE PERIOD OF TRANSITION: 1973-1979

The circumstances which surrounded the takeover in 1973
by the military junta meant that the new regime's policies and
actions were initially informed by pragmatic, short-term
considerations.   The junta's principle and most urgent task
was to impose 'order' and to 'normalise' the country's
activities.   Very soon, however, the type of society envisaged by the new military government became clear.   From the
beginning, changes in the economy were imposed which completely altered the country's established line of development.
Central to the military junta's conception of its historical
task was the introduction of a neo-liberal economic model
characterised by an economy 'open to the exterior', that is,
open to foreign capital and goods; by the liquidation of un-
profitable national industries;   by the reduction of the role
of the state in order to turn it into a 'subsidiary state';
and by the promotion of a privileged role for private capital
and the free market.

The political model which was adopted envisaged an
authoritarian military government which would ensure the
domination of the country by the armed forces for many years
to come.   Only a sharply limited political pluralism would be
tolerated according to which just a few groups would be
allowed to exist and develop.   The authoritarian regime would

determine which groups would operate politically and under
what conditions; there would be no free and open interplay
of diverse democratic forces as had characterised earlier
Chilean practice.

A social model was adopted which ended the population's
broad participation. Instead, the government promoted apathy,
conformism and unquestioning obedience to authority, thereby
transforming the people into passive subjects rather than
active, participatory citizens. Furthermore, the market
mechanisms imposed by the economic model were to shape and
orientate the social life of the country at all levels.
Though its role would be much reduced in many respects, the
state would be strong and would guarantee a 'natural' social
order whose mission was to safeguard and defend the nation
from the external enemy:

> 'The Government of the Armed Forces and Civic Order has
> assumed the historic mission of giving Chile a new insti-
> tutional form which reflects the profound changes which
> the contemporary epoch has been producing. Only in this
> way will it be possible to give our democracy a firm
> stability, purifying our democratic system of the vices
> which facilitate its destruction, but also rising to a
> new improved challenge in order to fully enter a brave
> new world.'[4]

The period between 1973 and 1977 mainly featured the
destruction or 'freezing' of existing social and political
organisations by purging the country of internal enemies and
by launching a massive and bloody persecution of the supporters of the previous regime. While the economic model was
imposed from the beginning of 1975, other structural changes
appeared more slowly; in fact, it was not until the government felt that it had fully consolidated its position that it
issued the Constitution of 1981. Up to this point, the
regime had needed a period of maturation in which it was
necessary to organise and develop an effective repressive
apparatus, to install a group of experts known as the 'Chicago
Boys' who were to run the economy and, above all, to secure
the pre-eminent position and power of one member of the junta,
General Pinochet. It is within this overall context that
changes in education should be understood, changes which were
shaped by the economic principles of the neo-liberal model
and constrained by the limits imposed by the strongly authoritarian government.

After the 1973 coup, the educational apparatus, along
with other services, had to be restructured and purged of all
'conflictive' elements and of all opposition to the new
military order. All educational institutions throughout the
country suffered military occupation. A network of military
authorities and representatives was established parallel to,

or replacing, the civil-administrative staff.   At the same
time a rigid hierarchy of functions was set up and a system
was imposed whereby posts were filled by a closed, secret
system of appointment rather than by the former method of open
public competition.   All the participatory practices and such
organisations as student centres and teachers' unions were
abolished, as was the Consejo Nacional de Educación (National
Education Council).   In this way, an authoritarian educational regime was created which persists to this day.

After this period of 'ordering' and 'cleansing', the
government decided to commission a diagnosis of the educational situation of the country.   The results of this evaluation
showed that, in administrative terms, there was too much
centralisation; a duplication of functions; weaknesses in
the structure and organisation of the educational system; and
a shortage of qualified personnel in the different areas of
administration.[5]   In view of these finding and in order to
begin the process of educational transformation, policies of
decentralisation were formulated, and were implemented through
the regionalisation and reorganisation of the country's
internal governmental structure.   Regional Ministerial
Secretariats were created (through Decree Law No. 575, 1974)
which were linked to the structure of regional government
headed by the Intendant, the highest authority representing
the government in each region.   It should be noted, however,
that:

> 'The process of decentralisation at the beginning of the
> regime was primarily linked to aspects of rationalisation
> and political manoeuvring and not to privatisation as
> would be the case later.'[6]

At first, the decentralisation sought to disperse the administrative functions which were held to overburden the state,
but the state would retain the same features of ultimate
control in the running of the country's educational system.

Educational policy during this period manifested a high
level of universality and was basically assertive in character.
The overall orientation of the educational system was shaped
and defined by means of decree laws, internal circulars and
official documents.   Alfonso Bravo, in a study based on this
documentation,[7] has observed that one of the most prominent
themes has been patriotism and its particular manifestations.
According to the ideology of the military government, patriotism is one of the most noble sentiments, relegating to
secondary positions such values as justice, solidarity, and
freedom.   Moreover, according to Bravo's study, love of
country is closely associated with the authority of the regime
and with the institutions created by Chile's military rulers.
Patriotism has entered education through the contents of each
subject, into which new elements and structures have been

introduced.

A second prominent theme of the official documents of the
period, according to Bravo, is 'verticality'. This idea
emphasises the need to create a clear, precise locus of
authority and command at every level and at the same time to
destroy the participatory and consultative organisations
which, as transmission belts, would disturb the absolute verticality desired. Gradually, the military regime came to
impose its educational policies and changes in accordance with
the principle of verticality, inviting no discussion or interpretation but demanding immediate obedience and implementation.

The third outstanding theme is that of school efficiency.
Since the military government had from the beginning declared
its intention of improving school efficiency, it implemented
a system of higher standards regarding the qualifications
needed to obtain promotion from one educational level to
another. In addition, the criteria and requirements govern-
ing failure and repetition were stiffened. In this way the
educational process was turned into a series of obstacles
which accentuated the selection function of education in
Chile and increased the rate of drop-out from the system.

The educational process became more selective, so that in
the medium-term social stratification would be deepened.
During this period, the school curriculum experienced only a
partial transformation and the process of decentralising the
educational system was geared essentially to the administrative fragmentation of the state's educational apparatus. In
practice, the state continued to control and orientate all
facets of educational change. By the end of 1978, the regime
had succeeded in its attempt to bring various social forces
under control and to 'purify' the educational system.

THE PERIOD OF CONSOLIDATION AND INSTITUTIONALISATION: 1979-
1982

This period witnesses a clearer definition of educational
policy. The military regime found itself completely secure
and facing the need to adapt the structure, functioning and
contents of education to the requirements imposed by the
global model shaping Chile's development. Concrete measures
were taken which deeply transformed the country's educational
system. New curricula for primary and secondary education
were devised and implemented, and higher education was destined for a thorough renovation. All these changes were
enacted within an authoritarian framework which governed the
entire process of transformation and which imposed its own
particular contradictions and limitations.

In March 1979, the restructuring of the educational
system was heralded through the so-called 'Directivas Presidenciales sobre Educación Nacional' (Presidential Directives
on National Education).8   These Directives announced a series

167

of measures and clarified the government's new criteria concerning education. The military government hereby assumed the responsibility for the formation, within future generations, of the type of Chileans most suited to the regime's vision of the country. Education constituted the principal instrument for achieving this.

The general orientation of educational policy and the level of participation and freedom which the educational system would allow were to be regulated by the ideology of the military government, as expressed in the Declaración de Principios de la Junta de Gobierno (Declaration of Principles of the Government Junta). The declared intention was to combine and harmonise neo-liberal ideas and Western Christian humanism with the authoritarian and nationalist orientations embodied in the doctrine of National Security. A policy of decentralising the educational system was therefore enacted whose purpose was to turn the state into a lender of educational services. The state is no longer conceived as an agent of development, rather, 'future educational expansion will be sought preferably in private initiative'.[9] Thus, educational development will be reserved for private enterprise, for in the 'Directivas Presidenciales', General Pinochet was clearly telling the Minister of Education that it was the intention of his government to progressively privatise education and that the government would support the private sector in the performance of its educational task. The state, however, would retain its rule-setting and supervisory duties.

This series of ideas and policies forms the context within which the educational changes occurring during this period obtain their meaning. Particularly important was the policy of decentralisation, understood as a process of privatisation, which became one of the central pillars of the process of educational modernisation in Chile. In order to achieve the desired educational changes, the transfer of state schools to the municipalities was begun. The existing system of educational financing, according to which the government awarded a fixed annual sum to each school, was replaced by one which provided that a type of subsidy was awarded for each enrolled student. Incentives were offered for setting up new non-fee-paying 'private' schools that were subsidised by the state under this new system.

The Process of Municipalisation

The transfer of schools to the municipalities constituted the central factor in the adaptation of the educational system to the new educational requirements of the regime. However, it must be emphasised that this process does not represent a way of achieving a genuine decentralisation of the system. One of the first acts of the military junta on coming to power had been the dissolution of municipal government and the

abolition of the democratic election of local councillors.
The military government assumed the right to appoint the
mayors and abolished all community and autonomous participation in policy-formation. In fact, the municipalities ceased
to be an organ of policy-formation in order to become an
executive agency for policies designed at higher levels of
government'.[10]

The mayor, as the representative of the central government, makes decisions on its behalf. The former spontaneous
involvement and participation of the community in the running
of municipal affairs has ended and this has contributed considerably to the growth of apathy and scepticism regarding the
search for solutions to local problems. Furthermore, the
mayors are not only dependent upon and accountable to General
Pinochet but they are also absolute rulers within their
municipal boundaries. All local public officials are
appointed at the absolute discretion of the mayor, whose power
is shared with no other social institution at that level.
According to one commentator:

> 'The changes in community administration do not imply the
> generation of a relatively autonomous power; they can be
> better interpreted as a stage in the process of privatis-
> ation imposed by authoritarian capitalism.'[11]

In the middle of 1980, a Decree Law (1-3063) was issued
according to which state schools, hospitals, and other services belonging to the public sector began to be transferred to
the municipalities. The respective ministries retained their
powers of technical supervision and control. The so-called
'process of municipalisation' was thus set in motion. The
government has tried to justify these changes by appealing to
various arguments, which have been conveniently itemised by
Egaña and Magendzo. The government's basic arguments in
support of municipalisation are as follows: (a) through
municipalisation, the process of decentralisation is deepened,
thereby allowing greater efficiency in the solution of problems; (b) municipalisation improves the rationalisation of
educational administration by leaving the Ministry of Education with only the normative duties of supervision and control
to fulfil; (c) more social participation will be made
possible; (d) municipalisation will allow an improvement in
the quality of education to be achieved; and (e) teachers'
salaries will improve by virtue of the greater availability of
resources at the disposal of the municipalities; (f) furthermore, the occupational opportunities of teachers will be broad-
ened for they will be able to select the municipalities they
will work for in accordance with their interests and aspirations.

However, as we shall see, none of these arguments has
been borne out in practice. The municipalisation of education

was rapidly introduced on a large scale between 1980 and 1982,
with no stage of experimentation in certain districts as had
been originally suggested.   In March 1982, however, when the
country began to be affected by a grave economic crisis, the
process of municipalisation was suddenly stopped in its tracks.
At that point, 84 per cent of Chile's schools had been transferred to the municipalities and about 200 schools were await-
ing transfer, subject to an evaluation of the strengths and
weaknesses of the municipalisation process.[13]

The 'Directivas Presidenciales' had also announced the
widening of the policy of subsidisation (via state funding
according to the level of pupil enrolment) to non-fee-paying
private education, and a lending policy was devised for the
benefit of private businesses wishing to open new schools.
Moreover, these policies reaffirmed the government's desire to
continue with the process already initiated of transferring
technical-vocational schooling to the private sector.   Thus,
it became clear that the objective of modernising the educational system basically meant that it would be privatised.
In fact, the process of municipalisation ultimately envisages
the transfer of municipal schools to private hands.   The
Ministry of the Interior has advised the country's mayors that
they should not become too attached to the business of running
schools but, instead, should leave open the opportunity for
their eventual take-over by private interests:

> 'The municipality cannot create nor maintain a static
> situation at the local level, since that would undermine
> the policy of subsidisation that the government has
> wanted to implement.'[14]

In the 'Directivas Presidenciales', General Pinochet also
emphasised that the focus of the state's responsibility in
education was upon the primary level; it was also acknowledged that all Chileans have the historic and legal right to
primary education not only in terms of access but also in
terms of its effective provision.   By contrast, no state
responsibility was admitted regarding secondary and higher
education, which are considered 'exceptional' in character.
Only the more highly qualified students were destined for
secondary education; to this end, entry standards were to be
raised considerably.   Those who gain entry, furthermore, must
sustain a high level of effort and achievement.   Other educational developments would depend directly upon private initiative.   An example, already noted is the case of technological
institutes, where the training of medium-level technicians was
to be conducted by private enterprise.

Changes in the Chilean School Curriculum

Changes in the curriculum can best be appreciated in

historical perspective.   In 1929, at the same time that six
years of primary education was made compulsory, a common curriculum at the primary level was introduced for all the
country.   This meant that, regardless of the pupils' socio-
economic backgrounds, the contents of school materials, subjects and experiences, as well as the length of each course
of study, were the same for all pupils and for every primary
school in the country.   Primary education thus served to some
degree to reduce social inequalities and basically to integrate all citizens into certain shared cultural patterns.   The
later reforms of 1948 and 1965 followed the same line of
development towards a common, uniform basic education for all.
On gaining power, the military regime broke with the country's
historical tradition of development through its reform of
primary education.   In accordance with its aims and precepts,
the military government introduced a diversified curriculum
for primary schooling.   In addition to various general objectives, certain minimum objectives to be achieved were also
established, namely, knowledge of how to read and write, basic
arithmetic, the history and geography of Chile, and elementary
notions of natural science.   These minimum objectives also
included knowing one's duties towards the community and the
values upon which a national consensus had traditionally
existed.

The flexibility of the curriculum was established in such
a way that only two subjects, spanish language and mathematics,
were compulsory until the fifth year of primary school, when
social science was also made mandatory.   If a pupil failed to
achieve the required standard in these basic subjects, it was
possible to suspend some branches of the flexible curriculum
in order to reinforce the pupil's study of the compulsory subjects.[15]

According to new plans, there are curricula differences
between state and private schools.   In the state schools, the
metas mínimas (basic educational aims) are very limited and
education is considered solely as a device for securing conformity to the system, training the pupils to fulfil the
'presidential ideal' of becoming good workers, good citizens
and good patriots. If material conditions permit, state
schools can offer other subjects up to a maximum of ten.
Private schools, on the other hand, are obliged to offer a
full curriculum, that is, a minimum of ten subjects.   In this
way, primary education is shaped by the circumstances existing
in a free economy, which means that inequalities in the quality and length of study are bound to arise.   A state monopoly
of primary education is out of the question.   On the contrary,
it is maintained that, in a society like that desired for
Chile, several types of basic education must be made available
so as to accord with the diversity of expectations and material conditions among those who 'consume' educational services.

In general, the curriculum is highly simplified.   The

programmes of study of each subject, for example, furnish only
objectives, with no specification of methodological criteria
as had been the case with the replaced programmes.   The curricula are also flexible in that they are adaptable to the
desired model of society.   On the other hand, such subjects
as history and geography implicitly or explicitly raise a
series of judgements, interpretations, or values through which
the regime's ideology is imposed.

In December 1981, a Decree Law (No. 300) was issued which
established a new curriculum for secondary education.   There
is only one collection of common objectives covering the
entire span of secondary education, with no differentiation
between state and private schools.   Differentiation only
appears during the last two years of secondary schooling, when
a choice is made between scientific-humanistic and technical-
vocational tracks.   There are also changes in the contents of
different subjects and in the length of study they require.
The evolution of enrolment, using 1964 as a base-year, is
shown in Fig. 1.

Only the pre-school and secondary levels have continued
their historical pattern of growth since 1973.   Pre-school
enrolment almost doubled between 1973 and 1982, while secondary schooling grew at a slower pace.   Both primary and
university levels suffered a decline compared with the expansion enjoyed prior to the military coup.   In 1982 there were
253,566 fewer students enrolled in primary schools compared
with 1973 and there were 24,392 fewer university students in
1982 compared with 1973.   The patterns of growth of enrolments and of rates of schooling during the last three presidential administrations are clearly distinguishable, as Fig.
2 shows.

In June 1981, the Catholic Church, the only public voice
strongly opposed to the military regime, issued a pastoral
letter which expressed its anxiety concerning the changes that
had occurred in Chilean education.[18]   In this letter, the
Catholic bishops called attention to the government's emphasis
on individual effort and competitiveness; to the exaggerated
role of economic incentives in the motivation of students;   to
the complete omission of any explicit reference to the term
'democracy' within the new school curricula;   to the lack of
any reference to a critical attitude;   and to the excessive
preoccupation with National Security which limits the new
curricula and takes education dangerously close to a type of
ideological control over the students.   The bishops observe
that, as there is no community participation at the local
level, nor any participation by teachers and parents at the
school level, the reform appears to be a deeply authoritarian
measure which aims to impose a specific political system upon
the country.   Moreover, the bishops recorded their concern
over the process of municipalisation which transfers schools
into private hands with no clear indication of effective

Changes in the Chilean Educational System during Eleven Years
of Military Government: 1973-1984

Fig. 1: Enrolment by Educational Level, in Percentages[16]

Years	Levels			
	Pre-School	Primary	Secondary	University
1964	100	100	100	100
1970	133.9	135.4	212.5	233.3
1973	205.0	153.7	313.7	441.5
1982	402.5	136.8	371.7	360.7*

*Corresponds to 1981

- - - - -

Fig. 2: Rates of Growth by Governmental Periods, in
Percentages [17]

Rates of Growth/Annual Average	1964-70	1970-73	1973-81
Total Enrolment of Formal System	6.21	6.54	-0.03
Population from 0 to 24 Years of Age	1.67	1.11	1.07
General Rate of Schooling	4.64	5.06	-1.06
Enrolment in Pre-School Education	5.43	16.26	7.62
Enrolment in Primary Education (1st-8th Grade)	2.17	3.29	-0.60
Enrolment in Secondary Education (9th-12th Grade)	11.54	9.34	0.71
Enrolment in University Education	12.25	22.23	-5.70

ownership nor what the pre-requisites are for opening a
school.   These considerations raise the danger that an un-
suitable group or persons, motivated by political or economic
interests far removed from genuine educational purposes, might
secure control over many schools.

CRISIS-MANAGEMENT: 1982-1984

From the middle of 1981, Chile's economic system began to
disintegrate and the effects of this collapse were quickly
felt at all levels of national life.   The military government
entered a phase of recurrent crisis-management, but this by no
means signified the imminent fall of the regime.   The government's main task during the past two years has been to survive
at whatever cost;   as a result, most of its central economic
principles have been abandoned.   Chile's experiment with the
free market economy has been a profound disaster:

'The most significant phenomenon of 1983, and one which
serves as a general backdrop to the events occurring during the year, is the complete failure of the regime to
solve the problems arising from the disintegration of the
economic model imposed by the Chicago team.   Neither the
crisis of the external debt, nor the collapse of the
financial system, nor the recession, nor the massive increase in unemployment, nor the lack of investment, nor
the growing levels of poverty and misery could be handled
with even a minimum degree of success.'[19]

In fact, in 1983 the rate of unemployment, including the
Programa de Empleo Mínimo, PEM (Minimum Employment Programme)
and the Programa de Ocupación para Jefes de Logar, POJ (Employment Programme for Heads of Families), reached at least 30 per
cent at national level, that is one out of three Chileans
available for work were unable to find employment.   Furthermore, the number of industries which went bankrupt in 1982 was
greater than the total during all the previous years since
the military government assumed power.[20]
This crisis has affected the educational system in a
variety of ways.   First, the military government has been
obliged to further reduce public spending.   This, along with
the growth of unemployment, the fall in income levels, and
many other factors, has served to increasingly isolate the
government and to encourage diverse social groups to openly
declare their opposition, not only to government policies, but
also to the regime itself.   The government has been forced to
suspend the process of municipalisation regarding education
for financial reasons.   Second, the freezing of the amounts
of subsidy induced serious problems in the functioning of
'municipalised' schools and subsidised private schools.   In
addition, the state has been unable to provide appropriate

redundancy payments to teachers transferred to a new employer,
the mayors;   as a result, the municipalisation process has
been discontinued.   Finally, unemployment and the drop in
income levels have also had a direct impact on education.   On
the one hand, it became difficult for many people to afford
the various types of fees and payments required but, on the
other, the stability, security and dedication of teachers have
been badly affected by unemployment.   Since the main component of educational spending is teachers' salaries, many owners
of private schools and many mayors have resorted to such
practices as dismissing well-qualified teachers and replacing
them with less qualified and less experienced teaching staff,
or increasing the number of hours on teachers' timetables.
Moreover, the capacity of students from low socio-economic
backgrounds has been affected dramatically and their educational performance has deteriorated noticeably.

Thus, gradually the economic crisis has demanded the
correction, suspension, or termination of certain aspects of
educational policy in the face of numerous contradictions
between the economic model and reality, between theory and
practice, and between policy intentions and the actual consequences of their implementation.   The government has been
forced to appoint a Comisión Interministerial (Educación-
Interior) with a view to reconsidering some of the measures
taken and to examining the difficulties that arise in practice
between the purely technical-pedagogical function and administration.   President Pinochet intervened directly to stop
what he consideed the irresponsible creation of new university
careers which unjustifiably inflate the number of student
applicants.   The Ministry of Education has been obliged to
abandon its usual role and it now intervenes actively and
directly in various educational matters.   It would seem that
the old idea of the Estado Docente (Teaching State) had at
least fulfilled some important educational functions;   by
comparison, neither the privatisation of education nor the
application of the free market model to education have proven
capable of organising the educational development of the
country.

The Effects of Municipalisation

As has already been seen, the process of municipalisation
ultimately aimed at transferring state education into private
hands, as Decree Law No. 1-3063 made clear.   The suspension
of this process also meant that privatisation could not take
place in the way planned, due partly to strong criticisms
emerging from within the schools themselves.   However,
privatisation has been pursued not just through municipalisation but also through the creation of new schools under the
stimulus of state subventions.   A comparison between 1980 and
1982 is revealing:

Changes in the Chilean Educational System during Eleven Years
of Military Government: 1973-1984

> 'According to figures provided by the Superintendia de
> Educación, out of a total of 13,581 educational units,
> 21.4 per cent (2,909 units) were private and 78.6 per
> cent (10,672 units) were public.   In 1982, by contrast,
> out of a total of 13,904 educational units, 29.7 per cent
> (4,112 units) were public and municipal.'[21]

In other words, in less than two years, private education grew
by 41 per cent.   The new subsidised schools had become an
excellent business.   The <u>Asociación Gremial de Educadores de
Chile</u>, AGECH (Professional Association of Chilean Educators)
has on numerous occasions denounced the 'Taiwanisation' of
education, that is the way in which education has been com-
mercialised like a cheap commodity.[22]   According to Marcelo
Castillo, the policies of the military government have been
shaped by the free market model, and educational policies have
been no exception.   However, this orientation has taken a
different form due to the subsidisation of education whereby
the state provides a monthly payment of 1,300 pesos (US$13)
for every pupil enrolled in a private school.   The state is
only concerned with the average rate of pupil attendance as
recorded in the attendance registers.   In practice, little is
known about what goes on inside the private schools - the
quality of private education is not monitored closely.   As a
result, it is known that poorly qualified persons, whose
primary motivation is to set up a profitable business, have
been allowed to establish schools.   Certain unorthodox
practices have begun to appear: attendance registers have
been tampered with; promotion rates have been falsified; and
teachers who refused to 'play the game' were liable to be dismissed.   AGECH has regularly received denunciations of such
practices.

Moreover, just as the economy contains various large
economic groupings, a number of educational conglomerates have
also appeared.   One example is the <u>Conglomerado de las
Escuelas Libertadores H.C.</u>, which maintains 28 schools within
the more densely populated and poorer zones of Greater
Santiago.   It is estimated that the conglomerate receives a
state subvention for 28,000 students.   About 700 teachers are
employed by this group.   Other educational groups include the
<u>Conglomerado de las Escuelas Galvarino</u> and the <u>Conglomerado de
las Escuelas Romo</u>.   All of these are family businesses and
their founders are usually from low socio-economic backgrounds.
Before setting up their own schools, they were often ordinary
teachers in some outlying school, with varying levels of
schooling to their credit.   The amount of profits which these
educational businesses make is remarkable: 'Just one of these
complexes with 1,560 pupils receives 1,950,000 pesos per
month'.[23]

The municipal schools receive the same amount of subsidy
per student enrolled and the mayors run the schools within

their jurisdiction like one of their own businesses. Teachers
are among those who have suffered most from this situation.
AGECH and other institutions often denounce the abuses committed by many mayors towards teachers under their authority. In
practice, teachers who are transferred to the municipalities
lose all the guarantees granted by the state, becoming a
source of relatively cheap educational labour. Many teachers
have been dismissed without cause, many have had their contracts amended arbitrarily. Holiday rights are ignored, the
number of required teaching hours per week has been raised to
over thirty, and salary scales which take years of service
into account have been abolished. These changes have effectively destroyed the professional status of many teachers, who
have come to share the same conditions of employment experienced by other workers in the private sector of a free market
economy. All this has created a growing, large-scale condition of job insecurity, with all that this implies for the
exercise of a teacher's profession.

Thus, through the process of municipalisation, the state
has awarded the private sector and the municipalities a share
in the most controversial and lucrative aspects of educational administration, namely, the financial aspect. In this
way, the regime has fulfilled one of its main educational
aims - to make education an economically more viable, and
profitable enterprise.

Finally, municipalisation has also created a more unequal
distribution of education. Those municipalities enjoying a
high average socio-economic level also enjoy a higher level of
educational investment, with obvious implications for the
quality of education:

'Differences exist with regard to average expenditure per
student, it being observed that while in Providencia
average spending reaches 1,657 pesos, in Renca it is only
813 pesos, that is, less than half of the former.'[24]

So the criteria which the government applies in distributing
its resources do not respect the needs of different school
populations, and therefore this allocation of resources offers
no compensation for the lack of educational opportunities
suffered by a growing proportion of the population.

The Effects of the New School Curricula

The changes which the government has implemented through
the so-called modernisation of the educational system did not
follow the historical trend of educational development. They
were designed neither to extend proven achievements nor to re-
medy existing deficiencies, nor did they introduce any new
ideas into actual pedagogy. The curricula changes did not
take into account the concrete reality in which they would be

implemented, and furthermore they completely ignored the
educational community. As a result, the new curricula soon
required substantial modifications.

At the primary level, the reform of the curriculum aroused numerous criticisms, created many problems, and secured few
achievements. Consequently, in 1984 a new Decree Law (No. 6)
was issued, according to which the primary curriculum ceases
to be flexible: all the country's schools must now offer, as
a minimum requirement, all the subjects indicated in the new
plan of study. The former restrictions on the educational
aims (metas mínimas) of state schools were thus eliminated.
The only degree of flexibility which is allowed is the time to
be devoted to each subject, with the exception of spanish
language and mathematics. Certain minor modifications were
also introduced, for example, a second language in the seventh
and eighth grades, which illustrate the lack of logic and
coherence in the new measures which have little practical
relevance to the urgent need to improve the educational system.
Changes have also been introduced in secondary education which
though partial in nature, tend to affect the curriculum in its
totality and overall rationality. The number of hours for
certain subjects has been increased. In addition, certain
optional subjects have now been made compulsory. However,
the contents of the study programmes remain unchanged.

Today, there is a widespread concern that the quality of
education is far from satisfactory. As a result, and as part
of overall educational policy in recent years, the government
has created the Programa de Evaluación del Rendimiento Escolar,
PER (Programme for the Evaluation of School Efficiency) in
association with the Catholic University. PER has concentrated on producing an annual evaluation of the cognitive and
effective objectives throughout the Chilean educational system.
This evaluation has been conducted on a massive scale, covering 85 per cent of the country's primary school population.
Its aim is to obtain objective information which could be used
by the educational system in order to improve the quality of
education. Objective tests are administered at the end of
the fourth and eighth grades of primary school throughout
Chile. This evaluation has been carried out in 1982 and 1983
and it is necessary to continue the programme for some years
more. However:

> 'The Prueba de Evaluación del Rendimiento Escolar PER
> (Evaluation Test of School Efficiency) which measures the
> efficiency achieved after eight years of basic education
> furnishes results described as 'a failure' by ex-Minister
> M. Madariaga. After eight years of instruction, many
> children do not know how to write figures, do not read
> satisfactorily, and only just know how to add.'[25]

Even worse, this situation has become serious in the higher

grades of primary education because the earlier grades do not
provide the child with the solid foundation essential for
further educational advance. Figures derived from the <u>Prueba
de Aptitud Académica</u> taken at the end of the fourth year of
secondary education also failed to indicate positive progress:

> 'In the private, fee-paying establishments, one out of
> every 8.3 pupils does not obtain the 450 points which
> constitute the minimum for university entry; in the
> private schools receiving state subsidies, this proport-
> ion is one out of every 3.3 pupils. And in the state
> schools, one out of every 2.7 pupils.'[26]

Pinochet's former Minister of Education, Gonzalo Vial,
has observed that while education in Chile is quantitatively
satisfactory, in qualitative terms it still has a long way to
go. According to Vial, the education provided is mediocre.
In fact, repetition and drop-out rates continue to be very high.
Out of 100 children who enter the first year of primary education, only 40 finish the eight years of primary school and
about 20 complete secondary education.[27] According to the ex-
Minister, mass education is a collective effort which implies
a huge mobilisation of people and resources for an extended
period. Consequently, any substantial improvement in the
immediate future of Chilean education can only be conceived
in terms of the direct intervention of the state on a grand
scale. As there is no private agency which can effectively
fulfil the role of the state, it is therefore necessary that
the state, in association with the community, assumes its full
educational responsibilities.

However, according to the latest available figures,
actual educational expenditures by the government constitute
only 4.03 per cent of the National Budget. Health takes up
5.04 per cent, while Defence absorbs 15.4 per cent. In 1984,
it is planned that Defence will continue to receive 15.4 per
cent, while Education, Health and Public Works will absorb
only 12.7 per cent between them. Moreover, according to the
magazine <u>Cauce</u> in January 1984, Chile spent US$70 per capita
on education and US$11,247 per soldier.[28]

CONCLUSIONS

It would seem that the possibility is remote for changes
to occur permitting a genuine improvement in the different
levels of Chilean education. The crisis which the country is
experiencing is so deep, extensive and pervasive that, no
matter which indicator one looks at, Chile seems to be going
backwards. The disaster which befell the economic model has
generated a deep social crisis, in which more than a million
Chileans are unemployed.

It is almost impossible to detect any sign of educational

progress during the eleven years of military rule.   The im-
position of a neo-liberal economic model in Chile has had
grave consequences for the rates of schooling; for the social
distribution of education; and for educational efficiency.
One recent study shows that, between 1976 and 1981, the average length of schooling among Chile's population decreased
from 8.1 to 7.5 years.   In 1981, almost a quarter (23.8 per
cent) of the population was composed of illiterates and people
with between one and four years of primary schooling.   The
inequality of educational distribution in 1981 is shown by the
fact that 6.8 per cent of the population up to 12 years of age
had only 0.2 per cent of the total years of schooling, while
another 6.1 per cent accounted for 15.1 per cent of this
schooling.   Between 1977 and 1982, the average rate of
schooling amongst young people between 15 and 19 years of age
fell from 8.8 to 7.8 years.[29]   It is also the case that during the nine years between 1974 and 1982, the evolution of
enrolment in primary and secondary education decreased by an
annual average of -0.6 per cent, in contrast with the previous
ten years during which enrolment increased at an average
annual rate of 5.9 per cent.[30]

As is widely known, it is not enough to have broad access
to the educational system.   The historical problem of Chilean
education has been the failure to secure a high level of
retention, especially for children and young people from
middle and low income backgrounds.   The military government
has not only failed to solve this problem; it has actually
presided over a considerable increase in school desertion and
a noticeable decrease in the average growth rate of schooling.
Within the educational system, there has been a clear increase
in social discrimination through different educational programmes for different socio-economic sectors.   In addition,
a determined attempt has been made to secure absolute ideological control over education, linked to the dictatorship's
strong emphasis upon authoritarianism, verticality and the
deliberate, organised inhibition of critical and reflective
capacities.

The private sector has demonstrated its inability to expand and improve the educational system along the lines laid
down by Pinochet's 'Directivas Presidenciales', thereby revealing the neo-liberal project to be not only un-historical
as far as Chilean conditions are concerned but also incapable
of effective implementation.   The government's educational
perspective refuses to recognise the social responsibility of
the community to provide, improve and transform education.
This refusal dooms any programme of educational change under
this regime to failure.   Many social sectors consider education to be a right and not simply a commodity to be bought and
sold in the market place.   Furthermore, structural social
conditions continue to severely constrain the ability of the
educational system to solve the problems which it faces.

Changes in the Chilean Educational System during Eleven Years
of Military Government: 1973-1984

It is clear that the problems of Chilean education do not
stem simply from the military coup, but Pinochet's government
has exacerbated the discriminatory, authoritarian and manipu-
lative aspects of education, and has destroyed the historical
tradition and social context within which earlier generations
of Chileans had sought answers to Chile's educational problems.

REFERENCES AND NOTES

1. For a useful overview of the Frei Reform, see Calvo, C.
    et al (1983), Chile: Comprehensive Liberal Reform, in
    Simmons, J. (Ed.), Better Schools: International
    Lessons for Reform, Praeger, pp. 121-147.
2. For further elaboration of this point, and for an analy-
    sis of education during Chile's last three administra-
    tions, see Aedo-Richmond, R., Brock, C. and Noguera, I.
    (1981), Politics and Educational Change in Chile:
    1964-1980 in Broadfoot, P., Brock, C. and Tulasiewicz,
    W. (Eds.), Politics and Educational Change: An Inter-
    national Survey. Croom Helm, pp. 209-227.
3. However, had the Escuela Nacional Unificada, ENU (Nation-
    al Unified School) programme been fully implemented, a
    qualitative break in the country's educational tradi-
    tions would probably have resulted.
4. Decree Law No. 1, 11 September 1973.
5. OEA, (1982), La Regionalización en el Proceso de desar-
    rollo global de Chile, in La Regionalización educativa
    de América Latina, Revista Internacional de Desarrollo
    Educativo, No. 88, Año XXVI, p. 14.
6. Egaña, L. and Magendzo, A. (1983), El Marco Teórico-
    Político del Proceso de Descentralización Educativa
    (1973-1983) PiiE (Programa interdisciplinario de
    investigaciones en Educación), p. 40.
7. Bravo, A. (1976), Interrogantes en la Educación Chilena,
    Revista Mensaje, No. 251, pp. 368-372.
8. Pinochet, A. (1979), Directivas Presidenciales sobre
    Educación Nacional, in Bases para la Política Educa-
    cional 1979, Presidencia de la República, División
    Nacional de Comunicación Social.
9. Carta Pastoral de Comité Permanente del Episcopado (1981),
    La Reforma Educacional, Revista Mensaje, No. 300, p.
    366.
10. Hevia, R. (1982), Cambios en la Administración Educacion-
    al: el Proceso de Municipalización, PiiE, p. 25.
11. Ruiz-Tagle, J. (1981), Un nuevo poder? las Municipali-
    dades, Revista Mensaje, No. 299, p. 266.
12. Egaña, L. and Magendzo, A. (1983), op. cit.
13. Ibid., p. 61.
14. Fernández, S. (1980), Discurso en el Segundo Congreso de
    Alcaldes, Diario El Mercurio, 12 Noviembre.

15. Fernándes, S. (1980), Planes de Estudios de la Educación
    General Básica, Revista de Educación, No. 79.
16. Nuñez, N. (1984), Educación y Regimen Autoritario: El
    Caso de Chile: 1973-1982, Signos, Revista de Educación
    y Cultura, No. 1, p. 8.
17. Ibid.
18. Carta Pastoral, (1981), op. cit., pp. 366-372.
19. Garreton, M. A. (1984), 1983-1984: El Regimen Militar
    Chileno en la Encrucijada, Revista Mensaje, No. 326,
    p. 36.
20. Mellen, P. (1983), Un balance de la situación económica
    Chilena del año 1982, Revista Mensaje, No. 316, pp.
    42-45.
21. Mellen, P. (1984), Las subverciones en el banquillo,
    Revista el Pizarrón, No. 27, p. 52. (Note: this
    journal is published privately; the names of the
    contributors of articles are omitted.)
22. See Castillo, M. (1984), La Educación se 'Taiwaniza',
    Revista Cauce, No. 8, pp. 28-29.
23. Ibid., p. 28.
24. Egaña, L. and Magendzo, A. (1983), op. cit., p. 64.
25. Castillo, M. (1984), op. cit., p. 29. (Note: The total
    results for the country as a whole for 1983 have yet
    to be published. The only known results are those for
    each school in particular.
26. Vial, G. (1984), Educación Chilena: realidades e ilusi-
    ones, Discurso de inaguración de las VII Jornadas
    Nacionales de Cultura, Noviembre 1983, in Revista el
    Pizarrón, No. 27, p. 38.
27. Ibid., pp. 38-42.
28. Vial, G. (1984), Los gastos militares, Revista Cauce, No.4,
    pp. 18-20.
29. Briones, G. (1983), La Distribución de la Educación en
    el Modelo de Economía Neo-Liberal: 1974-1982, PiiE,
    p. 61.
30. Revista el Pizarrón (1983), No. 23, p. 22.

Chapter Ten

ARGENTINA: HIGHER EDUCATION AND POLITICAL INSTABILITY

Nick Caistor

Higher education thrives on stability. If in a country there is uncertainty and uncontrolled change at all levels - the economic, the political and the social, as well as the academic - then the universities and colleges may be exciting or despairing places to be, but teaching and research are the first to suffer. Over the past decade, Argentina has had nine presidents, and a dozen education ministers; inflation has never been under an annual rate of 100 per cent, and on at least two occasions being six times higher; the political stance of the country's leaders has swung from full-blooded left-wing idealism to right-wing populism to bloody free-market militarism, coming to rest for the moment at least in November 1983 in social democracy. In the midst of all this, a student population which has reached as high as 500,000 [1] has sought professional education and research facilities that would train the nation's lawyers, doctors, scientists, archi-tects. It is not only a rare lecturer who manages to com-plete a career in university teaching, but it is an extremely lucky student who can complete his or her four or six years in higher education under the same government, with the same university curriculum and administrative system, or indeed the same accepted concepts about the purpose of education.

The problems for higher education in Argentina go back for more than a decade, however. Most observers situate the watershed in 1966. This was when the armed forces first broke into the campus of Buenos Aires University claiming as is their wont that the university was a breeding ground for 'subversion'. For several years prior to 1966, both country and university had been enjoying a rare period of relative calm under the government of Arturo Illia; academic matters had largely been left to the university authorities. This was a particularly strong period for the exact sciences and scientific research, and in the late 1950's and early 1960's, sociology and economics had become university degrees - as too had psychology, a rarity in Latin America and still absent from the university in Spain, where the Franco regime consid-

ered it anathema.   The principle of university autonomy in
Argentina, first proclaimed in 1918 at the provincial University of Cordoba, which was founded as early as 1613 by the
Spaniards, was paramount by the early 1960's.   The students
of 1918 demanded a say in the running of both the administration and the educational principles guiding the universities.
They were fighting against things which have not changed a
great deal in the intervening sixty-five years:

> 'poor instruction, almost exclusive emphasis on learning
> by rote from obsolete texts, inadequate libraries, ab-
> sence of practical training, and teaching methods
> 'characterised by a narrow dogmatism which contributes
> to the isolation of the university from science and
> modern learning.'[2]

With the victory of the autonomy movement, university
affairs were governed by tripartite university councils
consejos universitarios made up of students, staff and graduates.   They appointed not only the head of the university,
the rector, but in some cases the lecturers as well.   This
involvement of the students in the running of the university
is what opened the door to the institution becoming political
in the sense of being a force for change in society.   Also,
as Einaudi points out:

> 'when there is no respect for political and civil liber-
> ties in the country at large - the university becomes
> the haven for the opposition, which uses it as a guaran-
> tee against persecution.'[3]

Such a privilege, which derives ultimately from medieval
concepts of immunity, is obviously intolerable to any authoritarian government, and so it proved in Argentina in 1966,
when, on what became known as the 'noche de los bastones
largos' (night of the long sticks) several faculties in
Buenos Aires were invaded.   Illia's government soon gave way
to the far tougher military rule of General Onganía, and many
university lecturers were dismissed.   This saw the start of
a massive drain of talent abroad, whilst many others returned
to professional practice, which was far safer, more stable,
and more lucrative than university teaching.   This was the
start of a damaging split between academic and professional
life which is all the more harmful in a country such as
Argentina where a university degree is often a professional
qualification as well, and academic study tends to be far more
vocationally orientated.   This was well described by Nasatir
in his study of the attitudes of Argentine university students
as compared with their North American counterparts in the mid-
1960's.[4]

The Ongania military regime banned all political activity

and student union groupings, repealed university autonomy,
and appointed its own rectors and deans. A thorough educational reform plan, which concentrated mainly on the primary
and secondary school levels, was presented in 1968, but it was
still being tentatively developed in 1971 when Onganía himself
was ousted. The main concern in higher education during
these years was to make it as 'apolitical' as possible, which,
as one commentator at the time wrote: 'means they should
continue to pursue the government's policies'.[5]

Discontent with military rule was widespread, and
Onganía's successors - Generals Levingston and Lanusse - came
to the conclusion that the only way out was to let Juan
Domingo Peron back into the country. He had been the dominant figure in Argentine politics since 1945, and still had a
massive following. He had been expelled by the military in
1955, to the great relief of the upper and middle classes who
had seen their position in society threatened by his labour-
based populism. However, it was their sons and daughters who
went to the universities, and were there influenced by the predominantly left-wing ideas that were current in Europe, the
United States, and the developing world itself in the late
1960's and early 1970's. This was particularly so in the
social science courses which became increasingly popular, and
by 1975 for instance accounted for 20.6 per cent of total
students enrolled in higher education.[6]

Given the lack of a political alternative on the Left,
these students decided that Peronism, with its guaranteed
roots in the 'people' - the 'masses' - was the best vehicle
for the expression of their revolutionary ideals. Students
were prominent alongside workers in the demonstrations against
military rule and the Left was solidly behind the Peronist
stand-in candidate Hector Cámpora when elections were permitted again in 1973. Cámpora won a clear victory, and his
left-wing advisers suddenly found themselves in positions of
real power. Student militants and young Peronist academics
were thrust into the running of the universities, under education minister Jorge Taiana.

The first thing that they rejected was the idea of
university autonomy. They argued that a state should plan
its future resources carefully, and that therefore the universities must be closely tied in with the central planning of
the Argentina they were trying to build. The university
could not be a place of privilege, it must serve the community.
It could not be the 'apolitical', 'positivist' university of
the military regimes, but must aim to be 'fully integrated
into national reality'. All the subjects taught, even mathematics and the exact sciences, had to be explicitly related to
the outside world. The university councils now included the
non-academic staff, and could appoint and dismiss the teaching
staff. To try to make the institution less of a middle-
class preserve, the 1973 Peronists abolished any kind of entry

restrictions for students, at the same time spreading teaching hours further through the day and evening so that more working people could benefit. This was significant in that approximately half of Argentina's student population are part-timers who also have a job.[7] They attacked the idea of the teacher 'distributing knowledge' to passive students: learning was seen as a collective process of research, and of course all education was political - so the emphasis was put on practical work and discussion, which in fact often degenerated into endless political debate. The university was 'para y del pueblo' (for and of the people), which meant that the walls of its immunity were to be torn down with students and staff going out to apply their knowledge directly in the community. The chemistry department in Buenos Aires, for instance, began to produce cheap medicines in order to challenge the influence of the multinational drug companies.

The university became a force for change that was completely out-of-step with the rest of the country, where the internal contradictions of Peronism were becoming all too apparent. Indeed, on the return of Peron himself (2 June 1973) a gun battle broke out between left and right-wing supporters which resulted in 200 deaths. The left-wing militants in the universities and elsewhere who had considered themselves the 'servants of Peron', now found they were betrayed by their own master, who was unwilling, or unable, to press forward with the socialist revolution they sought. Following Peron's death in 1974, his widow, Isabel Martinez de Peron, took the government even further to the right. She soon appointed a reactionary education minister to take over from Taiana,[8] and removed the rector of Buenos Aires University. The whole country slid deeper into chaos from 1974 to 1976. Many more academics left to work abroad, and although student enrolments reached a record in 1975, the number of graduates did not increase significantly. Those Argentines not directly involved in the political struggle were more or less waiting for the next military coup.

When it did come, on 24 March 1976, it followed the line of its predecessors in Chile and Uruguay earlier in the decade in identifying the universities, and the education system in general, as one of the main areas for attack. The first phase of this was physical repression: the invasion of campuses, the arrest and 'disappearance' of lecturers and students identified with the Left. Faculties were closed all round the country, and departmental staff sacked en masse. Beyond the terror, a campaign was conducted to prove that the autonomy of the universities had been used to create 'subversive cells'. One such example took place at the University of the South, in Bahia Blanca, where seventeen lecturers from the economics department and the university rector, Victor Benamo, were arrested. More than forty others were accused of complicity, in what was described as a huge and

carefully concerted plot to implant Marxist ideology in the
university, and to use that as a base to spread subversion
through all the universities of the country. The local chief
of police brought out carefully prepared diagrams to prove
that the whole affair had been a plot directed by the Universities of Colorado, Grenoble, Louvain, Mexico and Paris in
conjunction with those in Warsaw and Bucharest. The only
proof offered for the allegations was the bibliography issued
by the lecturers, which included such books as The Open Veins
of Latin America by Eduardo Galeano, short stores by Julio
Cortazar, the Education Law of Romania, and a number of books
from the 'subversive' Mexican publishing house, Siglo XXI,
which was forced to close its operations in Argentina. The
following justification was given at the time by the regional
army commander, General Vilas:

> 'It is necessary to destroy the forces which sustain,
> train, and indoctrinate the subversive delinquents and
> these are to be found in the universities and the second-
> ary schools.'[9]

In the University of Cordoba itself, the birthplace of
the autonomy movement, the Air Force led the repression.
They compiled black lists of lecturers and students considered
dangerous, then set about eliminating them either by swoops on
university residences, dismissal with accompanying threats, or
kidnapping. All the teachers in the History and Psychology
faculties were dismissed, and overall about half of the staff
were sacked. Throughout the country, up to 2000 university
teachers were sacked in the first three months after the coup,
either under Law No. 21,274, which gave the military junta the
right to dismiss any civil servant they wished, or under Law
21,276, the new University Law:

> 'Article 7: It is forbidden, within universities, to
> both teaching and non-teaching staff, to engage in any
> indoctrination, propaganda, proselytism, or political
> or trade union activity.
>
> - - - - -
>
> Article 12: Any activity against, or disagreement with,
> the basic aims and propositions of the process of
> national re-organisation is incompatible with the carry-
> ing out of university teaching or any other academic
> activity.'[10]

Students who had enrolled in 1974 had to start their
courses again. All the attempts to widen the social function
of the University were of course swept away. University
autonomy was revoked: it was the leader of the first military
junta, General Jorge Videla, who himself appointed the rector

of Buenos Aires University.   The most suspect faculties,
sociology and psychology, were closed down.

Beyond the repression, an attempt was made to define what
the armed forces considered to be the university's proper role.
As in their economic policies, their ideas were not so much
novel, but rather a return to the traditions of another era.
Economics Minister José Martinez de Hoz sought to return the
country to being the world's provider of beef and wheat, and
renouncing the attempt to make Argentina a powerful industrial
force.   Indeed, national industry was placed a poor second to
opening up the Argentine market to its more advanced competitors.   In a similar way, it was made plain that the promise
of social mobility which had been one of the main attractions
of a university education for Argentina's youth, and the hope
that this training of new professions would advance the
country, were now at an end.   Education Minister J. J.
Catalán, speaking at the end of 1977, described what he and
the junta wanted higher education to provide:

> 'A lucid ruling class to point out to Argentina its
> goals, to determine how to achieve them, and to transmit
> to the rest of the population by its example and pres-
> tige, the political ideas necessary to guide the Nation
> in its best interests and in accordance with its noblest
> ideals.   To form this ruling class is the task of the
> most clear-sighted.   Many of them are here today (he was
> speaking at a Rotary Club reception).   Our schools and
> universities must also contribute to this effort to form
> a ruling class by the stimulation of youth within the
> guidelines of our great traditional values.'[11]

For the first time, a numerus clausus was introduced,
with first-year entry in subjects such as economics, medicine,
and engineering limited to 1,000, less than a quarter than
that of previous years.   Many subjects, such as librarian-
ship, information science and social anthropology, were taken
out of the universities altogether.   On the academic level
itself, a strict distinction was now made between teaching and
research, with the latter being hived off into separate
institutes which were favoured with special funds.   In many
cases, the universities returned to the conditions that the
students at Cordoba had rebelled against sixty years earlier:
rote learning;   inadequate or non-existent libraries;   and
out-of-date, traditional teaching.   The numbers of students
competing for university places fell sharply in 1977 and 1978.

The military governments also tried, following their free
market economic principles in the field of education, to
reduce the burden it placed on state expenditure.   The following table shows how government spending on education and
culture compared with those on defence and security between
1970 and 1978.

Fig. 1:   Government Expenditure on Culture and Education:
          as a Percentage of Total Government Expenditure

Year	Defence and Security	Culture and Education
	per cent	per cent
1970	17.5	17.1
1971	17.7	17.8
1972	15.4	18.9
1973	13.8	17.3
1974	12.7	17.9
1975	13.5	16.3
1976	15.6	10.0
1977	15.2	9.5
1978	15.5	10.9

Source: Tedesco, J. C., Braslavsky, C. and Carciofi, R.
(1983), El Proyecto Educativo Autoritario, Argentina 1976-
1982, p.93.

- - - - -

As well as this direct reduction of funding, they pursued
a federal idea of returning education to each of the provinces, thus increasing still further the gap between the
relatively rich seaboard and the poorer interior.   A parallel aim was of course the encouragement of private institutions of higher education, which in fact in these years became
for the first time more prestigious than their state-run
competitors simply by having greater financial possibilities
and, in many cases, better staff.   Staff in the government
institutions were demoralised by strict bureaucratic and ideological control;   also by increasingly inadequate salaries,
often paid so late that inflation had already cut their value
by half or more.

By late 1980, the military regime was floundering, and
found itself without a coherent strategy for dealing with any
of its problems, and education was no exception.   When
General Galtieri's desperate attempt to win popularity by re-
taking the Malvinas/Falkland Islands in 1982 ended disast-
rously, it was the end for the armed forces' government too.

The deterioration that had taken place within education
was lamentable.   Few figures were published to show exactly
what had happened to Argentine education in the second half of
the 1970's.   Education as a field of study had been removed
from the university syllabus, so that little or no research

189

into education had been carried out for nearly twenty years.
Nor was there much debate about education from the two main
contenders for the return of Argentina to civilian rule: the
Peronist party, and the Radical party, led by the eventual
successful candidate for the presidency, Raúl Alfonsín.   The
two parties were too busy attacking the armed forces' record
in government, trying to score points off each other, and
looking for ways of dealing with the chronic economic mess to
be able to put forward well-defined plans for the future of
higher education.

However, the Radical party did attract the support of a
large sector of the middle class, those who had experienced
university in the early 1960's.   They had since made their
way in professional life, not wishing to get involved in the
turmoil of the academic world.   Alfonsín persuaded a substantial number of them to show a renewed interest, and it was
this type of adviser whose views have been put into practice
since his victory at the polls in October 1983. The Education
Minister chosen, Carlos Alconada, had also been the minister
under Arturo Illia in the early 1960's.   The idea seems to
have been to somehow erase the memory of the chaotic instability of the intervening eighteen years, and to start afresh
as though 1984 were 1965.

The problems facing the new university authorities are
immense.   The legacy from the years under military rule is
daunting.   Firstly, there is widespread pressure to eluci-
date the fate of the 2,000 students and staff who 'disap-
peared' during those years.   The new generation of students,
who are once more admitted on to the university councils, and
to engage in political activity on the campuses, are continuing to demand that the military be brought to account.
Then there is the question of the teaching staff.   How far
can the new university authorities carry out a 'purge' of all
those seen as compromised by having been given their posts
under the military regimes?   There is considerable pressure
from the staff who lost their jobs between 1974 and 1982 to
regain their jobs automatically without delay.   There is also
a pressing need to reform all the syllabuses, which have become completely out of touch not only with the 'national
reality' but with all the advances made internationally in the
various fields during the last decade.   Students too who were
expelled from the university are demanding their places back,
and to have what they had already studied credited by the new
authorities.   The principle of restricted entry has of course
been swept away, and the faculties are swamped with students
trying to catch up.   The opposition Peronists are busy
attacking the Radicals for having no real plan for education,
accusing them of simply engaging in an ad hoc day-to-day
pragmatism.   As usual though, it is the economic problems
facing Argentina that condition all the others, and though the
provisions for education have been increased, the 600 per cent

inflation expected again this year makes a mockery of planned
expenditure. It also makes the so greatly desired political
stability seem just so much wishful thinking.
   To an observer used to the British system of higher
education, there are many things in the Argentine counterpart
which contrast. The fact that the successful completion of
secondary school gives students the right to go to university
to study whatever they like is alien to our tradition, and a
clear example of the lasting influence of the French model in
many of the Latin American states. On the practical level
it seems only to compound the problems of attempting to plan
for the future of not merely the universities, but society as
a whole. The political questioning of the role of the
institution from within, and the real power that students
have enjoyed in the debate about the running of the universities are also very different from Britain. Perhaps most
surprising of all, however, is the way in which the belief in
education, the desire for knowledge and a willingness to teach
have survived the incredible political and economic vicissi-
tudes of recent years. This tells us something of the place
of 'the university' in the formation and development of
Argentine society, and the contribution of education to
inertia as well as change.

REFERENCES AND NOTES

1.   The British Council Educational Profile (1978) provides
        basic information about higher education in Argentina:
        'At present the country has 76 national universities,
        half of which have been set up during the last 8 years.
        There are in addition 23 private universities (mostly
        Catholic and fee-paying), 4 provincial universities and
        the Federal Technical University which has its head-
        quarters in Buenos Aires and departments in all the
        major cities. Approximately 2.2 per cent of the popu-
        lation is in higher education. About 89 per cent of
        those students are in the universities with 11 per cent
        in higher education institutions (of which 8 per cent
        are in teacher training). Of university students 85
        per cent attend the national universities and the
        largest (Buenos Aires) had 227,086 enrolled in 1975
        (42 per cent of the total enrolment which in that year
        was running at 536,959).
2.   Einaudi, L. (1972), University Autonomy and Academic
        Freedom in Latin America, in La Belle, T. (Ed).
        Education and Development: Latin America and the
        Caribbean, University of California, p. 611.
3.   Einaudi, L. (1972), op. cit., p. 616.
4.   Nasatir, D. (1972), Education and Social Change: The
        Argentine Case, in La Belle, T. (Ed), op. cit., p.
        697-8.

5.   Orgaz, J. (1970), <u>Reforma Universitaria y Rebelion Estudiantil</u>, Ediciones Libera, p. 73.
6.   British Council (1978), op. cit., Appendix, p. 3.
7.   British Council (1978), op. cit., p. 13.
8.   Jorge Taiana was arrested in March 1976 and held for several years without trial in La Plata jail.
9.   Press conference (July 1966), Bahia Blanca.
10.   Amnesty International (1977), <u>Repression against intellectuals in Argentina.</u>
11.   Reported in <u>La Opinión Semanal</u>, 11-17 November 1977.

LIST OF CONTRIBUTORS

Colin Brock - Chairman of the International Education Unit at the University of Hull Institute of Education.

Dr. Hugh Lawlor - Senior Lecturer in Education at Nonington College, Dover, Kent.

Ruth Aedo-Richmond - Research Student at the University of Hull Institute of Education.

Pilar Aguilar - Research Student at the University of Hull Institute of Education.

Dr. Nigel Brooke - Coordinator of Integrated Rural Development Projects at the Secretariat of State Education, Minas Gerais, Brazil.

Nick Caistor - Researcher on Latin America for the magazine Index on Censorship.

Professor Erwin |E. Epstein - Professor of Sociology at the University of Missouri-Rolla, USA.

Dr. Roger Garrett - Lecturer in Science Education and Curriculum Development at the University of Bristol School of Education.

Ines Noguera - Coordinator of Primary Programmes at St. George's College, Santiago, Chile.

Dr. Rosemary Preston - Research Fellow in Sociology at the University of Leeds.

Dr. Gonzalo Retamal - Regional Officer for the United Nations Refugee Programme in Central America.

Mark Richmond - Lecturer in Economics and Communication Studies at Humberside College of Higher Education, Hull.

INDEX

194